Out of Sight

Out of Sight

Crime, youth and exclusion in modern Britain

Robert McAuley

WILLAN
PUBLISHING

Published by

Willan Publishing
Culmcott House
Mill Street, Uffculme
Cullompton, Devon
EX15 3AT, UK
Tel: +44(0)1884 840337
Fax: +44(0)1884 840251
e-mail: info@willanpublishing.co.uk
website: www.willanpublishing.co.uk

Published simultaneously in the USA and Canada by

Willan Publishing
c/o ISBS, 920 NE 58th Ave, Suite 300
Portland, Oregon 97213-3786, USA
Tel: +001(0)503 287 3093
Fax: +001(0)503 280 8832
e-mail: info@isbs.com
website: www.isbs.com

First published 2007

ISBN 10 1-84392-196-0
ISBN 13 978-1-84392-196-7

British Library Cataloguing-in-Publication Data

A catalogue record for this book is available from the British Library

Project managed by Deer Park Productions, Tavistock, Devon
Typeset by TW Typesetting, Plymouth, Devon
Printed and bound by TJ International Ltd, Trecerus Industrial Estate, Padstow, Cornwall

Contents

List of illustrations

Acknowledgements

First, respect to the young men and women who took part in this study, plus the staff at the Project, Gateways, and the Nova Centre. The world is theirs. Thanks to my supervisor Dr Janet Foster for her thoughts, ideas, support and tolerance. Thanks also to the Cambridge sisters of mercy: Belinda Brookes-Gordon, Nina Cope, Amanda Matravers and Alison Wakefield. Dr Loraine Gelsthorpe, Professor David Downes, Dr Ben Bowling, Dr Graham Steventon and Dr Allison Liebling all helped me through the writing process, as did all the staff at Warwick Sports, 'specially Greg. I am also indebted to Maureen at the Institute and Julie Powley, David Thomas and Dr Padfield at Tit Hall. Thanks also to the Economic and Social Research Council, Trinity Hall and the University of Cambridge, Institute of Criminology for their assistance and guidance. Finally to Brian Willan, and everyone at Willan Publishing, I thank you.

For Dad, Maria, and Janet

Introduction

Nova is a housing estate on the edge of Ford: a big city in the north of England. Compared with other areas of Ford, Nova's residents face greater hardships, unemployment is disproportionately high, as are crime, ill health and mortality (ODPM, 2004). Local people are also disadvantaged in education; in a survey conducted just before my own fieldwork only 1 per cent of a random sample of 300 residents had a further or higher education qualification. *Out of Sight: crime, youth and exclusion in modern Britain* is about young people's experiences of living in Nova, and with the stigma surrounding this poor community.

During twelve months of interviews and participant observations with a group of 33 young adults living in Nova, I recorded local perceptions of the estate across Ford. Nova gained disproportionate attention in the local media, and reports usually focused on crime, including burglary, drug distribution and vandalism. During the early months of my fieldwork, one family began to appear regularly on the front cover of the *Ford Evening News*. The Quinns had been the first council tenants to receive an exclusion order, following complaints about the family's eldest sons Andrew and Michael. Several neighbours had written to Ford City Council and the local press claimed the two brothers were 'terrorising the neighbourhood'. When the *Ford Evening News* picked up on the story, council officials gained a High Court order preventing both men from going within a mile of the estate. As the young men were removed from their mother's home, the event triggered a debate in the local press about 'youth crime' in Nova. Readers of the *Ford Evening News* mentioned worklessness, poor parenting and welfare dependency as reasons for Nova's reputation as a problem estate. Truancy, gang membership and drug abuse were also cited as factors in what many believed to be a 'tendency' towards crime among Nova's young adult population.

It is true that almost half of Nova's population are young people, living alone or as families in properties owned and rented by Ford City Council. Young people I met and introduce later also describe how crime is a 'pattern' in Nova. Outside of Nova, however, it seemed that few people were willing to understand the cause and direction of that pattern. Instead, as young people themselves told me, outsiders simply 'assumed the worst' about all of Nova's youth. Listening to young people's accounts of persistent exclusion, in employment, training and at school, stigmatising residents of this poor community had become interwoven into the culture of the city. Many young people I met in Nova described exclusion as 'the life', and the term seemed to define how young people grew up as objects of suspicion in the eyes of Ford's affluent majority. Over the forthcoming chapters, young people describe Nova's history of exclusion, running parallel with the urban regeneration of Ford during the 1980s. All of the 33 young people who took part in this study were children at that time and described being demonised in school and then in local labour markets for being members of a poor community. That began when Nova, a new estate originally built to house industrial workers, experienced mass unemployment during the 1980–1 recession.

Masking poverty

Like many industrial cities, Ford survived de-industrialisation by re-building its former manufacturing districts into retail and science parks. In Nova, regeneration resulted in Gemini Park, an assortment of retail outlets and hi-tech industries (see Picture 1, p. 3). Gemini Park, however, has done little for the people of Nova: unemployment and crime remain high while household incomes, and the estate's built environment, deteriorate. It seems the only lasting achievement has been the polarisation of Nova from the rest of Ford and the ghettoisation of younger residents within the estate.

During my fieldwork, one of Nova's public amenities, an employment advice and activity project for young residents, was forced to close. Local youth agencies felt that allowing young adults to socialise at the Project was 'unconstructive'. I describe the closure of the Project, where I met most of the young people who took part in this study. The closure seemed to represent the symbolic exclusion young people describe in this study. Even though the Project enabled young people to search for work and skills as a community, youth agencies felt that young people had to be tackled on an individual level. Young people describe the successive failure of similar initiatives because of the way Nova's young adults were perceived as inherently bad. In my account of the closure of the Project, I argue that initiatives designed to target 'socially excluded' youth can easily become a masquerade of crime; objectifying young people living in a poor community to justify a consumer lifestyle. Alison Young (1996: 15) describes how 'Seeing the Other is a form of

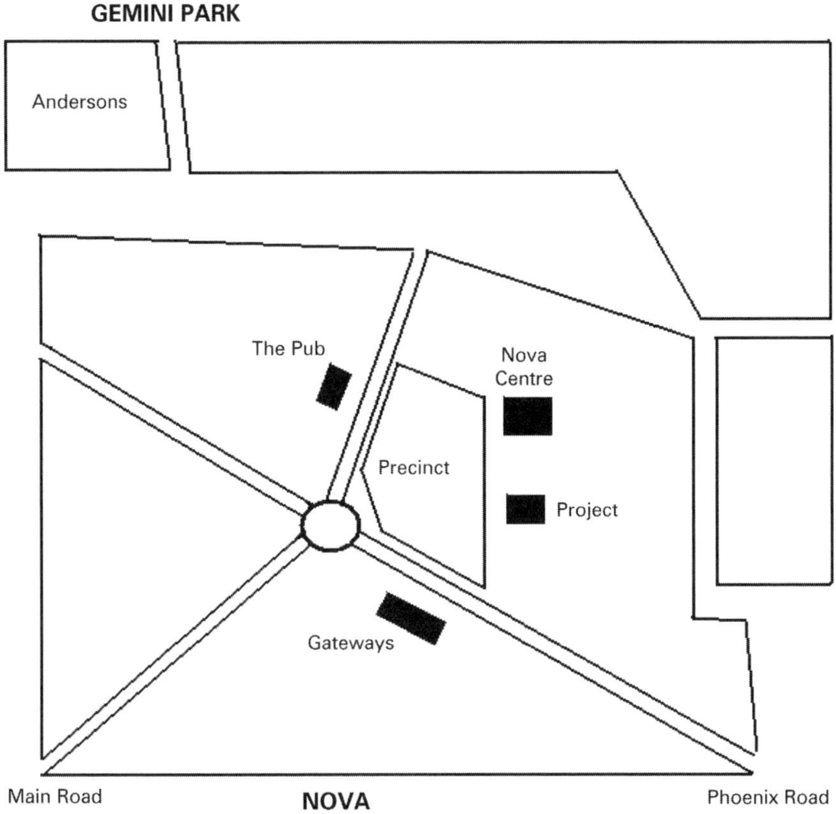

GEMINI PARK

Main Road	**NOVA**	Phoenix Road

Picture 1 Map of Nova and Gemini Park

self-reproduction. In looking at or for the other (the criminal), we represent ourselves to ourselves.' This process often characterises young people's accounts of exclusion in this study.

Out of Sight describes how 'the life' of a poor community is objectified in a consumer society, and how thinking about crime prolongs the exclusion of already poor communities. Nova's young adults also describe how realities of poverty are hidden by the reputation silently imposed on Nova, whereby a community with a strong work ethic is looked upon as members of an underclass.

Will Hutton (1995: 719) highlights how Britain is now a '30–30–40' society: 40 per cent are 'the privileged' in jobs that provide full holiday and pension rights, 30 per cent are working in insecure jobs, while the remaining 30 per cent of the working population are unemployed. *Out of Sight* describes how the new social divisions created during Britain's urban regeneration were hidden through a masquerade of crime played out during the 1980s and 1990s. In addition, the consumer society that developed during that period has redefined policy on employment and crime to help justify a consumer lifestyle.

Nova's economic exclusion is sustained by workfare, a policy initiative devised during the 1980s to help those communities worst affected by de-industrialisation. Workfare policies were often implemented in tandem with urban regeneration initiatives like Gemini Park, whereby former manufacturing workers were encouraged at job centres to take jobs in new service industries. Many of the young people I met preferred 'working for yourself' to avoid what was commonly perceived as slave labour. The tragedy was that 'working for yourself', even when individuals were successful, only compounded the stigma associated with young people living in Nova.

Twenty-four seven society

My aim in *Out of Sight* is to show how these realities remain hidden by a society driven by consumption. The increasing expense of further and higher education has meant that people living in poverty and with no financial assets can easily become trapped in a 'no pay, low pay' cycle of temporary jobs (see Giddens, 2000). While workfare is principally just, living in Nova and being consigned to work in Gemini Park resulted in what was effectively a slave mode of production. Young adults describe Nova's workfare merry-go-round, involving years and for some people decades of cyclical employment and unemployment. Young people's accounts of the workfare merry-go-round also underline how a consumer lifestyle now defines today's work ethic. Higher education qualification and private pension schemes have both been promoted over the past 25 years as access to a consumer lifestyle. In Chapter 1, I show how a consumer lifestyle is a private existence, constituted through a circadian cycle of desire and satisfaction. A society in which lifestyle is valorised over the life of a community is one reason why the body time of the consumer society stands as such a contrast to the social time young people represent in these pages. All of the young people I met survived by believing in a collective work ethic, creating a community where young people earned respect among themselves. The tragedy was that young people faced exclusion because mainstream British culture is now defined by consumption, the antithesis to the work ethic that bound Nova as a community.

Jock Young (1999) refers to an increasingly exclusive society, and young people's accounts of exclusion in this study often stemmed from a need to exclude. Chapter 1 describes how exclusivity is defined in a consumer society through the consumption of crime. Living in poverty is today seen through television and computer screens as entertainment, such is the nature of the medium. In a consumer society such as ours, poverty is also the negative or excrement in a cycle of seduction and satisfaction that defines the consumer lifestyle. This cycle is sustained through communications, the crosshairs of the consumer society: through them images of community become objects of hatred and desire to justify a society in which consumption is an end in itself. The masquerade of crime is defined by the 'war on terror', a war in which the human face of one community has been criminalised to secure our freedom to consume. Economic crime is subject to the same process: the realities of living in poverty and surviving together described by young people here is now an image, for most people, of gangs and anti-social behaviour.

Outline

Out of Sight begins by describing how thinking about crime became interwoven into Britain's consumer society. Young people then describe in their own words the consequences of that process: a chaotic and violent social world overshadowed by crime, drug abuse and desperation. The key to understanding the often-inexplicable process of ghettoisation that young people describe in this study is the closure of the Project. This is why the event is the foundation of this study. I spent a year with a group of 30 young adults aged between 18 and 30 in Nova, gradually getting to know people and listening to individual experiences of exclusion. This process began in Nova's main shopping precinct at the Project, a drop-in centre where young people went each weekday to look for a way off the workfare carousel. Chapter 2 describes the Project and its importance for the young adults I met. In interviews I conducted with young adults at the Project just before it closed, each person describes a place free from suspicion and discrimination. In Chapter 2, I also describe going to the Project, where I listened to young adults talk about searching for a better job, and a normal life free from the stigma of crime.

Exclusion, at school and in Nova's local economy, meant that many young people had grown up imprisoned within the area; the majority of young adults I met had not been outside of Ford apart from school day trips. For many, the only holiday young people had been on was while at school, and then usually for just a day. Workers at the Project would do anything they could to provide a break away from Nova, even for just a few hours. Chapter 2 ends by describing the effect the closure of the Project had on young adults.

Chapter 3 describes the Precinct, a close network of streets around Nova's main shopping arcade. Conditions are very poor in the Precinct and young people are most concentrated there. Chapter 3 is an account of how young people survive the poverty and terrible living conditions that characterise the area, and explores the relations between work and crime in 'the life' of the Precinct. Young adults I met at the Project describe living in the Precinct in their own words, and of coping with debt, cold and hunger, whether people are in work or unemployed. The Precinct is described as a private prison, a place where a sense of confinement and desperation multiplied after the closure of the Project. The economic realities of being excluded also became worse: the Project had closed at the start of winter and young people describe trying to survive on a minimum wage or state benefits. It was during those winter months that I gained an insight into the culture of community young people shared to maintain a sense of hope and self-respect.

Chapter 4 focuses on the meaning of 'the life' for young people, how individuals maintained respect living 'the life', and how living as a community resulted in continuing exclusion. If anything, 'the life' was the decision to live and work on your own terms. Young people describe maintaining respect 'workin' for yourself' and 'findin' an earner'; a culture built around constant innovation young people lead to survive the death associated with temporary jobs, benefits poverty and debt. 'The life' enabled young adults to maintain hope in the future, working free from the workfare merry-go-round that characterised Gemini Park. Without the representative social space that was the Project, 'the life' meant being exposed to consumer society, as an enemy within it. Even though young people were hard working and resourceful, living in Nova meant being denied financial services because of the stigma that surrounded the estate. Young people describe the importance of respect and self-respect as protection against the consumer society.

Chapter 4 concludes by depicting what happened when young people were unable to maintain self-respect and lost hope in the face of exclusion. This chapter covers the winter months of my fieldwork, the most harrowing time when I saw young people trying to maintain self-respect. Continually eroding young people's self-confidence were the stigma of crime and the impossibility of gaining skills and qualifications that could secure a permanent job. That sense of exposure only underlined the importance of the Project as a social space interwoven into the public life of the estate.

The closure of the Project was felt throughout Nova, even among residents who rarely went there. As the Project closed, I met older residents who were attempting to build a new social space, one that could address an experience common to all residents: educational disadvantage. Recession and exclusion had not only broken the connection between school and work for young people. When the factories around Nova closed at the start of the 1980s, older residents who worked in Ford's manufacturing industries were left with skills that were no longer required. Chapter 5 charts the battle to build a new Project. Residents involved in that process and young people who used the Project describe the difficulties of trying to gain skills and qualifications while trying to survive in a low-paid, insecure labour market. I also show how outside agencies translated the realities of Gemini Park's workfare merry-go-round as apathy on the part of residents themselves to acquire new skills. What followed on the ground was a struggle between local residents and outside agencies to create what eventually became Gateways: a local education and employment-training centre. Community groups were able to make Gateways a facility that represented the problems faced in Nova's local economy.

Chapter 6 describes how residents were given that power following a change in policy and society. Gateways' success was aided by the election of the Labour government in 1997, a moment when people generally started to believe in society. In Nova, that optimism resulted in the building of a new shopping arcade, after years of trying to persuade businesses back into Nova. Then, one year into the new millennium, that feeling of optimism and opportunity vanished following the attacks on 11 September 2001. Chapter 6 ends by identifying how, following the 'war on terror', the idea of community once again became demonised as a threat to society.

At the heart of young people's experiences of exclusion were the images of crime imposed on their poor community. Chapter 7 is a retrospective on young people's history of exclusion; how the realities of poverty described by young people in Nova have been steadily eclipsed by images of crime, in the news, on television and in video games. The chapter shows how crime has become an inexplicable and necessary threat in the consumer society. I describe how communication technologies, including the consumption of television and the press, convert young people's experiences of living in poverty into an entertainment based around crime.

Chapter 1

A mugger's paradise

This study begins by identifying the context for young people's experiences of exclusion: Britain's consumer society. I show how a consumer lifestyle gains its definition thinking about crime. I also pinpoint how communications – television, personal computers and mobile technologies – screen out poverty by allowing consumers to imagine poor people as criminal. But first I want to describe the physical set on which the masquerade of crime is played out. This chapter charts the physical creation of Britain's consumer society, specifically the redevelopment of cities into theme parks organised around the pursuit of a consumer lifestyle.

The dominant explanation as to why crime persists is that Britain's cities contain communities where people, including families, are intolerant of work. The idea of an underclass has no bearing on people's experiences of poverty, nor is it intended as an explanation for crime. Instead, this is the masquerade of crime in a consumer society. It is consumed by people in a landscape where everything appears available, including work.

The unusual suspects

Even though crime has been a reality of the industrial city for three centuries, thinking about crime is embedded in the consumer society. Crime's function in defining a consumer lifestyle links back to the transition from a manufacturing to service economy in many cities (see A. Young, 1996; Lea, 2002). For many people this meant an end to earning money through production and a move to a working life organised around making money from other people; through services provided to others either locally or in other parts of the globe. Because many people chose to operate this way in order to live a consumer lifestyle, the result is that other people appear as objects: characters in a theme park. Since the start of the 1980s, consumer industries have remade cities, applying one standardised landscape. Gemini Park is one piece of that, a series of geometrically organised ornamental sheds built in the 1980s along Ford's border. Throughout this study, young adults describe 'the life' of poverty people are forced to lead in Nova because of the nature of work in the local economy and the perception consumers in Ford have about people living in council estates. As a consumer society, Ford is a microcosm of the world we now live in, divided between individual lifestyles and communities forced to survive in poverty.

Everyone I spoke to in Nova described exclusion as a dialectic experience, of segregation within and from school as a result of the stigma surrounding the children of Nova. After being expelled or discouraged from staying on, young people described being confined to Gemini Park by workfare policies designed to get young people into work. Later, young people describe the difficulties of trying to gain skills and qualifications while being forced to work unsocial hours and for minimum wages. The circle of exclusion was completed when young people tried to work together outside of Nova's local service economy; working together, all became demonised as a gang.

Working poor

The significance of exclusion in the consumer society stems from the changing nature of work over the past 30 years and its effect on people's perception of society. When one looks at contemporary culture, people with a degree of affluence do not aspire to live as part of a community. The consumer society is defined by what Jameson (1998) describes as a perpetual present: each day organised around a circadian cycle or body time of seduction and consumption (see Adam, 1995). The result is a society made up of images or objects, instead of social relations, outside of which are poor communities such as Nova.

In Britain today, poverty is the antithesis to a consumer lifestyle because work, for many people, no longer has a social meaning. In Nova, people still believe in work because for the past 30 years poverty has stalked the estate. In the following chapters, young people describe searching for money to buy food and pay for utilities and growing up in families facing the exact same hardships. Because labour has always been the only way to survive poverty, the continuance of poverty and exclusion explains why a work ethic remains so important in Nova. Work is the foundation for the community young people describe in the coming chapters, of 'earning' to gain respect and self-respect within their community. Linden, my main sponsor in Nova whom I introduce in Chapter 2, described the importance of work for everyone living in what remains a very poor community: 'See, everyone I know is unemployed but there's one group of people that are unemployed that just do nothin'. Sit around all day, fuckin' in front of the telly. And there's lads that I know that get up and go to work.'

For almost all of the 30 young people I met, 'working is a value in its own right, a noble and ennobling activity' (Bauman, 1998: 5). Yet the realities of work in Nova's local service economy are temporary jobs and incomes that only create poverty. Young people explained how employers in Ford have a negative attitude to people from Nova, an attitude that stems from the belief that Nova exists as a culture of crime. This study concludes with an examination of the idea that poor communities are inherently criminal. My concern here is how Ford was gradually divided between an affluent consumer society and poor communities.

Residents I spoke to who were born before the 1970s described how Ford's culture used to be socially progressive. Andy, a youth worker who I introduce in Chapter 2, described 'a buzz around the place' when Ford itself was at the centre of the post-war boom. Young people I met in Nova were children at that time, and grew up when Nova's local economy collapsed. After the recession, many described how Nova's social fabric disintegrated under the weight of mass unemployment: also, how within Ford, residents were gradually perceived as a collective danger. For many young people I spoke to that process began at school during the 1980s, when Nova began to experience mass unemployment. Many of the young adults I spoke to described being stigmatised at school for belonging to a community responsible for its own downfall. Jimmy, who I introduce in Chapter 2, described his own experience at Greaves, Nova's feeder secondary school, 'see at Greaves, it was like two sides of a fence. Those who went to the school were either from Greaves Park or Nova. But the kids from Greaves Park were middle class. See if you lived in Nova, the teachers looked down on you; they never gave you a chance. After the third year, I stopped goin'.' Greaves Park is a residential area neighbouring Nova.

Growing up in a poor community

Nearly all the young adults in Nova talking about growing up described a feeling of belonging to Nova. Yet, this was the 1980s, when class was felt to be at odds with a burgeoning free market society. Anthony Giddens (1991: 197) identifies how, to survive de-industrialisation, economies began to require societies of individuals: 'Market-governed freedom of individual choice becomes an enveloping framework of individual self-expression.' People living in areas worst affected by de-industrialisation, such as social housing estates, were unable to be part of the consumer society. Instead, as young people describe later, being part of a community was the only way to survive. This is why, in the consumer society, life appears split between a consumer lifestyle and poor communities.

Nova was built on a belief in community. Many of Nova's first residents had migrated to Ford, often with nothing but a suitcase, so people had to get on to survive. Steve, a close friend of Jimmy who I also introduce in Chapter 2, told me how his parents, like many of the young adults I know in Nova, migrated to Ford.

> Steve: Yeah, I grew up there. Me mum and dad are from Ireland and they moved here, to Nova. That's it, I was born in Ford.
> RM: Nova was the first area they came to?
> Steve: That's it; they never lived anywhere else after that.

In Nova, culture continues to be defined by a collective belief that people can overcome poverty, and, listening to residents of all ages, that feeling also characterised Ford up until the 1980s. Ford's burgeoning manufacturing economy was the reason why many people came to the city. The fact that people had migrated to the city, often from other countries, meant that being part of a community was vital. People and families from Ireland, the Caribbean, Poland, the Asian subcontinent, Eire, Scotland, Wales and other areas of England all moved to Nova during the post-war boom in the 1950s. Like the formation of a constellation, Nova was created by people with one overriding desire, for a better life in Ford. Then at the end of the 1970s, when most of Ford's factories closed, the city's peripheral social housing estates, of which Nova is the largest, experienced economic collapse. As the public life of estates such as Nova became eclipsed by poverty, unemployment, crime and violence, it seemed as though the rest of Ford retreated into a private culture of consumption.

Through the looking glass

Growing up during the 1970s, the idea of society seemed to decline in parallel with the disintegration of Fordism (see Gellner, 1983). Recession had real consequences on society: as the cost of living rose and production levels slumped, unemployment, especially long-term unemployment, rose sharply. In many areas including Ford, the problems stemmed from an over-concentration of manufacturing industries. When manufacturing collapsed in Britain at the end of the 1970s, it was inevitable that heavily industrial cities such as Ford would experience the brunt of recession.

11

In the first three years of the 1980s, the region lost 319,000 jobs, or 14.3 per cent, again the highest loss compared with any other region in the area. By February 1983, there were 46 unemployed adults for every vacant job in the region – a higher number than in any other region. In April 1983, Ford City Council estimated 39,000 people were claiming unemployment benefit, a rate of 16 per cent, which was higher than the rates in several areas with Development Area status, such as Merthyr Tydfil, North Tyneside and Dunfermline. By the time of the next recession in 1989–91, Ford's Economic Development Unit predicted a net loss of 7,000 jobs between 1991 and 1993. Once again, many of these jobs went from what remained of the city's manufacturing base. After 1991, most major manufacturing firms in Ford made further redundancies. In August 1991, a large vehicle production factory announced 1,490 redundancies while Ford's last remaining colliery closed. As with the recession of the late 1970s, subsequent slumps had a disproportionate effect on already economically deprived regions such as Ford. Alongside other regions where manufacturing sustained whole communities, such as the north of England and parts of Wales, levels of poverty and unemployment here remained disproportionately high. Worst affected were social housing developments such as Nova that had been purposely built to supply factories with labour (see Power, 1993, 1997; Morris, 1995).

Unemployment has always been a feature of industrialisation: the problem in Britain is that we live in a society that grew accustomed to consumption during the 1960s. This was why the global economic crisis of the 1970s had such a profound effect on British society along with other affluent societies of the post-war period. To prevent social disintegration, former industrial economies across Europe and North America had to sustain consumer demand even though goods that had characterised the post-war boom – from cars to domestic appliances – were now too costly to produce. Many succeeded by transforming cities into a commodity through the creation of retail parks and shopping malls, mainly to try to attract tourism and business investment. As a result the urban landscape of many cities was redrawn. The production of goods sold in cities now occurred in other parts of the world, though concept design and service industries remained. As young people describe in the following chapters, what followed was the steady disappearance of working-class culture from now post-industrial cities such as Ford. The city's transition to a post-Fordist economy meant that factory jobs were replaced by what young people I met refer to later as 'shit work'.

In many former industrial areas such as Ford, labour demand divides between highly skilled specialist industries, such as finance and telecommunications. Usually to maintain these industries there has also been a proliferation of 'bad jobs' (see Sassen, 1997). Lash and Urry (1994: 12–30) describe the creation of 'core' industries in their study on the creation of Britain's post-industrial economy:

> This information-saturated, service-rich, communications-laden core represents a major shift from the older order's central cluster of Fordist industries. It is in this new core, and not in the restructured older manufacturing sectors, that the most significant processes of flexible specialisation, localisation, and globalisation are developing.

Alongside the development of this core has been a growth in hotel and catering trade, office work, leisure time and entertainment, service trades and commerce, cleaning and maintenance. These ancillary sectors are characterised by jobs that are labour intensive and require few qualifications, are badly paid and offer no career prospects (Benassi, Kazepov and Migione, 1997). They also characterised Nova's local economy; for example, in a study carried out by Ford City Council in 1992, researchers interviewed 300 local residents, 73 of whom were employed. The nature of the jobs held by the 73 (33 men and 40 women) gives a picture of employment opportunities in the area and the skills necessary for these jobs. Firstly, compared with other areas of Ford, Nova residents were under-represented in managerial and professional occupations and over-represented in service occupations such as care assistance and kitchen and bar staff. Although almost as high a proportion of women worked as men, the survey found that many of these jobs were part-time and poorly paid, such as cleaning, school meals assistance and care assistance. Respondents were also asked how long they had worked in their present occupation. One in eight workers had been in their current occupation for less than a year.

Being poor in an affluent society

Changes in the nature of work in Ford have led to a radical shift in the nature of work and poverty. From a city where the bulk of the working population was employed in manufacturing, de-industrialisation meant that many people had to specialise, often through providing services to others. Others were lucky, working in so-called 'core' industries such as teaching, local governance and administration (see Kumar, 1984). This is one reason why Ford appears such divided city, carved up into sites of consumption, residential districts and socially excluded communities. However, the division now appears to be essential to the city economy: creating labour markets where jobs prevent people from breaking even. This is how the young people I met define poverty, a condition I experienced myself when I worked for three months in Nova's local economy.

Gemini Park, a retail park built during the 1980s on the edge of Ford, characterises the workfare merry-go-round young people describe in the following chapters. This open-air shopping mall was intended to regenerate Nova's local economy after the recession of 1980–1. At the centre of Gemini Park is a ring road: on the left, a collection of anonymous office buildings practically invisible next to the gaudy retail park on the right. Even though the area itself looks completely familiar, the social divisions that operate there are as bad as those described by Frederic Engels (1845), Charles Booth (1889–91) and George Orwell (1937) in their accounts of poverty during the industrial period. Because of the way Gemini Park is organised, as a world of consumption, the extremes of poverty and wealth are invisible.

People I met from Nova who work in Gemini Park lived in poverty because no one could earn enough money to live. However, because Gemini Park's service industries literally dress people as characters, no one sees this. The retail side of Gemini Park is open 24 hours, though consumers rarely see the system required to make that possible. During my fieldwork, I worked at Anderson's, a large supermarket on the perimeter of Nova. Anderson's forms part of Nova's local labour market. There I, like everyone else, was required to wear an outfit that, in its design, gave the impression that I was a service provider: black tie, white shirt, black trousers, shoes and a nametag. Everyone had to appear impeccably dressed with just two outfits, so you continually had to wash one while wearing the other. This was just one of numerous hardships people endured working in Anderson's that together resulted in incomes less than state benefits. Depending on people's age, employees earned approximately £3 to £4 an hour. I earned just over £400 a month and after rent and utilities found it difficult to find money for food. That was only after working at Anderson's for three months. Young people described working in these industries after leaving school at 16, often because teachers assumed young people I met were either lazy or incapable.

All that remained was Gemini Park, which typifies Britain's urban regeneration, an edge city made up of large multinational retail stores and anonymous hi-tech industries. Most financial businesses are call centres or administration facilities for leading high-street banks. The jobs available in both sectors are radically different. In Gemini Park, the majority of work available in superstores is very low-paid and often temporary. Jobs usually involved working as checkout operators or maintaining stock supplies for customers. The financial service industries usually employ people with forms of knowledge denied to Nova's residents: programming skills and software production. Many of the people who work in this sector were graduates and came from other parts of Ford or from outside the city itself. However, these glaring inequalities are invisible because of the way the world within Gemini Park is designed (see Picture 1, p. 3).

Nova's local service economy

Gemini Park is an urban redevelopment aimed at a consumer society: a cultural enterprise symptomatic of the McDonaldisation of Britain's post-industrial cities during the 1980s. Based on the success of the restaurant chain, McDonaldisation became a blueprint for urban regeneration in North America and Europe. In the case of Ford, it seemed that local areas with high rates of unemployment were identified. Then the local landscape was re-created to look rural, in an attempt to eradicate any sign of Ford's industrial past. Completed in 1985, Gemini Park has helped beautify Ford's southern edge, covering over the derelict landscape and literally obliterating Nova itself from the horizon. Once shoppers began to flock in on a weekly basis, Gemini Park then became Nova's local economy, albeit a cosmetic one. The problem in Ford is that most people are living on average incomes leaving companies to chase demand. To ensure everything available is not only affordable but also abundant, employees are paid minimum wages and with little prospect of promotion or increased remuneration.

Seen in a historical context, McDonaldisation is more than just urban regeneration. George Ritzer (2004) describes how the shift towards a mass consumer society has had a profound effect on the lives of affluent people. Ritzer (2004: 2) describes how, 'McDonaldisation affects not only the restaurant business, but also education, the criminal justice system, health care, travel, leisure, dieting, politics, the family, religion and virtually every other aspect of society'. Because the goal is to enable people to consume habitually once society is structured by the rules of McDonaldisation, it starts to consume itself.

To appreciate how poverty is consumed in retail parks, we need to understand how time is constructed. Consumer time involves looking, selecting and purchasing in places that look alike no matter where they are. Moreover, when one looks at the average consumer lifestyle, the laws of McDonaldisation potentially determine every aspect of existence. First, our existence, like McDonald's, is efficient: 'consumers are hungry and need to be full' and the company achieves that in the fastest possible way. Second is what Ritzer (2004) describes as 'calculability' where everything – time, money, product – coheres to strict measurements. Third is predictability: every McDonald's product tastes the same and every McDonald's worker looks the same in a worldwide operation consisting of 30,000 outlets in 119 countries. Finally is the control: of workers, food, drinks, light, air.

In a consumer society, people define their lives as reflection of themselves, which is why the consumer side of Gemini Park was built to function as a scrapbook of images: a village clock tower, mock rustic architecture and hanging baskets filled with flowers that never fade. This is why within Gemini Park nothing seems real: none of its buildings arose over time or in harmony with the local environment, as Nova's public amenities have. Gemini Park took over a year to construct, designed as a pastiche of rural America. As a retail park, no one appears to share that fantasy, or attempts to build a community around consumption; instead, everyone walks oblivious of one another. At five o'clock and at weekends many of the people employed in Gemini Park's business district go to the Cotton Club. The place itself echoes the rest of Gemini Park, what Baudrillard (1988: 143–4) describes as a digital space involving 'the meticulous reduplication of the real'. Inside you are in Old Orleans: red and white striped table cloths, free shots of Bourbon, and Dixieland Jazz. The Cotton Club has an extended bar and closes early in the morning. Many of the young professionals who worked in Gemini Park were regular customers and would spend most weekends there.

I went to the Cotton Club, and most of the young affluent clientele dressed in what seemed like a costly replica of the dress code young people in Nova lived by: sportswear, trainers, caps and woollen hats. During the early months of my fieldwork, Jason and Chris, who I introduce in Chapter 2, had obtained application forms from the Cotton Club and asked if I would act as a referee. Working in the Cotton Club, alongside working in Anderson's, means working in poverty while potentially being subsumed in a dialectical process. Judging by the way people dressed at the Cotton Club, customers appeared to be seduced by images of socially excluded young people. In Chapter 4, I argue that such manifestations of consumer culture help mask the master relationship the Cotton Club's clientele have with the people of Nova. Yet this was only made possible by the creation of Gemini Park, a theatrical set where the masquerade of crime is played out. Workers at the Cotton Club were dressed in identical outfits designed to blend into the Old Orleans feel and atmosphere of the restaurant. Like other retail outlets in the area, consumers could escape from the society and poverty surrounding Gemini Park, simply by travelling into it (see Picture 1, p. 3).

Ordinary world

Going to the Cotton Club felt like being part of a degenerate culture, possibly the effect of the consumer-orientated urban regeneration initiative generally. As retail parks smoothed away recently demolished factories to sustain consumption, consumers themselves began to use crime as a way of making sense of the consumer lifestyle that characterised the 1980s. This is why young people in this study do not talk about crime as a part of their lives. As members of a community, young people experience the world through Nova, instead of an individual world of possessions.

This consumer society seems antithetical to the world of community that young people described, and the design of areas like Gemini Park set the stage for those divisions. Changes in urban space such as the creation of retail parks and shopping malls allow consumers to inhabit an unreal world, and to believe that people living in poverty are a threat. The belief is constituted through media technologies such as the Internet, televisions, telephones and cars, which give consumers mastery over society. Chapter 4 describes how human existence becomes an entertainment when seen through these forms of communication technology. Images, by their nature, are objects even when they depict people. Yet, paradoxically, these technologies allow consumers to be more socially connected than ever before. However, as a society, each consumer exists alone since all we are able to perceive are fragmented images. These images include the people we love, including our families. Because all these people appear as images, no one is real to consumers. People seem real because, as in Disneyland, we can place ourselves into the fantasy world. Communication technologies give us mastery over everything we see and hear, though only in a preconditioned consumer environment. Like the corporations that make up Gemini Park, Disneyland and Disney itself is an industry that profits from making us feel good, and making us feel good requires a vast empire. Disney's stores are spread throughout the developed world while its factories in developing countries make goods for a fraction of their retail price. Yet, in Disneyland as in Gemini Park, the human face of poverty created by the company is masked.

The masquerade society we now live in is made of images; a consumer imagining a world that feels real even though what we are feeling is individual, predicated by our own desires. Even entering Disney stores typifies the consumer society; even entering as members of a group, reality disappears because we all become lost in a private fantasy. Even though each character is universally recognisable, recognition takes place in the mind's eye and at different speeds. In the case of the gangster, because each person constructs their own fantasy in different ways, not only does time become distant, it is impossible to distinguish where we are in a world with no 'peculiarities of place' (Byers, 1998: 247). This is why, as I show in Chapter 4, communities of young people living in poor urban areas have become globally recognisable as delinquent. Ford, like many other cities, resembles Disneyland, where most of the population exists in a private fantasy that spills out into the city itself. Why we feel so uncertain in these places is because everything and everyone come at a price.

Belonging to a community, living there, and being with other people, we are subject to human nature, the pain of rejection, failure, getting things wrong. By contrast, a consumer lifestyle only creates a world of individuals: 'One listens to reggae, watches a western, eats McDonalds food for lunch and local cuisine for dinner, wears Paris perfume in Tokyo and retro clothes in Hong Kong; knowledge is a matter for TV games' (Lyotard, 1985: 76). Lyotard (1985) describes a society of individuals caught in a crystal maze, of cars, planes, malls and leisure centres. The consumer society, however, is not a society but a masquerade involving collections of silent characters to produce a world where poverty appears as a culture of crime. Nor is the consumer society progressive. In the following chapters, young people describe how the consumer society around Nova is dependent on people living in poverty and under the stigma of crime. This dialectical process may explain why young people's experiences of poverty seemed so intractable.

Crime as status

During Britain's industrial period, cities were places of production and work, visually very different from the landscapes of pleasure and consumption we see today. Working-class people manufactured goods, while the city itself was organised by a bourgeoisie, resulting in a productive, albeit unequal, relationship. Marx (1818–83) and Engels (1845) described how the city's working class generated wealth working in factories owned and run by a burgeoning middle class. Creating its own exclusive territories within the city meant those with wealth could maintain a middle-class lifestyle. Boundaries existed – usually legal – to prevent working-class people from getting in. In the 'Great Towns' chapter of *The Condition of the Working Class in England*, Engels (1845) was one of the first sociologists to identify how people from different social backgrounds had to co-exist. In his account of Manchester, Engels (1845: 85) described 'an instinctive and tacit agreement' between different classes, as the social foundation for this industrial city. Listening to young people's accounts of exclusion in Nova, Ford's city culture was constituted through stigmatising poor communities. Given the antagonistic relationship between Nova and Gemini Park, that change had its roots in the urban regeneration of Ford into a consumer society.

To survive de-industrialisation many of Britain's cities became cultural enterprises, profiting from the sale of goods made in other parts of the world. This had a profound effect on class relations within former industrial cities such as Ford. From what had been an agreement between Ford's middle classes, status gradually became personalised. Firstly was the growth of higher education, which gradually became currency in the consumption of a consumer lifestyle. The use of communication technologies then replaced social capital as the mechanism through which people achieved status (see Bourdieu, 1984: 77). Today in many so-called 'core' industries, working relationships only take place in the canteen, if there is one (Lash and Urry, 1994). On a more fundamental level, people generally became less concerned with the social significance of work, more on what was available within the burgeoning world of leisure. Driving the post-industrial economy was consumption, and to sustain consumer demand cities were re-created into playgrounds.

Changes in the urban environment also reflected how the sight of poverty could potentially affect sales. One consequence of the serious social problems that arose during the recession of 1980–1 was an increasing anxiety about crime and an urban underclass that many believed to be emerging at that time (see Auletta, 1982; Murray, 1990). To ensure consumer spending at a time when many cities were disintegrating, initiatives such as Gemini Park were built, in such a way that poverty and industrial decline became unnoticeable (see Foster, 1999). Over the past 30 years, the public places of cities have been gradually paved over to appear as one (see Charley, 1995). Based on my research in Nova and subsequent studies I have conducted, the 'privatisation' of cities has also radically affected the ways in which people from different economic backgrounds experience one another (Dixon, Levine, and McAuley, 2004; see Wakefield, 2004).

Welfare and workfare

Many young adults in Nova described being excluded as a social as much as an economic experience, of being perceived as an object of suspicion, particularly in semi-public places such as Ford city centre and Gemini Park. In Chapter 3, young people describe being perceived as anti-social for congregating together, also as an economic threat to retail businesses through 'hanging around'. The danger that surrounded Nova's young adults seemed to suggest that, in a consumer society, people are only respected through being able to participate as active consumers.

For J. K. Galbraith (1992) the idea that communities of poor people constitute cultures of crime is 'deeply functional' in a consumer society. In *The Culture of Contentment*, Galbraith (1992) describes how the image of poor communities as criminal gives an affluent society purpose. For Galbraith (1992: 18–26), the culture of contentment can be defined by four determinants. First is 'the affirmation that those who compose it are receiving their just deserts'. Second, 'short-run public action . . . is always preferred to protective long term action'. Third, 'the state is seen as a burden'. Finally, 'we are tolerant of great differences in income'. Using a term that became a prototype to 'the gang', Galbraith (1992: 31) argues that the 'urban underclass' created by the transition to a global economy: 'is integrally part of a larger economic process and, more importantly, it serves the living standard and the comfort of the more favoured majority'. Low-paid jobs with short-term contracts are necessary to sustain Ford's economy as many companies leave once they have found a cheaper source of labour (see Sassen, 1997; Benassi, Kazepov and Migione, 1997). Alternatively, as in the case of retail facilities, companies themselves were taken over by larger multinationals that then outsourced labour from other areas.

People I met in Nova, young and old, described how the estate became enslaved once Gemini Park was built. During the 1980s, local people were expected to work there for a minimum wage or face the withdrawal of state benefits, even when employers refused residents secure jobs. Many of the young people I met chose to live and survive together and subsequently became stigmatised as a culture of crime by youth agencies. The result is what I describe as the workfare merry-go-round, a seemingly endless cycle of temporary employment and unemployment. As a policy implemented during the 1980s, workfare means that welfare recipients work, 'be prepared for work', or have benefits withdrawn altogether. Because unemployment in Nova ran between 40 and 80 per cent of the adult population at the start of the 1980s, the policy affected every working adult, whether employed or not (Corbett, 2003: 113). In Chapter 7, I argue that economic and social policies designed to target young people living in deprived urban areas are based on a principle of evil. Their implementation, as the next chapter identifies, usually resulted in young people being seen as depraved and subsequently being treated inhumanely. In Chapter 2, young people describe working in Gemini Park as a degrading experience: trying to survive on £100 per week while being stigmatised for working in menial jobs by customers and employers. Often it seemed young people were defined in those terms to justify and sustain Ford's consumer culture. Like the consumption of goods, this was a circadian process beginning with a desire for young people living in areas such as Nova to fail. Then, when individuals lose hope, and fall prey to crime and drug abuse, I believe that many people free from the realities of poverty and exclusion gain a sense of satisfaction.

Poverty, culture and crime

Oscar Lewis's (1976) work is central to the idea that a culture of crime begins in a community where poverty and unemployment are high. Lewis's (1976) 'culture of poverty' thesis is that when communities experience unemployment, families develop criminal tendencies. This culture of crime then becomes self-perpetuating over time: 'by the time slum children are aged six or seven they have usually absorbed the basic values and attitudes of their subculture and are not psychologically geared to take full advantage of the changing conditions or increased opportunities that may occur in their lifetime' (Lewis, 1968: 110).

In a consumer society, Lewis's (1976) thesis clearly has a logical circularity: in a world of plenty, poverty is a matter of individual or family responsibility. The empirical basis of Lewis's (1976) work came from his fieldwork in the urban slums of Mexico and Puerto Rico. His thesis, however, can be traced back to the Chicago School of urban sociology and the work of Robert Park (1925), in which natural areas generate their own culture, which then becomes self-perpetuating over time. Yet, while Park (1925), like many working within the Chicago School, emphasised the influence of wider factors including racism and other forms of discrimination, Lewis (1976) focused on the lifestyles of people living in poor urban areas. Unlike the Chicago School, who were working in the middle of the depression, Lewis (1976) was conducting his research on poor communities at a time when North America was at the centre of a post-war boom. By this point America, and Europe soon after, had become what Debord (1967) described as the 'society of the spectacle', a world where everything and everyone had been reduced to a commodity (see Barthes, 1972).

When one looks at the moral panic surrounding Mods and Rockers in Britain during the early 1960s, it seemed Debord's (1967) society of the spectacle was beginning to define modern British culture. That is, within a burgeoning consumer society images of deviance were starting to function as mass entertainment. Lewis's (1976) culture of crime thesis is so effective because, within the context of a consumer society, consumers can objectify poverty. As I have already suggested, a consumer lifestyle, what is principally a degenerate existence, can only make sense contrasted with images of community or collective action. The value of images of poverty is that they have what Baudrillard (1988) describes as a destiny, because the images are empty, or signify a lack of value, people can seduce themselves into believing *they* are real.

When the consumer society was in crisis at the start of the 1980s, Lewis's (1976) 'culture of poverty' thesis became the foundation for extensive social policy through Europe and America (Greenstein, 1991), particularly in policy on housing. John Lea (2002: 86) describes how the culture of poverty thesis was implemented in social policy after the Second World War: 'Relocation to new housing estates would break down the old community norms through new forms of living space in flats based on the nuclear family rather than collective community.' Lea (2002: 87) also identifies how the culture of crime thesis influenced criminal justice policy: 'Appropriate therapeutic regimes to assist the process of "growing out of crime" could be imaginatively devised.' *Crime and Modernity* (2002) identifies the effect the culture of poverty thesis had on criminology at a time when modernity itself was in crisis. As British society became a mass consumer society, economic crime, even though rates were diminishing, was becoming integrated into consumer culture: the most graphic instance being the Great Train

Robbery (see Read, 1978). Like Lewis's (1976) work on poverty, mainstream criminological research on young people and crime, from the late 1950s until the present, has to be seen in the context of the affluent society. For instance, with the majority of his sample in full-time employment, Mays (1954, quoted in Roberts, 1987: 91) found that 'work was primarily a means of acquiring money to purchase the pleasures and enjoyments of the city'. For Parker (1974: 69), secure employment also enabled an easy transition into adulthood as jobs were 'easy come, easy go'. Like 'the lads', Parker's (1974: 67) 'Boys' would become adults through full-time work: 'They felt the role of adult was not far away; once they had a job and plenty of money to spend they could assume conspicuous consumption habits that would put the seal on their adulthood.' Reading research on youth crime during the post-war boom, studies seem to have pinpointed a tension between the proliferation of a consumer lifestyle and the transition from school to work.

The difference between now and the post-war boom is that for young people living in communities ravaged by de-industrialisation, there is no transition from school to work. During the post-war boom when Britain fulfilled Galbraith's (1985) definition of *The Affluent Society*, the collective transition from youth to adulthood was starting to disintegrate into a culture where consumption was an end in itself. In his ethnographic study on young people's transition from school to work, Downes (1966: 236) identified a sense of fatalism among working-class adolescents:

> What has been achieved ... is an opting-out of the joint middle- and skilled working-class value-system whereby work is extolled as a central life-issue, and whereby the male adolescent of semi- and unskilled origin is enjoined either to 'better himself' or 'accept his station in life'. To insulate themselves against the harsh implications of this creed, the adolescent in a 'dead-end' job, in a 'dead' neighbourhood, extricates himself from the belief in work as of any importance beyond the simple provisions of income, and deflects what aspirations he has left into areas of what have been termed 'non-work' (rather than leisure).

In *The Delinquent Solution*, Downes (1966: 134) identified a growing frustration with 'traditional' working-men's pubs and clubs and 'official' middle-class sponsored youth clubs predicated on a 'delinquent sub- culture pushing the legitimate values of "teenage culture" to their logical conclusion'.

Too much too young

Research on youth crime through much of the post-war period is characterised by an objectifying, distancing approach. Compared with the social upheavals experienced during the 1930s, at time when researchers themselves seemed to be much more involved in the social world of the city, by the late 1950s 'youth' and crime were beginning to be categorised as anti-social (see Park and Burgess, 1925; Polsky, 1971). My argument is that this context of a mass consumer society greatly affected researchers on young people and crime. At the heart of the post-war boom it must have seemed transparently obvious why young people became engaged in crime, because young people themselves did not have a sufficient work ethic. What was less obvious was the way in which consumerism was beginning to erode the importance of work for an increasingly contented affluent society. Sadly, when one looks at policies directed at anti-social behaviour, the idea of a culture or subculture of crime remains even when that world of full employment has disappeared. What also remains left out of the 'culture of crime' thesis is an acknowledgement that thinking about crime, alongside criminology itself, are now elements in a consumer lifestyle.

According to young people I met in Nova, crime is a matter of survival. Workfare and the chaos it imposes resulted in a breakdown in traditional family formations and trans-generational unemployment. Yet, throughout the 1980s, policy, influenced by the culture of crime thesis, literally pretended that work still had value in keeping young people out of crime. The conflict was manifest in the constant repackaging of the Youth Training Schemes (YTS) (see Williamson, 1997: 124). The workfare policy was implemented in force following the withdrawal of benefits for 16–17 year olds in 1988. By 1992, the British Youth Council (1992) estimated that 30,000 young adults each year still refused to participate in the YTS (see Craine, 1997).

Social exclusion

One of the reasons why the cultural explanation of crime appears logical is that it provides us with an objective explanation of the subjective experience of working for poverty. Today in criminological research young people and crime are explained through the imagery of the 'gang'. In *Youth Crisis: Growing Up in the High-Risk Society*, Nanette Davis (1999: 265) describes how the gang is the cause of poverty experienced by young people in deprived urban areas:

> Gang problems arise in American communities because of entren-
> ched poverty and few or no legitimate opportunities. They flourish
> in areas of high residential mobility and striking urban decay.
> 'Underclass' youth, those who are most economically and socially
> divided, are most likely to be attracted into gangs at an early age . . .
> The gang phenomenon reflects weak community, neighbourhood,

and family structure, wherein young people seek identity and social connections among street peers that may involve full-time criminal lifestyles.

Implicit in Davis's (1999) account is that the gang destroys the work ethic available to young people at school, as does belonging to a poor neighbourhood. Though again, the concept of gangs echoes Lewis' (1976) thesis, in that it provides a cultural explanation to what in Nova were deep-seated structural factors embedded in Britain's urban regeneration. The situation young people describe in Nova is that work creates poverty because residents generally were classified as a shipment of cheap labour during the 1980s. In addition, policy continues to remain influenced by cultural explanations such as 'gangs', and listening to young people's accounts in Nova, their application only seemed to sustain exclusion.

Why policy is important is that it gives our fears about young people and crime credibility. Young people in Nova described how the culture of crime thesis was applied the moment you started school, often because people living in Nova belong to a poor community. In 1992, Ford Council conducted a survey assessing the educational qualifications of Nova's working population. Of a random sample of 273 residents, 28 per cent had no formal qualifications and a third of 16–19 year olds sampled were without formal qualifications. The survey also shows how people in Nova continue to be disadvantaged in school and employment training. Over half of all households on an estate of 3,500 were in receipt of state benefits. Only 40 per cent of households had a car compared with 67 per cent nationally, while 43 per cent of households were without a telephone (compared with 13 per cent nationally).

Stitched up: exclusion at school

For all the young adults I spoke to, both primary and secondary school were perceived as the root of each person's experience of social exclusion. Many young adults I interviewed had left at or before the age of 16, or were required to leave. Many of the young adults I met in Nova felt they had been unable to gain or even aspire to qualifications because of a lack of understanding and encouragement from teachers. Primary and secondary school teachers were often outsiders, and were perceived by most interviewees as having a limited conception of what it was like growing up on the estate. It seemed that while many failed to appreciate that the jobs available in Nova's local economy only sustained poverty, others simply labelled children as delinquent. Listening to young people's accounts of exclusion, the process of exclusion each child was subject to at school seemed to operate at a more psychological level, compared with the social class divisions described by Engels (1845).

The likelihood of being poor during the industrial period was predicated on which family you were born into, or who you became. This was a trans-generational process whereby the availability of work gave everyone living in the industrial city the opportunity to earn a living for themselves and their families (see Thompson, 1968). I described above how the consumer society could only be preserved through the re-creation of cities into consumer cultures. The fact that Ford's poor communities were singled out in this process, the likelihood of experiencing exclusion in childhood and adolescence related directly to people's area of residence. This was one of the most detrimental consequences of de-industrialisation in the city, whereby unemployment affected generations of people in communities purpose designed to supply industry with labour. In addition, the options available to people growing up in such areas during de-industrialisation were limited even further if urban regeneration involved 'private property' developments such as Gemini Park (see Foster, 1999).

Compulsory youth training

All but two of the 30 young adults I spoke to described how they were faced with two options on leaving school, training schemes or service industry jobs in Gemini Park. Because training schemes and service industry jobs only paid minimum wages, all of the young people I met said they had to remain living in Nova, while undertaking what many described as 'shit work'. Many young people referred to the situation as a Catch 22: after the withdrawal of benefits for 16–18 year olds in 1986, young adults not 'participating' in post-16 education were compelled to take up a training programme (see Carlen, 1996; Pearce and Hillman, 1998). As a result, very few young people have the opportunity to obtain solid skills. Among the 30 young adults, only one, Hannah, successfully completed a vocational course as a dental technician after leaving school. Many other young adults I spoke to described how local employers used trainees as a cheap source of labour. Slim, a 17-year-old man I introduce in Chapter 2, described the work available to young people from Nova:

> Mechanic, leisure centre, factory work, fixin' bikes, dry cleaners in town, packin' crisps, bricklayin'. I either got sacked or laid off. I was happy doin' them but it was just the money, £35 a week. You've paid your mum a tenner (£10) and then you've gotta get a bus pass goin' to work and then you've got about £2 left to yourself at the end of it.

In Nova, and in other social housing areas along Ford's periphery, consumer developments seem to thrive on poor communities as a cheap, reusable labour supply. One must also acknowledge that areas such as Gemini Park supply a growing demand for what appears to be largely superfluous goods. As we demand infinite choice, this system can only operate by enslaving millions of people to poorly paid work. That occurs in the developing world, where global corporations exploit local populations to make the goods that fill retail outlets. Many developing countries are exploited as clothing manufacturers by many of the world's leading sportswear companies: UNICEF (2005) recently estimated that 210 million children aged between five and 15 are in full-time employment. In so-called developed countries, many post-industrial cities now function as service providers to these companies. Like Nova, social housing areas built to supply industry with labour now suffer high levels of unemployment. In addition, areas themselves are in close proximity to sites of consumption such as Gemini Park. Ford is now an outpost of this global network; distributing goods made in the developed world and providing services that ensure commodities circulate. Alongside children in the developing world, people in areas such as Nova are paid what is legally required and with no prospect of professional development.

Combined with workfare, the effect of the redesign of cities into consumer zones is that employment appears plentiful. According to figures from the Office for National Statistics, unemployment fell by 7,000 between June and August 2005 to 1.42 million. This leaves the number of people in work at a record high of 28.76 million, the highest total since records began in 1971 (Madouros, 2005). So why, when labour markets are experiencing a gap in applicants, do certain areas continue to suffer social problems such as unemployment, crime and victimisation? It can only be that people themselves are inherently criminal.

The value of crime in the consumer society has to do with its instantaneity: consumers, through the media, can believe poor people are the cause of crime in the blink of an eye. The concluding chapter of this study identifies how imagining crime has been made easier and more exciting with technology. I also show how in today's media-saturated consumer society, the screen has become an invisible boundary between affluence and poverty.

Working in a service economy

Ford's public places now form a crystal maze of consumption, and that world was made possible through the mass production and consumption of televisions, personal computers and mobile phones. The result is a personal world of communication technologies, through which thousands of people now exist. As commodities in a world of commodities, these devices allow people to live as a seduction between individual desires and the world before them. Listening to young people's accounts of exclusion, the transition to a private world of information seems to have speeded up the process of exclusion itself. As young people describe later, outsiders to the area 'immediately assume the worst' when confronted with a group of young residents.

Communications today give people mastery over the visual world. The nature of consumer culture suggests that many people choose to use that power to create a masquerade of crime, instead of engaging with other people susceptible to it. This is why, as I describe in the following chapter, very few studies are produced involving researchers' conversations with people living in poverty. Academics seem to prefer to be seduced by the image of the gang as an explanation for crime, instead of recording people's experiences of poverty. Working within higher education, I speak to many people employed as ancillary staff, who describe living in desperate situations. At the same time, people I work with pontificate about the need for social change while remaining oblivious to people around them. The situation young people describe in the following chapters highlights how the consumer society is simultaneously blind to poverty and seduced by crime.

Room 101

Living a consumer lifestyle requires wealth, which global financial institutions are now happy to provide people with, so long as individuals prove themselves to be secure investments. That means being committed to oneself, and having the freedom to invest in oneself. Ownership of property is the main method through which people achieve entry: signing a mortgage agreement, we become literally locked into our own existence. Like Winston Smith in George Orwell's (1949) *Nineteen Eighty-Four*, we are forced to confront our worst fear in room 101. Though ours is a room we have created for ourselves. We use communication technologies initially designed to sustain the global economy – even in the event of nuclear war – as a method of entertaining ourselves. As entertainment is all that remains in an affluent society such as ours, we become pornographers of our own existence, using images to create wallpaper communities.

Images have always been the medium through which we sustain a visual perception of the world. Looking, 'we believe that we see this reality before us as a solid structure in which every individual element has its assigned place, and in which its relation to all other parts is exactly determined. The fundamental character of all reality lies in this definite relationship.' Berkeley's (1709) theory on how we perceive the world remains precise, though today many people circumvent the intolerable through technology. Even though we still interact socially, technology makes everything into our own image. In purchasing technology, we gain mastery over our own perception. So, over time, using technology to experience the world means realities that cannot be mastered, such as human decay, are slowly pushed off the map of people's experience.

Inhabiting a city without communication technologies or today's saturated skyline meant that people living in poverty were part of everyone's life. In his research for *The Condition of the Working Class in England*, Engels (1845: 120) met and listened to people living with poverty, including Reverend Champney, a preacher in London's East End. Reverend Champney described the poverty endured by people living in the area because of unemployment:

> At the gates of all the London docks hundreds of the poor appear every morning in the winter before daybreak, in the hope of getting a day's work. They await the opening of the gates; and when the youngest and strongest and best known have been engaged, hundreds cast down by disappointed hope, go back to their wretched homes.

In the context of today's affluent society, Engels' (1845) account seems arcane; not only in the squalor endured but also in the sheer multitudes of people made poor by the industrial revolution. However, during the first four months of my fieldwork, I witnessed the same scenes of desperation and poverty each day at the Project.

Now people can escape these realities of poverty in retail parks, where every aspect of sensory perception is controlled, or simply by changing channel. We believe that such extremes of poverty are restricted to cities in the developing world. Not only are we separated from the present, but also from one another. In seeing images of crime without experiencing people's experiences of poverty, the relationship between both is broken; all we are left with are thieves and young single mothers. Seen alongside the transition to a consumer society that is all we see, as these are the characters we fear the most. Why most people fear crime relates to the way in which many of us work for ourselves to pursue a consumer lifestyle. In addition, those fears are justified through the way policy replicates crime, as a threat to avoid. In Chapter 7, I argue that policy on crime operates as a system of care for consumers, thereby sustaining this cycle of fear and suspicion.

Trying to gain an understanding of poverty and crime by consuming (and destroying) images only degrades our knowledge and people's experiences. To begin with, images of poverty displayed on screens and monitors are by definition objective. Added to that, media technologies are designed to achieve the most sophisticated representation possible. This is achieved through the speed at which images can be produced and received. Paul Virilio (1989) uses the analogy of modern warfare to describe how this occurs. The speed at which one army can survey the terrain greatly enables their ability to capture land from 'the enemy'. The same rule applies to representations of poverty and exclusion. Engels (1845) spent two years investigating the conditions he describes, conditions that can now be imagined in an instant. Rosalind Coward (1994) identifies how poverty was stylised in the media following the urban disturbances of the early 1990s: 'The 1990s image of the council estate, with its gangs of alienated youths, abandoned mothers and violent homes, drug dealing and drinking and violent crime, is an update of an earlier vision of the dark side of Britain's social landscape. Today's commentators speak in truly Dickensian terms.' The images Coward (1994) describes are objects, not people's subjective experience of living with poverty and its consequences. Even though Coward (1994) is criticising stylised representations of poverty, the passage remains a seductive explanation for crime. In a society driven by consumption, consuming the image of the council estate enough times, this cartoon strip gradually defines people's attitudes about the causes of poverty and crime.

Crime and consumption

Imagining crime enables us to remain consumers without having to reflect on the poverty consumption creates. If one surveys contemporary culture, especially television, crime has achieved value status: a superficial negative to justify positive consumption. Writing on the rise of consumerism, Lash and Urry (1994: 61) describe how, 'whole areas of lifestyle and consumer choices are freed up and individuals are forced to decide, to take risks, to bear responsibilities, to be enterprising consumers'. To adopt a consumer lifestyle, and for that to be effective, having principles can only limit the art of our own seduction. And because policy is subject to the consumer society, social ethics, such as recent debates on respect, have to appear as entities alone, no longer aspects of human subjectivity. In Nova, my research with young people reflected a community that everyone was subject to; if young people did not work, as a community, individuals would perish.

When one considers debates on anti-social behaviour and yob culture, morality is a commodity alongside every other commodity, to be consumed at election time. The consumer society is governed by what Lash and Urry (1994: 61) refer to as 'reflexive accumulation': people accumulate habitually to the point where we can no longer distinguish people from objects. This is the process whereby young people in groups become gangs; youth policy is not simply governmental but an interaction between consumers and state. With the creation of a mass consumer society at the start of the 1960s, social policy on young people was gradually packaged to cater to consumer demand. The process was perfected during the 1980s in Britain and the United States through the conception of an 'underclass', which was programmed into the consumer society; much like a virus (see Blackman, 1997; Alexander, 2001). Robbie, who I introduce in Chapter 3, described being subject to suspicion the moment he started attended primary school:

> But a lot of people out around 'ere, y'know the mums and dads and everythin', they said they shouldn't hang around with me. Don't hang around with him he'll get you in to trouble. But it really weren't that, y'know what I mean it was because I was bored; I never had anythin' to do. And the old bill like, all the time they were just always havin' a go. From an early age they knew me, from a very early age. I first got into trouble with the police when I was about ten, ten, or eleven.

Many community workers I spoke to in Nova told me that failing to listen to young people's experiences of exclusion and crime was the main reason why the relationship between both was so poorly understood. In a paper on the inability of researchers to understand the experience people face living in socially excluded communities, Janet Foster (2002) applies the term 'people pieces'. Foster (2002) identifies how the failure of research reflects the fact that little research is conducted in areas suffering from poverty and exclusion. As a concept, 'people pieces' is symbolic of the importance of sticking together. All of the young people I met saw their life and identity embedded in Nova, reflecting how everyone is subject to a community and a society: we all are. Yet, listening to young people's accounts of being excluded from the world outside of Nova, each person's experience reflects how excluding poor communities has become part of British culture.

Chapter 2

Nova

Nova is a patchwork of 4,000 council houses, low-rise flats and municipal squares, built in the early 1950s, like many of Britain's social housing estates, to accommodate labour for the post-war recovery (Power, 1993, 1997). The function of the estate explains why first-generation residents were migrants. For many people, visitors and residents, Nova's entrance is a big traffic junction off Ford's primary southern exit road. On the left is a line of eighteenth-century mining cottages: not preserved like some living museum but lived-in and dilapidated. The eight cottages, originally ten, were built around a colliery settlement, long since disappeared. Directly opposite are one of Nova's three takeaways – Fryday's – and a post office/off licence. At a distance, the junction resembles the beginning and end of an industrial revolution. The cottages and the takeaway also mark the entrance of Main Road, Nova's main route into and out of the estate. Winding along and down past residential houses, Main Road then starts to become populated by social housing constructions – houses, low-rise flats and municipal buildings. With their sandstone colouring and cornered shapes, every structure is in line with the undulating landscape. Only when you get to know people do you see how Nova's design and cohesion lies hidden behind cars too expensive to fix, crumbling plaster and barricaded properties beyond repair. At the centre of the road is a large primary school, visible behind big iron railings. After Nova Primary is another set of traffic lights, another takeaway, and The Cedars, one of two public houses on the estate. If you continue down the road, Nova ends at a third traffic junction. On the horizon beyond is Gemini Park, twinkling under tall clustered lights.

Nova's central traffic junction is a crossroads and Main Road is cut in two by Phoenix Avenue. Turning right and going north takes you into the more sparsely populated Nova Heights. South at the junction leads down into the Precinct, Nova's community centre. Taking either direction puts you on Phoenix Road and when I started my fieldwork, Phoenix Road's southern route went straight into Nova's original shopping arcade. The arcade resembled an ocean liner, its stern moored against a big grassy island. Standing in front of the island was The Hand Maiden – known informally as 'the Pub' – directly behind her, the Nova Centre, Nova's main community centre. Then there was the main arcade, spread out before both like an auditorium. If you stood in the Pub's car park, you stood before the Precinct's façade: a row of shops broken by two gaps where shops could have been in their place, two corridors, lined with railings, and behind them mostly barricaded shops. All that remains down these two alleys are the Precinct's floral arrangements, set out in large circular basins situated in differing sizes between the shops.

There was a time, older Nova residents said, when the Precinct was a safe and popular place to meet and shop. Until the end of the 1970s, there was even a cafeteria. During the recession of the early 1980s, however, the Precinct quickly became derelict and abandoned. Walking around the arcades you could see that the Precinct's original design was intended to provide a communal focal point on the estate with its pavement amphitheatres and floral terraces. Looking back, however, it seems that Nova's modernist planners failed to envisage the collapse of Ford's manufacturing economy. The Precinct's main arcade had been intended as a space where people could interact as a community. Then came the 1980s, and Nova disappeared under the brave new world of Gemini Park. What had been intended as the regeneration of the local economy resulted in the steady desertion of local businesses from a community felt to be unprofitable. Shop holders who did stay were often core businesses like the bakers and newsagents, but they found it impossible to compete against the multinationals who had moved in down the road.

The Precinct had been scheduled for demolition at the start of my fieldwork, yet four shops remained, an off-licence, a post office, a chemist and a mini-market. The only other buildings still functioning were a tiny municipal library and the Project, a drop-in centre. Both were almost invisible at the far end of the Precinct, at a distance from the shops.

The Project

When I started my fieldwork, I soon discovered that having somewhere to go in Nova, to meet friends and talk, is central to surviving poverty and exclusion. For Nova's young people, that place was the Project, a converted shop at the end of the arcade, where I met many of the young people who took part in this study. In this chapter, I introduce those I met and describe the importance of the Project as a haven from exclusion. It also describes the closure of the Project and its effect on young people's everyday lives.

When it was open, limited funds meant that the Project was free from the corporate identity that defines many youth centres: the freedom allowed young adults to make the Project their own. The Project itself was much smaller than the Nova Centre, made up of two rooms and a toilet. The Project's walls had mellowed through sunlight and nicotine, except the back wall covered in a colourful mural painted by young people. The mural depicted a day in the life of the Project, a couple playing cards, and the cards swirling into an arc around the people. Beneath the couple, an older man reads a newspaper and a group of young men and women play pool. The first time I went there, the mural was like a reflection of the day itself. At the centre of the main room was a young African-Caribbean man circling the table in brilliant white Reebok Heritage trainers, dispensing balls effortlessly. Everyone else sat and watched, along with Andy, his opponent, seemingly resigned to defeat. The only furniture was a collection of plastic school chairs and wooden tables. The tables were littered with the day's papers, and decorated with graffiti, cigarette burns and coffee rings.

Many of the young people I met at the Project had jobs and others went there to look for work: the workfare merry-go-round on which everyone I met was stuck. At the time, the Project was the only local resource where there was no distinction between staff and young people. Because everyone who worked at the Project acknowledged the problems all residents had to face, no external pressure was applied to the mostly young men and women who went there. However, among external youth agencies at that time there seemed to be a shared belief that allowing young people the freedom to socialise unsupervised at the Project was unconstructive. As a result, the centre had been scheduled for closure before I started my fieldwork. Later I describe that sad process, when the Project was demolished along with the old arcade, leaving a hole in Nova's public life. Anyone who used the facility was assured that they could go there, chat, have a smoke or a cup of tea, or just retreat from the hurricane of pressures blowing outside the door. At that time, projects aimed at young people living in Nova were often designed to produce objective results: a percentage gaining a qualification, work placement or job. The importance of the Project was as a place where young people in Nova could go and survive as one. Later I describe how outside agencies tried to impose a new, fundamentally different Project, one that sought to engage with young people by isolating individuals. One of the Project staff identified how that strategy always failed because professionals were unwilling to appreciate the significance of community as a defence against exclusion.

Uncle Sean

The Project opened at 9 a.m. every weekday as an advice centre for local residents. People in need of advice had to make an appointment. At noon, the building became a drop-in centre offering subsidised cups of tea and coffee, free local and national newspapers and a game of pool or table tennis. As I discovered during my initial meetings with staff, most of the people who went there were young adults aged between 16 and 30, coming in during time off work. A free phone and free local papers also made the Project a good place to look for a job or usually just a better one. Young men and women would chat about vacancies, lessening the inevitable introspection that looking for work entails. The Project managers were Eddy and Sean. Sean practically ran the Project as Eddy was constantly hassled by paperwork. Eddy was approaching retirement, a small plump man who, despite his enthusiasm for young people, was growing weary of the external pressures. Even though young people who came to the Project were saddened at the prospect of its closure, many felt Eddy deserved the break. Sean in contrast was a rock for many young people in Nova, big, tall, with a positive attitude. Sean worked for years as a children's worker at the Nova Centre, which is why almost every young person who attended the Project knows him. Next, were the co-workers: Mathew, a tall slim African-Caribbean man, straight out of university like myself, and divided between optimism and frustration; finally, there was Andy, Caucasian, quite short and thinning on top, who was studying at Ford University for a Masters degree, and kept fit through the other programmes he ran for young people.

On my first day Andy was playing pool with Antoine, who was off work for a week, along with Chris, Antoine's best mate, a slim, well-dressed Caucasian man approaching 20 leaning against the wall. At the window, sitting on a chair tilted against the glass was Martin, a young, good-looking African-Caribbean man aged 22. Martin was one of the people I became closest to and his experiences and insight helped shape this study.

In the back room Tracy and Catherine, both in their mid-20s, each of medium height, sat talking while Eden, Catherine's five-year-old daughter, and Tracy's seven-year-old son Dane burst around the room with energy. As I walked into the back room Sean turned around from the sink and smiled hello. I soon discovered that almost all the young men and women who come into the Project had known Sean when they had attended the activity groups he organised at Nova Centre. Young people also grew close to Sean passing the Project each afternoon on their way home from school. The roads linking the Precinct, where many of the young people I got to know lived, with Nova's three primary schools, all seemed to connect directly in front of the Project window. Every weekday at 3 p.m., the street outside the Project became filled with a tricolour of tiny children and parents.

Sean always seemed to be there for people: everyone knew where he lived and had his phone number. The depth of knowledge Sean had about what young people face growing up in Nova was reflected in the respect everyone I met gave him. The only time I saw Sean look disconsolate was when I asked him what would happen when the Project closed. He told me the Project's funding agency was trying to find another backer for a new facility, though his face showed little sign of optimism.

In retrospect, it seems the Project's popularity among young people was its downfall. Not defined by a strategy or targets meant that the Project, as a service, appeared on paper as if it was not providing one. This was the main reason why, after 15 years, it had to close. Yet the young adults who went there did so because it allowed them time and space to step off the workfare merry-go-round, if only for a few hours. Sean explained how over those years the Project became part of young people's lives, while schemes organised by outside agencies came and went. Previous initiatives had been unpopular through the way youth workers sought to impose restrictions on young residents. The result, through the 1980s and 1990s, was a spiral of short-lived projects where young people were coerced into programmes simply to produce results. The effect was that young people themselves felt that, in the eyes of outsiders, they were regarded as a local problem.

For Sean, the result of this lack of co-ordination was that many children in Nova grew into adolescence with a negative perception of youth and community workers. As Sean said one afternoon, 'one minute they are accommodating young people, the next they're telling them what to do'. During my afternoons at the Project, Sean also identified more deep-seated factors, including Ford's economic decline and the effect that had had on the resources available for deprived areas. Provision for young people in Nova had been transferred from local government to an amalgam of private and semi-private agencies.

Born and bred

Working as an assistant in a children's playgroup at Nova's main community centre, Sean had an insight into the relationship young people had with their families, and described the effect exclusion had on children's lives. Sean explained the pervasive realities of living in a community associated with crime: separation, domestic violence, parents who experienced mental or physical health problems, drug dependency and imprisonment. Sean described how, in families scarred by these problems, young people grew up angry and the anger was often expressed at school. When that happened the barriers young people already faced echoed into adulthood. Nova's young adults are incredibly strong and only a few of those I got to know became totally alienated or lost hope inside. Sean said the majority of young people were strongly motivated by a sense of family. Of course, some young adults I got to know had young children themselves, which Sean suggested gave young adults someone to love who also loved them back. However, many young adults I met were also unloved as children, at home, at school or sometimes at both. One afternoon at the Project, Pele, tall, Caucasian and blessed with a devilish smile, explained how teachers at his secondary school insisted that his mother taught him. This was after Pele had already been placed in 'the Unit', a separate building at Greaves Secondary School for pupils who were regarded as problematic:

> Pele: Yeah. At Greaves, they used to have a little class where you didn't get allowed out at break times. They used to put me in there, write out loads of lines and that (laughs). They called it the 'the Unit'. They also used to get me mum down to school, she used to teach me. They put me in a separate classroom and she used to teach me and then she'd go back to work again and the next day she'd come back down again. She had the afternoon off to teach me again.
> RM: Your mother wasn't a teacher in a school?
> Pele: No, she'd just come down to keep me out of trouble.
> RM: Did she teach you?
> Pele: No, I just used to sit in a library and that where it was quiet. I just used to read and do me homework and she used to tell me what to do. The teachers would tell her what needed to be done and she'd just say do this, do that. Then as soon as she went, I'd be off again.

For many young people, frustrations stemmed from experiences at secondary school, and many adults described their anger at not being able to continue into further education. For Pele, that anger spilled into adulthood. I noticed that Pele, who went to the Project every day, suddenly stopped attending. I asked him why:

> RM: I saw you in The Project just when I started going in there but then you disappeared. Where did you go?
> Pele: Oh yeah, well it's a long story. See I'd gone out on the lash [drinking] one weekend. I was fuckin steamin' I'm tellin' ya. Anyway, it was Saturday night and we were trying to get a taxi home. Anyway, yeah we got a mini cab and me and me mates. And then he [cab driver] stopped, Asian bloke he was, and says we've gotta get out 'cause were causin' too much trouble. Yeah, so that's when I got into a fight with 'im and I hit him. Then after

that I went on the run for a few months. Then after about a year, the old bill caught me and I got sent down for three months; that was in the Young Offender Institution.

Through my observations at the Project and then listening to Sean, I began to understand why young men and women were filled with rage and frustration. Pele and other young people, particularly young boys, described being treated differently, often inhumanely, by teachers. Research reveals how growing up in a socially excluded community can be a barrier to further opportunity. Gorard *et al.* (2002) identified how the choice of schools available to parents and children living in poor areas could also be a barrier to educational achievement. Describing the effect of school selection, Gorard *et al.* (2002: 370) note, 'In effect, social segregation between schools is increasing, leading some disadvantaged schools into a "spiral of decline", and creating a clear system of winners and losers.' Local geographies such as wards show broad and deep divisions of participation chances: the 20 per cent of young people living in the most advantaged areas are five to six times more likely to enter higher education than the 20 per cent of young people living in the least advantaged areas. Maps of local participation rates reveal that many of the region's cities and towns are highly polarised. In one neighbourhood, almost no one goes to university, while in others 70 per cent of young people will enter higher education (Gorard *et al.*, 2002: 370). Spending time with young adults each day at the Project, I began to understand the emotional impact of exclusion; also the ways in which young people were able to survive through friendship.

Spirit of a community

Adults often criticise young people for their irresponsibility or reckless-ness. My own belief is that young people's sense of danger is a method of establishing who they are. In her study of crime and community in a deprived urban area, Janet Foster (1990) describes the transition from childhood to adulthood among the young people she interviewed. The form the transition took was from the 'public to the private' (Foster, 1990: 137). Foster identifies how young people left school, found work and developed relationships: 'The intermediate years, owing to preoccupa-tions with relationships, the assumption of adult status, and the new opportunities afforded by work, were characterised by a gradual shift away from the public sphere.' Nova was no different: Slim, for example, described the workfare merry-go-round many young people were trapped on; 'most of the jobs are shit; and all I'm getting off the dole is £70 a fortnight. I mean that's gone the first and second day you get it.' Jay explained where the money went:

See no one's really got an education in Nova. A lot of people with families. You've got your own place and you've got to pay rent which is say £40 and then you've got to pay council tax, your water, your gas, your electric. And then if you've got kids you've got to get the food and keep them clothed and what not else.

Jay identified the economic realities of the workfare merry-go-round: long hours, minimum wage, and few prospects for promotion.

Going to the Project was a way of overcoming these uncertainties as a community. Wasserman *et al.* (1998: 201) describe the importance of places like the Project, 'Because place attachment reflects a history of human interaction, it is shaped by the changing understanding people have of that interaction, and it is subject to retrospective revision in ways that are not always obvious to those who experience it.' Despite its limited resources, the Project provided free sources of recreation and the means to search for a 'decent job'. Sean, with Eddy, Andy and Mathew, all did what they could for the young people who came in. One day Olly, who I met and introduce below, came into the Project with a job application form. Olly needed a reference and Sean and Eddy were able to help. It was also in the Project where Sean introduced me to many of the young adults I interviewed. Below is a diagram of the three communities of young people I met by going to the Project.

Jason (18), white, tall, slim and always smartly dressed, came in to see his friends, Slim (18), and Olly (21). Slim and Olly were much shorter and looked more youthful than Jason, with his prominent good-looking

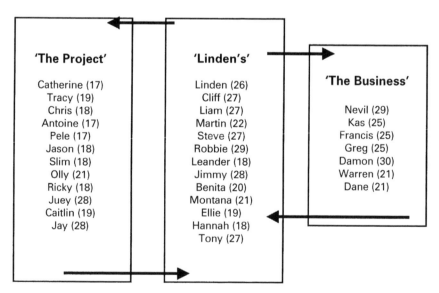

Picture 2   Respondent groups

features. Both were Caucasian: Slim, medium height and build, and Olly, short and stocky. All three were working for an employment agency. Many of the young people I subsequently met were registered with several agencies. Even though work was usually only for a few days at a time, agencies required young people to start immediately. The work itself was usually within Ford's service industries: restaurants, supermarket, or distribution warehouse. Being on call was one reason why Jason, Slim and Olly are always smart in their appearance. All always wore crisp clean shirts with short sleeves during that hot summer, with smart shoes, trousers or jeans. Even though the clothes young people wear cost very little, looking good was a statement of self-respect.

Olly, Slim and Jason were very close friends through growing up together and attending the same primary and secondary schools. Almost all the young adults I met went to Greaves. When friends had attended the same primary school, friendships were inevitably much stronger. Going to Nova primary school and Greaves secondary was one reason why Jason, Slim and Olly were so close. Pele (17) and Ricky (18) were friends of Olly, Jason and Slim. Both were the same age as Jason and Slim. Pele, tall, white, and slightly heavier than Jason, went to St Mary's, Nova's only Catholic primary school. Olly, who also boxed and played football at the Nova social club, also went to St Mary's. Olly then went to Hillcrest Secondary, a feeder school for Nova's neighbouring residential estate. These differences set Pele and Ricky slightly apart from the other friends. All of the boys, however, were usually together at the Project. Jason, Slim, Pele and Ricky were single at that time, and went to the Project because it provided an opportunity to meet young women who went there. Single young adults, whether in work or not, usually seemed to have more unstructured time and the Project gave a unity to the day. Slim and Olly both had partners. Vivian was Pele's girlfriend, Caucasian, and the same height as Slim. I never met Olly's girlfriend, though I saw Teresa and him together with their young son in the arcade occasionally.

Catherine (17) and Tracy (19) were both diminutive Caucasian women and each had a young son. The Project provided a break from David, who was Tracy's son, and Brad, Catherine's. I met both young boys on my first day at the Project. As I continued to go I quickly found how both could easily monopolise my time with their boundless energy.

Going to the Project each afternoon, I began to wonder why the young women who went there seemed to be more mature compared with the men. Having children may have been why Catherine and Tracy appeared less concerned about what others thought about them. Overall, the young men I got to know in Nova seemed to act as if they had more to prove. This was especially true of young Caucasian men, which I explore in Chapter 5. Chris (18), slight framed, Caucasian and good looking, and Antoine (17), African-Caribbean, tall and stocky, were all regulars at the Project. Both loved playing pool, and played together even though Antoine usually defeated any competitor. Sean and Andy also had difficulty extracting both from the table to allow others to play.

Caitlin (19) and Jay (28) were the final two of the twelve young adults I interviewed at the Project. Caitlin is Caucasian, medium height although she looked taller for being so slim. Compared with most of the young adults who went to the Project, Caitlin was more inclusive than the rest. Jason, Slim, Olly, Slim, Pele and Ricky all formed a close-knit group. Catherine and Tracy were inseparable, as were Chris and Antoine. Caitlin, however, was happy in anyone's company. Jason, Slim, Olly, Pele and Ricky all agreed to be interviewed at the Project. I was unable to conduct interviews with Catherine, Tracy, Chris, Antoine or Caitlin because they all disappeared when the Project closed. The Project's closure had a detrimental impact on the unity and stability of the young adults' social worlds generally. Even for young adults who were working at the time, most of the jobs in and around Nova involved unsocial hours. This meant that the Project was the only place to go. Bus journeys to Ford city centre on a regular basis were beyond the means of most of the young adults I met, working or not. The last member of the group I got to know at the Project was Jay, tall, Caucasian and slim. Jay was a decade older than the rest of the group and was close friends with Huey. Huey, Caucasian, tall though a lot heavier than Jay, worked in a local hotel. Huey worked nights and the Project allowed a relaxing time off. A week before the Project closed, Sean, Mathew and I drove Jason, Slim, Olly, Pele, Ricky, Chris, Antoine, Huey and Jay to a local park just outside Nova for a game of football. The game spelled the end of a beautiful summer and an invaluable resource for young adults in Nova.

After the Project's closure, young people were bereft of an intermediate safe space: somewhere to go on a weekday and not feel pressured to spend money. The Nova Centre, the estate's principal community centre, was only open to the public for three hours in the morning, a time when many young people were searching for work. When I was with young people between nine and midday, the hours involved waiting in job agencies for nonexistent jobs, working on training schemes, or queuing to sign on. It would be too easy to suggest that all that was required was another Project. Yet the Project's shared sense of community, which bathed each person who entered, had taken years to capture. The magic of the Project was no mysterious process, known only to people who live in Nova. It was simply a matter of giving young adults time, so everyone could weave the Project into history. Friendship also made the Project a place to go, as did the concern and empathy Sean and other workers have for young people. The historian Eric Hobsbawm (1997) describes the importance of these elements in history: 'ideally each generation copies and reproduces its predecessor ...'. Even though Mathew and

Andy did not live in Nova at that time, both were respected. In listening to young people, all four men also made the Project an intermediary between a hostile, mistrustful outside world and the volatile public and private culture of Nova itself. Despite the criticisms levelled at the Project by outside agencies, the initiative was not a comfort zone but a process. Friendship was the culture of the Project and it allowed young people to step off the workfare merry-go-round and feel at ease. When the Project closed at the end of the summer, friendship remained though the culture that filled the void could only be described as a helter-skelter of crime and drugs.

The rule of the street

By October, the Project had been reduced to rubble and young adults were forced to spend time in and around the place where they lived. For younger people, who had often just left home, that is 'the Pre' (the Precinct). Intractable poverty and a transient population in the Precinct also meant that it experienced high rates of victimisation. A similar picture, where a culture of violence dominated the public life of a community, can be found in Bourgois' (1996) ethnographic study of East Harlem in New York. As in Nova, a small minority, engaged primarily in the use and supply of crack-cocaine, controlled certain areas. Bourgois (1996: 34) refers to a 'culture of terror' at work in East Harlem within which the 'threat' of violence can engulf and enslave an already vulnerable community and result in a profound ideological dynamic that necessitates a distrust of one's neighbour. Being burgled in the Precinct could never be reported because of the culture of violence that sustained it. People who did report being a victim of crime were often subject to further victimisation. Warren, who I met after the Project closed and introduce later, lived in the Precinct. He said, 'People would like come round askin' for Rizla (cigarette papers) or somethin' and when you opened the door they'd case up your house'. When I spoke with Martin about living in the Precinct, he told me how an internal system of control had evolved to prevent burglaries proliferating:

> If anyone fucks you over, steals your video. You can't come into a lad's yard (flat) and steal his stuff, his video, his tapes. Anyway, if someone does that you get it sorted. One guy did something a couple of weeks ago and got thrown off one of those flats down there; you know those three-storey ones. He was hurt, though he didn't go to the hospital. If it was anyone else, they would have been injured but he took it. He was sore for a few days; he broke a few ribs.

Despite the dangers, crimes committed by residents on other residents persisted for reasons Jay described: 'more people are stealin' off each other. I mean usually it's just for a drink or summit. That's all they want, just a drink.' The volatility of the public and private culture of the Precinct was also reflected in the incidents of violence I witnessed between men and women involved in relationships. One afternoon I was chatting with one young man I had met at the Project in Nova's main arcade. Linden, who I introduce below, invited Christine, a tall and smartly dressed young Caucasian woman, to come over. Linden asked Christine how things where going and she explained she had just had an argument with her boyfriend. Christine then lifted her hair to reveal a deep curved scar above her eye, covered in stitches. During the argument, Christine said that her boyfriend had hit her with a broken beer bottle.

Talking to Jason, Slim and Olly about living in the Precinct, where all three did at that time, all told me they were reluctant to spend a lot of time there during the day. There were a high proportion of young people usually living alone in the Precinct and an equally high proportion of outsiders. That, combined with the multiple problems young adults had to face, made the Precinct a very chaotic world. Population turnover there was also very high. Many young adults I spoke to, some of whom lived in the Precinct, blamed the haphazard mix of people, usually young people from other parts of Ford, for making it an uncertain place. Jay described how young people who moved in were targeted: 'Y'know, they move in and they'll get targeted, they don't know anyone. But basically, no one's got anythin' in Nova. But they'll mooch [steal or deceive] them anyway just to see. If they ain't got a telly or video they'll just rob the washing machine or somethin'.'

After the Project, many young adults were forced to occupy that space, one where the susceptibility of being a victim of crime or drug use was much higher, as I describe in Chapter 4. Everyone I met through going to the Project seemed to disappear once it closed. It was only through meeting a young man who lived in the area that I was able to appreciate the hardships residents faced.

Linden's

After the closure of the Project, I spent most of my time with Linden (26) and Liam (27); Linden is a well-built African-Caribbean young man. Liam is Caucasian, and nearly as tall as Linden, though less muscular. Through his kindheartedness, Linden opened the door to the social world he and his friends shared, and to the importance of 'the life' in maintaining respect (see Whyte, 1945). Linden's world also revealed the dangers faced by young people trying to survive exclusion on their own.

Above all, Linden's world personified survival, and many residents regarded Linden as a 'top lad'. The term itself had little to do with gender, just a referent for someone well respected in and around Nova. Neither was being 'a top lad' related to violence or crime. Younger and older residents respected Linden because of his strength, good humour and compassion. Linden told me after the Project; 'Yeah see me, I know the top ones. I know the ones right down the bottom. I don't look at them any different really. I don't look at them and think "you're nothin' you are; I'm wanna the fuckin' lads": I'm not like that.'

Being accepted into Linden's world happened when he got a job at an engineering company on the other side of Ford. The job itself was characteristic of workfare: if Linden declined the job, working on a night shift six miles from Nova, his benefit payments would be stopped. To clock on at 6 p.m., Linden would have to leave his flat at 5 p.m., leaving at least an hour for the two buses. After finishing at 6 a.m., Linden then had to wait at least an hour until the first bus into Ford city centre at 7 a.m., and then catch another into Nova. Receiving just above the minimum wage, after travel and living costs, Linden would barely break even. When Linden told me about the job, I offered to take him to and from work for as long as I could. After three weeks, Linden was dismissed, after complaining to the night manager about the lack of heating.

One could understand how many young people, including Linden, tried to remain self-employed: Liam was the most successful in gaining regular informal work, making a living as a painter and decorator for people in Nova. Young people who went to the Project were often self-employed, usually after working in Gemini Park: it seemed like a good place to build social capital. During the Project's last week, I asked both how they felt about the closure. Liam said, 'it's shit really, there's nowhere else to go'.

In the weeks and months after the Project's closure, I spent most of my days in or around Linden's flat: Liam and Linden's other close friends lived nearby. Linden was very genial and his own flat was a meeting point for his friends chiefly because of its size; an architectural quirk as most flats in the Precinct consisted of box rooms. Being invited into Linden's, I met Linden's partner, Hannah, nearly six years younger. Hannah, Caucasian and beautiful, was in her late teens and worked at the medical centre in the Arcade. This meant we only usually met at night. The rest of Linden's friends tried to stay free of the workfare merry-go-round, 'working for yourself'. That meant all were restricted to Nova for most of the day and night. Only one of Linden's friends at that time, Jimmy, had a car, though he had difficulties keeping it running.

After the closure of the Project, the pub on the edge of the Arcade became the only alternative to being stuck indoors. As that summer came to a close, Linden (26), Cliff (27), Liam (27), Martin (22), Steve (27),

Robbie (29), Leander (18), Jimmy (28), Tony (28), Benita (20) and Montana (21) would sit outside in the car park listening to the jukebox. On those summer days, Linden's circle echoed Whyte's (1945) account of the street corner society. As Nova's skies became cold or overcast, the group would go inside, money permitting. Linden became an ideal sponsor, providing me with his phone number and saying I could phone or come around. Most of Linden's friends were in their mid-20s and grew up together in Nova. Cliff, Martin and Tony were African-Caribbean. Cliff and Martin are both tall and stocky, as was Tony, though he was more slender. Steve, Liam and Jimmy looked practically identical, medium-built, slim and Caucasian, while Robbie is the smallest of the group, quite slight and Caucasian. Appearance was incredibly important for all the young adults I met, a way of defying the negative stereotypes of outsiders. Linden and his friends dress in a Hip Hop style. In Chapter 4, I illustrate the importance of Hip Hop and R & B for men and women. Leander, Benita, Ellie, Hannah and Montana, all Caucasian, were slightly younger than the men in the group. Montana and Benita grew up together in another area of Ford and bonded at another school. When Montana was in prison, Benita told me 'we used to keep in touch, I used to write and go and see her', even though the prison itself was on the other side of the country. Benita was taller than Montana though both women, each Caucasian, looked similar in the clothes they wore; long leather overcoats, stylish boots, polo neck sweaters with a gold necklace. Hannah and Montana were just over five feet tall and Leander as tall as Benita, approaching six foot. Ellie was the tallest and the strongest. Like Benita and Montana, all four were incredibly smart and highly innovative in the clothes they wore. Benita and Montana shared clothes and jewellery, and liked to look similar, while Hannah, Ellie and Leander all expressed their own individual style.

After being introduced to Linden's friends, I tried to be with all as much as I could for as long as I could while trying to avoid being a nuisance. In the following chapters, I describe the social world Linden and his friends created for one another, and the ambiguous feelings many had about the consumer society that glistens on Nova's horizon. At the end of *Learning to Labour*, Paul Willis (1977: 194) concludes: 'At best, daily life, like art is revolutionary. At worst, it is a prison house. At worst, reflection, like criticism, is reactionary. At best it creates plans for escape.' Linden's friends made what must have been a daily prison house a revolution. The closure of the Project, if it could have been otherwise, was a chance entry into Linden's world. The closure also meant many of the other young adults I met became much harder to find. How deeply the closure of the Project affected everyone I will never know.

Nova: it's me; it's who I am

The Project was a social world inclusive of age, gender, ethnicity and dress: history was made there because the social world of the Project transcended age: older residents recollected their own experiences along with young adults, creating 'spatial stories' each day involving the life of a community (de Certeau, 1984: 118). Even though I never witnessed young people dissociating themselves from older residents, after the Project closed interactions between both groups vanished. Anne Power and Katherine Mumford (2003: 268) describe how 'Community brings strangers together and transforms a frightening sense of uncertainty into a more confident feeling towards the bigger world of the neighbourhood and beyond'. During my own fieldwork, transformation depended on a place where people could feel socially uninhibited. After the closure of the Project, up until the time of writing over six years after it ended, I have noticed that Nova's young adult population contained more strangers. It is not simply that there has been an influx of young adults from other areas; Nova's Precinct area has been characterised by a transient young adult population for the past 20 years. Instead, the noticeable non-interaction between young strangers seemed to reflect the absence of a social space where young people can get to know each another.

When the Project closed, young people were left with consumer culture. In Linden's world and the social worlds of other young people, a sense of belonging is sustained through culture: how you look, the music you listen to, the work you do, the car you drive, the lager you prefer, all became strategies to define each day because that was all that remained: culture. The Project provided its own definition, its own sense of belonging; walking in the door was reason enough to be there. When the Project was open, there was always hope of a better job because Sean, Eddy, Mathew and Andy fostered that promise each day. After its closure, the options of getting a secure job diminished. Young people's aspirations and the desire to express them continued; and as I describe in Chapters 3 and 4, after that point consumer culture took over primarily to survive against an approaching winter that turned out to be one of the coldest on record. After the closure, crime and drugs became strategies to survive being resigned to the Precinct, freezing temperatures, and a Christmas in poverty or, worse, in jail.

Survival of the fittest

While I drove Linden to and from work each day, he told me about his incredible life. Linden, like Liam and some of the other young men and women I met, spent his early childhood years in another part of Ford. Both Linden and Liam's parents had divorced and the boys had moved with their mothers to Nova. Even though this must have been an unsettling experience, Linden's account of how he adapted to it highlights how social he was. Linden described how he enjoyed school, especially Greaves, Nova's feeder secondary school. 'It was like the mix of people, the different people,' Linden explained, 'I never wagged [truanted] it once, not once. I had about two or three days off out of the whole five years. It was my mum, see, she was strict, really strict.' Linden left school at sixteen after winning a highly sought-after apprenticeship at a local car factory:

> Yeah, left school at 16. But within a week, I had a job. I got a job at Weston. See every year Weston would recruit 12 lads from 12 schools in the city. They'd send out application forms and then the headmaster of each school would select four people and get them to sit an exam. You 'ad to be brainy to get on the shortlist. An' I did. Sailed through the exam and got a job there. I worked there for four years.

During those journeys Linden described his time at Weston where he also 'wheeled and dealed' (sold goods informally) among other workers. Informal economies are common in many factories; Willis (1977: 54) describes the shop floor culture, 'amongst workers it is also the basis for extensive bartering, arranging "foreigners" and "fiddling"' (see Garfinkel, 1986). Linden told me how his time at Weston's included selling 'knocked-off' goods such as unlicensed alcohol, tobacco and cannabis. Such activities could have been interpreted as a sign of disrespect against his employers at Weston's. Work in Nova was regarded in relative as opposed to absolute terms. For young adults I spoke to, the experience of exclusion was being denied decent jobs and having to suffer exploitation and insecurity in the local service sector. Nearly all the young adults I met, including Linden, had worked or were working at that time in exploitative jobs. All young adults also described being exploited and discriminated against growing up in Nova. As I describe in Chapters 3 and 4, often exploitation was seen as a dialectical process among young people themselves. Linden also echoed the exploitation and prejudices against other African-Caribbean young men such as Martin and Tony, as I describe later.

Linden's frustrations were also reflected in a general belief, among everyone I spoke to, that crime was inevitable so long as young people continued to be excluded. Linden himself said, 'No, there's lads goin' out moochin' now. No, it'll never stop, [pause] it'll never stop.' 'Mooching' is not a term that refers directly to crime, but deceiving outsiders. The dictionary definition of the term is similar: 'A dupe, as in a confidence game' and outsiders were often seen as fair game for leading a consumer lifestyle. I asked Steve about his work experience in Gemini Park:

> I did once, I had a job when I was 17 when I first passed me drivin' test. I only lasted a month. It was drivin' the delivery pizzas. They'd used to phone up 'do ya want tomato'. I said 'I'll give ya fuckin' tomato on your pizza'. Used to stick me fingers up me arse then stick me hand right in it, in the garlic bread. Then I was in the van one day with me mate and he's grabbed the handbrake. It fuckin' span 'round and smashed into this old lady's car. Brought the van back, wheels all shakin' at the front. Bang, the sack, you wrote the car off.

Elements of a culture

Mooching signified collective enterprise, the economy of 'the life'. It was also working free from the workfare merry-go-round, and enabled young people to maintain self-respect by 'working for yourself'. Mooching is also a relationship with a society that denies young people a life; free from the objective shadow of crime that surrounds Nova. In his study *Outsiders*, Howard Becker (1963: 8) describes how deviance is created by society and that, 'rules tend to be applied more to some people than others'. Exclusion is a rule applied to young adults in Nova, particularly in relation to work. Being with Linden for long periods of the day and night, I was also able to gain an insight into how he and his friends collectively survived exclusion. When Linden lost his job on the workfare placement at the engineering firm, he, like the rest of his friends, had to find ways to make ends meet. With the Project, its free phone, newspapers, and all-important contacts now gone, young people now had only one another to survive.

For most of the twelve months I spent with Linden and his friends, apart from a few weeks at Christmas, all were without permanent work. Having to alternate between benefits or temporary jobs, Nova's workfare carousel barely allowed people to cover the cost of utilities such as gas or electricity. As a result Linden and his friends, like many of the young adults I met, survived 'dealin'', 'doin' a bit of business' or 'out on the shift': some ventures were legal, others were not, and the general strategy was trying to remain self-employed; to hold onto 'the life'. Compared with the irregular temporary work and restrictions imposed living on workfare, 'moochin' involved even more uncertainties and risks. As a way of ordering what Jimmy described as the 'fuckin' chaos' of 'the life', moochers had developed terms that seemed to encapsulate the contradictions of exclusion and poverty in a consumer society.

Linden and his friends worked together 'out on the shift', a phrase that echoes Nova's industrial past when young adults' parents would work the day or night shift at one of the big factories that surrounded the area. 'Out on the shift' encompassed any activity that enables young adults to generate ready cash. In short, any form of work other than workfare in which all monies are processed by the benefits agency.

All of Linden's friends, apart from Hannah who had a full-time job, were unable to obtain bank accounts. Many young people said how 'coming from Nova' was the main reason why banks refused to offer financial services. Atkinson (1998: 7) describes how 'the use by financial institutions of street postcodes for purposes of credit rating' results in the economic exclusion of entire areas. Many young people also had debts including rent arrears, hire purchase agreements, or County Court judgments that were often paid for by the benefits agency; extracted from either wages earned or income support payments. In this situation, one can appreciate the value of 'working for yourself' as a way of earning a disposable income. Steve described the debts he was facing at the time, mainly in the form of unpaid parking fines:

RM: How many fines have you had?

Steve: Thousands. But that was mostly for one time. One time in Nova, the police kept stoppin' us. They stop me, give me a producer, pull off, get in the car park, change 'round. Then they'd stop me again and give me another producer, the other copper on the other side. So there's two in one day. So, I went to court and I had about twelve producers in the glove box. And 'cause they kept changin' around they couldn't get done for harassment, sly bastard's y'know what I mean. Every time I was goin' to court I was getting £500 fine, £500 fine for arrestin' me. Every time I was walkin' out of court, I was comin' out with big fines. I 'ad about £7000 in fines.

RM: Have you paid them all off?

Steve: I haven't. I went to court for it and they knocked off £1,111. The screw says comin' out; he says 'you're better off doin' days' (a regular job). Now I've got a committal, that's either pay up or straight to jail.

RM: Does jail worry you?

Steve: Na, it's not one of the places I'd like to visit. I'd prefer to see Florida. Fuck the prison. A weekend in a police cell's enough for me.

During the time of my fieldwork, 'mooching' usually involved some form of deception or contravention of the law: selling unlicensed cigarettes, alcohol or other drugs. Working in this way was described in those terms, as valid work, whereby the effort young people put in was reflected in a disposable income even though, as I describe later, it can never be invested. The internal logic that work has for young adults reflects Becker's (1963: 8) account of how activities come to be defined as legal or illegal, 'A society has many groups each with its own set of rules, and people belong to many groups simultaneously. A person may break the rules of one group by the very act of abiding by the rules of another group. Is he then deviant?'

Because local jobs were perceived as superficial, working for yourself was given a strong work ethic. As a result, the end of the working day also had a deep emotional significance, a time to relax and think about tomorrow. Weekends in particular were a time to be worked for, as with any young person not intimidated by the city. Linden and his friends were together as a group though usually only at night, and normally at Linden's flat. These events were referred to as 'the session'; time off work spent getting together and relaxing. In the day the group divided into smaller groups, usually couples. This sounds tactical though its reality was just a reflection of the nature of friendships within the group. Close friendships were reflected in people, including Linden and Liam, living near one another. Equally, many of the young adults who went to the Project spent the day there in the company of best mates, who were often childhood friends. Being in couples or a threesome also reflected the ways young adults work. To earn money Linden, his friends and other young adults I met would move from one place to another in cars. That meant people were often confined to groups of two three or four. Yet, returning to the nature of friendships within the group, people will prefer to be with just a best friend as it reduces risks. The importance of cars, as transportation around a big city such as Ford and as a method of access, also restricted me in terms of who I could spend time with during the day.

Orpheus

The culture of the session involved music, a nice meal (Linden is an excellent cook), drug use (licit and illicit), television and video games rented from a local video library. Money permitting, people would go out to a club, and then go back to Nova for a session. The ritualistic nature of the session emphasised its importance as a way of bracketing off the world of work (see Giddens, 1991). As I describe in the following chapters, this social world seemed like a helter-skelter compared to the continuities of the Project. In Chapter 4, I show how age and experience were important in protecting young people from the stigma that surrounded Nova, though a clearly defined social space was of far greater significance. After the Project closed, Linden invited me out with his closest friends at that time, Tony and Leander. Tony, six foot, slim and contending with Martin for the best looking man in Nova, was seeing Leander at the time: 18, nearly six feet tall and striking. Tony and

Leander were Romeo and Juliet, desperately in love even though everyone said they were wrong for each other because of their explosive temperaments.

It was a Saturday night and everyone had enough money to attend Orpheus. Orpheus was Ford's primary dance club. It opened in 1986 and had been seminal in British club culture, being one of the first to open an offshore operation on the 'white island': Ibiza. Like Ford City football team, Orpheus developed an army of supporters, young workers in the service economy for whom the club was weekend salvation. The club's management style had always bordered on the illegal, a trademark of club culture generally despite the arrival of super-clubs in the 1990s – felt by many clubbers at the time as a sign of commercialisation. Yet, after pressure from the local city council and residents living around the club, Orpheus was subsumed into Ford University, which immediately installed a zero-tolerance policy on drugs. As the university was obliged to protect a large student body, the policy was understandable though its application seemed to affect everyone to the point where being thrown out of Orpheus became a tradition for students and local young people alike. Gradually and despite the loyalty Orpheus had inspired as a focus for the loved-up summers of 1988 and 1989, Ford's youth stopped going (see Haslam, 2001). In 2005, Orpheus was closed, seeming to represent another chapter in the colonisation of Ford's local youth culture.

Linden, Tony and Leander had intended to go to Orpheus. The night began at Linden's; just the two of us were there: Leander was at work, Tony 'out on the shift', and Hannah, Linden's partner, was out with her mates. Once dressed and after berating me for looking shabby, even though I had gone home to change for the evening, we set off into the freezing night for the Pub.

For a Saturday night, the Pub was empty: apart from the regulars in the bar, there were only five people in the lounge: an older couple I had not seen before, Jimmy, Baz and Dizzy. I knew of Baz and Dizzy, successful moochers like Jimmy, though this was my first introduction. Baz, Caucasian, massive and well dressed, was driving a BMW coupe at the time; financed by a then-emerging cocaine trade. Prices had fallen in line with a growing demand among Ford's new graduate market. Driving a relatively new exclusive car, Baz was highly conspicuous in Nova, mainly since he continued to wear sportswear and was incredibly big behind the wheel. When Linden and I joined their circle, Jimmy smiled while Dizzy, African-Caribbean, slim and suave – always wearing a nice suit over a T-shirt – nodded along with Baz.

Jimmy was naturally good-humoured, his smile infectious despite his granite features. Looking up, Jimmy produced a broad smile: 'Alright mate, how's it going.' The three of us then sat, while Jimmy continued his account of his recent trip to the continent. On his return flight, Jimmy had started chatting with a fellow passenger. Arriving back, Jimmy told me that he had helped the person through customs with an item of luggage: a sports bag. On arrival, Jimmy was asked by a customs official to open the bag: inside, among some clothes was a 'nine bar' (nine ounces of cannabis resin). Jimmy explained that the bag was not his, and was promptly released from airport custody: 'I ain't even got a criminal record,' Jimmy said. To this day, I have never been quite sure whether Jimmy was pulling my leg. After telling the tale, Jimmy went to the gents for a 'sniff' (line of cocaine). Linden whispered that, ordinarily, it was customary for people to do a line at the bar. That had stopped after the arrival of what turned out to be the Pub's final proprietor. After my fieldwork, the Pub was closed and demolished to make way for Nova's new arcade, described later. In its final months, fireworks were literally being set off in the Pub lounge, largely as a symbol of protest at the imposition of what were felt to be pointless rules. It was true that outsiders to the area rarely ventured into the Pub. Like the Project, many young people who went there felt that the Pub was representative of their own experience.

In being allowed into this very exclusive world, as a sign of appreciation, I went halves on a bag of cocaine with Linden, paying for most myself. After Linden procured the cellophane bag, we went off for a game of pool, to pass the time before Tony's arrival. Leander finished work at 11 p.m. and Tony had agreed to pick her up. When the balls were ready, Tony strode in, came straight over, and snatched the pool cue from Linden, who then went off to the toilet. In line with my pool skills at the Project, my time at the table was short-lived and Tony then racked up for a game with Linden. After organising the balls, Tony went over to an empty table, took a small cellophane bag from his pocket and emptied the contents of the bag onto the table: an entire gram. After lining up the white powder with a beer mat, Tony took it up both nostrils. Amazed, I went over and asked Linden in a whisper if he had just snorted amphetamine, staggered that someone could withstand or afford so much cocaine in one go. Linden muttered it was coke, that Tony never snorted 'whiz'; then shouted over to Tony, 'Recharging your batteries?' Tony nodded at the joke, rarely smiling.

As Linden and Tony played, I sat before the pub's massive TV screen, watching Terry Wogan; puzzled why pubs install giant plasma screens and then leave the sound off. I had already heard from other young people that Linden and Tony were excellent pool players, and the cue ball was flying all over the table. As they played, Tony kept glancing at the clock above the bar, and then as the second game ended both went to the toilet together. Returning, Tony came over and said that we all had to go with him to pick up Leander up from work. Just as he said this, Leander walked into the lounge and looked at Tony with a grin. As they began to talk to each other in hushed tones, Linden and I went back to the table. As we played, Tony came back and told Linden he was taking Leander home so she could get changed. He advised us to finish our drinks, as he would be back soon. Both then asked if I could drive into Ford; I had parked in front of Linden's and told Tony I would drive into the car park before he returned.

Outside the pub, in the neon darkness, a crowd of young lads had gathered. As I approached the door, one of the lads shouted, 'Alright, soft lad.' It was Olly, one of the boys who frequented the Project. I grinned in recognition: 'How's it goin'?' Olly told me that he was waiting for a cab to take him and 'the missus' to Orpheus. Despite the bitter cold, the four boys casually scanned the Precinct. One, an African-Caribbean boy I had never met who was around 19, speculated with his friend as to whether the landlord would give him a 'sub' (drink on credit). As Linden chatted aimlessly with the boys, a battered hatchback swerved into the lot, and out came Tony, who informed both of us that we were leaving. We had to pick up Leander who was at home getting ready and we would then go down town.

Travelling down the Lewis Road towards the city centre, Leander speculated as to whether we would get in. The time on the dashboard clock flickered 11.56 p.m., and Orpheus stopped allowing people in after midnight. The conversation then halted with the car when Tony ordered me to stop the car; 'there', he said, pointing to a cashpoint: we were now inside Ford's central business district. Parking just before a zebra crossing, both he and I got out. At the cash point I stood behind him as he leant over the screen, the reflection of his face showing an expression of intense purpose. As he slid the card into the slot, the screen delivered the message 'PLEASE ENTER YOUR CARD NUMBER'. Tony punched each button deliberately. A few seconds then passed while the number was verified. The menu offering a series of amounts then flashed onto the screen, causing him to punch the air with his fist. He then hit the key indicating the highest amount, £200. Tony waited again while the cash machine processed the transaction. The computer refused the transaction, telling Tony that there was only £95 left in the account. He was then automatically returned to the menu screen. He struck the 'OWN CHOICE' button. Tony then punched in '95' without hesitation. The card then popped back out of the slot followed by the steady appearance of a wad of £10 notes from the cash dispenser. Tony retrieved the card then the notes, turned round to me and grinned widely. I then went to the cash point, entered my own card, and made my own withdrawal. When I returned to the car, Tony had his head down behind the driver seat having more powder. As I got in the passenger seat, I noticed a police car approaching in the wing mirror. I whispered what was approaching though Tony continued, raising his head violently as the squad car halted directly opposite me. Inside were two men; one asked with a smile that we best move on; Tony then rolled the window down after quickly rubbing his nose with the palm of his hand. As the police officer asked us to move on, Tony smiled politely: 'Sorry I had to get some cash from the machine, we're just goin'.' The officer driving replied that if he did not move he would be taking out another £40.

Driving past university buildings, we approached Orpheus, identifiable by a crowd at the entrance. The club, like many distinguished dance clubs, resembled an indeterminate warehouse. We parked in the big municipal car park under the flyover then walked hurriedly towards the club with the minutes moving away from midnight.

Once inside and free from the cold, we all relaxed in the spacious ultraviolet foyer. At the reception desk, a massive chrome belt buckle, we each paid the £15 entrance fee, Tony paying twice, for himself and Leander. I noticed all three wince when they heard the price of the event; higher than usual because Pete Tong and Sasha were headlining DJs. We then ascended the stairs to the top floor, the ground shaking as we approached the speakers, positioned like upright coffins around the gallery. Each one visibly shook from bass-line thumping. As Tony and Linden pushed open the doors to the third floor we all disappeared in a cloud of sweet disco smoke, then cleared into the gallery room: empty at the centre to allow the 50 foot drop to the ground floor. The third floor of Orpheus was split level, like a circular auditorium: we all walked along the higher level, the easiest route through the strobe lights and jumping bodies to the bar at the back. It looked like pandemonium. While the dance floor itself was a relatively liberated space, accessing it or the bar at the other end was like every other club: a mass of people each lost in their own music. Everyone seemed to be dancing or moving to the beat of his or her own drum. Travelling along the narrow aisles surrounding the dance floor, it was impossible to avoid being elbowed in the face, back, or have your toes crushed. No one seemed to mind, though; that is the point of club culture: emotional abandon. Now that the university had taken over, there was also a strange mixture of soft and hard faces: undergraduates and die-hard members.

I also suddenly noticed a very distinct cultural geography, particularly when we finally reached the bar. Through the mist I recognised Steve, his gold teeth glinting as he grinned at Tony and Linden. Then other peripheral members of Linden's circle began to appear at the back of the room, standing composed like staff at an asylum. After several minutes of greetings, taking the piss and the furtive exchange of ten pound notes and cellophane bags, the four of us headed to the bar, where Tony bought us all a bottle of Bud. We then returned to the edge of the pit to watch the sea of humanity below: as the happy boys and girls twitched and cavorted, Linden and his friends chatted with one another as if Orpheus was an empty street. But there was continuity: people on the dance floor and podiums were sharing something that defines club culture, something secret but also public in the clothes people wear:

Kangol, Adidas and Nike Air, even though the ages stretch across 30 years. The only distinction was the stamina driving the teenagers: I felt tired even though I hadn't moved. After an hour, I noticed Linden sitting on the base of a circular podium. As he sat with his back to a sea of liquid silhouettes, he held a bottle of Budweiser in one hand swaying slightly. Linden was less inhibited than his friends when it came to partying; one night at the Pub, Hannah and I had to help carry him home. I am not being judgemental; later that night I was in a waltz with consciousness myself. Compared with his friends Linden was just more confident, as if his reputation in Nova acted like a halo. He had been to the United States: a man he knew was dying and wanted to see America before he died and asked Linden if he would be his guide.

Linden sat for several minutes as the rest of the party chatted, and then I suggested that we go to the toilet. We barged through towards the two black silhouettes standing frozen above each toilet. The gent's was like a ghost train; every five seconds a cubicle door would burst open and two or three blushing men would scurry out. We found one, closed the door, and then heard a male voice ask everyone to leave. The cubicle door then thundered and I opened it. A 'ninja assassin' stood before us, then swept past to inspect the toilet bowl, noting an upturned pint glass with a sigh of frustration. We were then escorted out. Behind the man's shoulder, I then saw Tony, smirking as he was washing his hands at the sink: 'where did you come from', Linden asked Tony as we were escorted out the gents. We were then on the fire exit stairs alongside two security guards, a man and a woman. The female security guard was very polite, ushering us both downstairs. The male guard, however, seemed to focus on Linden. People were milling around, Tony peeping through the fire exit door, when the male guard – dressed in a black baseball cap, army boots, black commando trousers and what looked like body armour – told Linden to remove his boots. The woman, dressed more casually, had seemingly lost interest and disappeared back into the crowd.

I tried to explain that I had been responsible, though the guard continued to insist that Linden remove his boots, simply, it seemed, to humiliate him. Linden, like many of the older young men and women I met in Nova, is physically very strong, and the tension was beginning to build. The guard then seemed to regain a sense of humanity, marching us down three flights of stairs before ejecting us into the cold early morning. We went back to Nova for a night of door knocking around the Precinct (see Chapter 5) while Leander and Tony spent the evening at Ford's most exclusive downtown hotel.

The chaos of that night seemed to underline the difference between the social space of the Project and the vicarious consumerism which now seems to define Ford's city culture. This was the first time I had entered Ford's night-time economy with Linden and some of his friends and for the first time everyone seemed marginalised in what was a very exclusive space. Yet, like Ford generally, there was no alternative but to compete through consumer culture. And since the only way many of the young people I met could participate was through crime that often felt like a zero-sum game. The paradox was that crime and drug use were ways of neutralising the tensions of exclusion that, when applied, only made young people more exposed to attack.

Going under

I first met Leander when she opened the door to Linden's flat one Monday morning. At the time, Leander was then halfway through an NVQ in Caring at a local nursing home. By the end of the first week in October, however, she had been sacked after telling an elderly resident to 'fuck off' when he tried to fondle her. By the middle of October Linden, who knew practically every dealer in Nova, told me Leander was buying heroin and crack-cocaine on a regular basis. Linden said at the time that both prevented her from holding a regular job. This was rare among Linden's friends, who were relatively in control when it came to drug use. Most of the money Linden and his friends made went into consumer culture, including drugs, though within the context of 'the (Hip Hop) life', this had a cultural significance (see Chapter 4). Leander still had aspirations rooted in Ford's public culture, including fashion and nightlife, though, at that time, she was becoming a private drug user.

In Linden's social world, people were rarely alone. Whenever I was at his flat friends would always arrive with close companions. This was usually for a chat over a smoke and/or drink, though very few people drank alcohol in the daytime. Through being part of this day-to-day world, I got to know Steve and Jimmy, Benita and Montana. Along with Tony, Martin and Liam, the seven represented Linden's circle. Sometimes members accompanied Linden 'out on the shift'. Jimmy, Montana and Benita all confessed to regular drug use, including heroin and/or crack-cocaine, though their decision to go 'out on the shift' was motivated by generating cash to go out as opposed to retreat inwards into drug use. During my time with Benita and Montana, both would go 'out on the shift' together, to fund new clothes, gold jewellery, music (usually Hip Hop, Rhythm & Blues and Dance Hall), going to clubs and dance halls, in addition to illicit drugs. Similarly, on the night I interviewed Jimmy, a family man, he said that he directed much of his income into his home and family. Steve, by contrast, had a reputation as a regular at local nightclubs and lap-dancing bars. Liam and Robbie, two white males, and Cliff, a tall stocky African-Caribbean man, had all spent time in jail and were no longer involved in activities that might entail further jail time. Liam described his plans, since leaving prison:

RM: Have you been tempted to go back into crime?

Liam: Oh yeah, everyday, particularly by you know who (pointing towards Linden's flat across the street). Na Rob, that ain't the answer, I just sign on and do a bit of paintin' and decoratin' on the side.

RM: But don't you get frustrated being on the dole?

Liam: Yeah, but it's better than jail. I'm tellin' ya man, me not goin' back to no jailhouse.

RM: Is there any work in Nova?

Liam: Na, not unless you've got a skill. That's what I'm gonna do now, a course in CNC (computer assisted) engineerin'.

Work and leisure

By being able to spend more time in Nova, largely through Linden's friendship, I managed to create a 'web of trust' among another separate group of young adults largely involved in illicit drug supply in and around Ford (see Douglas, 1976, quoted in Adler 1985: 19). During my fieldwork, I bought and sometimes used cannabis with Linden and his friends. This was a good way of establishing trust within Linden's group, and allowed me to gain access to members of 'the Business' (see Picture 2, p. 38). Cannabis use is also a highly communal activity, contradicting the stereotype of the lone user. Howard Becker (1963: 78) describes: 'A person will feel free to use marijuana to the degree that he comes to regard conventional conceptions of it as the uninformed views of outsiders and replaces those conceptions with the "inside" view he has acquired through his experience with the drug in the company of other users.'

It was only through knowing Nevil (29) that I was able to gain the confidence of quite a suspicious group. As most of the group are involved in selling drugs or unlicensed alcohol and cigarettes, suspicion is inevitable. This all-male group comprised Nevil (29), Kas (25), Francis (25), Greg (25), Damon (30), Warren (21) and Dane (21). The Business was a more stable social world compared with Linden and his friends, largely through the custodianship of Damon, whose age and experience put him as a patriarch within the group. Damon's social world does not require as much travelling and usually occurred at night, making 'the Business' less visible compared with going 'out on the shift'.

Approaching 30, Damon was the most successful and popular supplier of cannabis within and beyond Nova during the time of my fieldwork. When I met him, Nevil had just moved out of Nova and into his own home in the suburbs. Then, after several sustained periods in the company of Dane, Nevil and Greg, I was able to gain access to the rest of the group. All buy and sell unlicensed cigarettes and alcohol, usually obtained from mainland Europe. Like moochers, members of the

Business sometimes have to take jobs; some would claim benefits and be required to seek work while other people would work in 'shit jobs' to prevent suspicion from social services, the Inland Revenue or the police. Even though I conducted fieldwork for twelve months, I could see that in the longer term, people who never had a permanent job, such as Hannah, were left alternating between workfare and 'going out on the shift'.

Working in Nova

Unlike moochers, those involved in the Business had more to lose by opening their lives to an outsider. This is because of the inherent dangers involved in the storage and supply of illicit drugs, unlicensed tobacco and alcohol. For those out on the shift the threat of arrest was usually a distant prospect. Being 'out on the shift' involved travelling miles, sometimes hundreds of miles, from Ford. For dealers, however, being exposed was a daily, often hourly, prospect. Many young people I know who were involved in the Business are holding significant amounts of unlicensed cigarettes, alcohol or illicit drugs. A steady economy means members of the Business had greater opportunities, even though moochers were much more innovative (see Chapter 3). The indeterminate and more accelerated social world of moochers made it difficult to save any money that was earned.

Even though 'the Business' was a method of surviving poverty, being able to work in Nova means that life is less chaotic, whatever the venture. Members of the Business have more time because they already have a steady enterprise and are not forced to spend each day looking for a new venture. Also stepping into the consumer society means that people's sense of respect and self-respect is exposed to the stigma of crime, as Linden and Tony both described:

> Tony: No, well a couple of years ago we all 'ad BMWs and that.
> Linden: That was when moochin' first began and people were makin' thousands, fuckin' thousands. My first job, first time I went out on the mooch; I went out for two days. We went to Hornton for two days, I was the driver. I came back with £750 in two days. All I did was drive up there, stay in hotels, drink beer, had a whale of a time, listen to the stereo and come back with £750.
> Tony: Because that's the place it started from. Y'know what I mean, like a couple of years ago from the Pub there's about ten cars leaving everyday with three or four lads each. £5,000 a day each, bookin' into top hotels, y'know like, livin' it up and that, three or four days at a time.

By the mid-1990s, however, it seemed the world Linden and Tony both described was over. Linden explained why mooching had become more difficult, 'with cameras in the shops. Yeah, I've seen a couple of lads on Crimewatch. And I thought to myself, I was with you that day.' Tony himself referred to Ford as 'a surveillance city'. Becoming more visible was possibly another reason why 'the life' is so chaotic, as the following chapter describes. The internal use of CCTV within Nova seemed to make young adults I met feel conspicuous, though residential use may have a comparable effect on young people generally (Dixon, Levine and McAuley, 2004). During my fieldwork, cameras were already in operation within public and residential areas and I noticed people, including myself, conscious of being watched. Being visible is much less important for members of the Business. The nature of the Business, however, did not mean that it is without risk, just that the risks were different.

A bit of business

In selling unlicensed drugs, the risk of contravening criminal law seemed to result in a condition of economic instantaneity. In short, members of the Business appeared to have too much ready cash and taking drugs on a daily basis ensured that all were constantly spending. When I was with members of the Business, all appeared far more preoccupied with business compared with moochers. This almost manifests itself in a mindset or attitude similar to what could be described as being 'business-minded'. Moochers, even though they are entrepreneurial in their general outlook, are also aware of the need to relax, though for different reasons. Mooching was defined by a sense of cultural instantaneity because crime and drug use were simultaneously protections against exclusion and strategies for further exclusion. The dialectic was a consequence of consumer culture, an arena that moochers were forced to live in to survive. In contrast, members of the Business were far less visible: travelling at night and rarely within urban public spaces.

Differences in the type of anxieties felt by business members and moocher stem from surveillance. For Lyon (2001) technologies such as CCTV are simultaneously protective and punitive. He uses the example of an increasing trend among parents of installing CCTV cameras in the home to watch over their children. This means children are safer though they are also restricted in terms of how freely they can express themselves – smearing paint on walls, for instance.

When people are being watched and are aware they are being watched, they are inevitably objectified. Seeing-without-being-seen gives people behind the lens of CCTV cameras control over people. Not knowing the people they are watching also means that people in the street are little more than puppets. Moochers were aware of that, of being watched and selected from the crowd because they were perceived as dangerous subjects. It seemed that the only way moochers were able to survive the stigma of being constantly watched was through an attitude of defiance (see Blackman, 1997). On the day I first met Montana, she had just been released from custody. The day before, Montana had been accused by the manager of a clothing store of trying to obtain goods by deception. As two security guards followed her out of the shop Montana heard one of the guards call her 'scum'. With this Montana turned around and shouted at both guards and they grabbed her. Montana then began lashing out, striking both guards until they overpowered her. Eventually, Montana was held in the backroom. While she waited with one of the security guards, she struck out again. 'I fuckin' battered 'im', she said, 'I just kept smackin' 'im in the 'ead'.

Like a big tree

When members of the Business are trading in the illegal, doing so usually involves possessing an illegal commodity, making them subject to analytic surveillance. The obverse is true with moochers, who are culturally ubiquitous through their clothes, attitude and lifestyle generally. These logistical features of each group result in the divergent subcultures both live through; moochers perceived they had nothing to lose. What started out as a visible enterprise, even when moochers were not transgressing criminal law (i.e. hanging around in public), resulted in an equally visible culture. Business members are much less visible, as they have to be. Even though members of the Business, like moochers, were unable to invest, the benefits of economic instantaneity reflected itself in business members' social relations. As Chapter 3 describes, being unable to invest money, consumer culture – clothes, music and drug use – became protective armour against exclusion among moochers. Even though members of the Business were just as hedonistic as moochers, their subculture was far less conspicuous. No one in the business dressed ostentatiously, as moochers often did, even though the clothes moochers wore were relatively inexpensive. Business members also traded at night, spending the day either asleep, working in regular jobs or just relaxing.

What mooching and the Business, as culture economies, did share was an invisible tension between individualism and collective responsibility. Describing the culture of the shift, Steve explained, 'Nova doesn't have a pecking order, it was more like a big tree'. Everyone was just trying to stay on their own branch, trying not to fall off. Steve said: 'it's part of me, it's my life. I mean you could be there in the Pub skint, and then bang someone's says "here let's do this". Then you've got a pocket full of money, just for bein' there y'know what I mean. Listen it's not what you know these days it's who you know, it's not what you know.'

Caught on the workfare merry-go-round, young people's aspirations seemed to diminish over time. In the days of the Project, young people's hopes and aspirations were kept alive by the support and experience that Sean, Eddy, Mathew and Andy provided. When the Project closed, so did a social world: a place to believe in was replaced by what Jameson (1998) describes as the perpetual present of consumer culture. Culture is a disposable, since by definition it involves consumption. The Business and going out on the shift were constituted through buying, selling and spending, which meant there was nothing left to show for it. The impermanence of both worlds was summed up by Steve's metaphor of everyone placed on the branch of a tree, a perpetual present where it was impossible to accumulate capital. Steve said the 'the life' contained little future. Even though he loathed the thought of a local job, Steve told me, 'Yeah I've got to get a job, some poxy warehouse makin' tea. That's all I'm good at, makin' tea. Do these look like working hands to you (laughs) look at that, soft as a baby's bum they are.'

In our discussions Jimmy and Steve identified the merry-go-round on which almost every young person I met was stuck; also how its alternatives were just as limiting. This was 'the life' of exclusion, one with no alternatives. Tony concluded our interview describing living in Nova and living 'the life': 'I know everyone here and I can do business in Nova y'know what I mean'. In the next chapter, young people describe how 'working for yourself' is fundamental for surviving 'the life'. Even though the only guarantee in 'working for yourself' was freedom from the drudgery of workfare, 'the life' Jimmy described was enough to provide young people with a sense of respect.

Chapter 3

Work

Research and debates on social exclusion often portray its victims as dependent on society: if the state cannot protect the poor, they will turn to crime and drug addiction. This chapter shows how young adults worked as a community to compete within Ford's consumer society, and how crime and drug use were elements of both worlds. Young adults describe working within Nova's local economy, and earning less money than state benefits, to sustain what was a superfluous world of consumption. People, young and old, also described the economic realities of the workfare merry-go-round; a world of temporary employment that only drains what little money people are able to make working a week here and a few days there. This chapter describes how young people, to avoid 'going under', as Linden put it, innovate to sustain a history of their own.

Spending time with young people, I could see how friendships protected against the stigma outsiders tried to impose on Nova. I also gained insight into networks of local, usually informal opportunities that allowed people to hold onto hope and self-respect. Once young people started to try to live free from the workfare carousel, a dialectic process was initiated. Once young people gained a reputation as a working community, usually among benefits agencies and the police, and were seen as a gang through the clothes people wore, exclusion was enforced even further. In the next chapter, I show how the culture of the gang becomes a commodity in the consumer society, whereby a community is assumed to be a culture of crime, what I describe as the masquerade of crime. This process echoes through young people's accounts of growing up in Nova.

Life or death

'Working for yourself' was a term many young people used in discussions on the alternatives to workfare. Young adults also described how outsiders and outside agencies were hostile to young residents associating together in and outside the area. Through my own participant observations with young people, I saw the stigma surrounding young people as a dialectic process of social exclusion, whereby society created then objectified their subjective experiences of work (Denzin, 1994).

In the previous chapter, I described the cultural significance of 'the shift' and 'the Business'. For most young people I met, work within Nova's local service industries was equated with poverty, and working at one supermarket for three months it was difficult to refute that. Yet, the principle of workfare gave the impression that developments such as Gemini Park are a resource for jobs and a career. Becker (1963: 15) describes how 'a person may feel that he is being judged according to rules that he has no hand in making and does not accept, rules forced on him by outsiders'. His statement reflects the experience of exclusion many young adults described. Young people at the Project spoke of being excluded from school and work because of the association teachers and employers have about Nova, its young residents, and crime. The only way to maintain self-respect and survive that stigma was summed up by Linden: 'See, I've never been down and out, I can always find work. I can always make money.' Damon was filled with the same self-determination, expressed at an evening at the Cotton Club. He told me about incredible events while occasionally observing the affluent customers with disdain:

'Cause I never 'ad any money, never had any money for me or the family. Sitting eatin' baked beans out of tin and I thought 'that's it'. That's all it is see, that's why everyone does it, livin' on the dole or doin' a job and 'avin no money, can't go out, can't live like everyone else [Damon pointed his fork at the other affluent people in the room]. That's why I left the last job, by the time I'd paid the bills and bought food I 'ad nothin' left. It's like I said before; I can earn more money workin' for myself.

Even though Damon could make money, sitting in Gemini Park that night it was as if a screen existed between Nova and the consumer society. Consumers look into that glass; images of people trying to survive poverty becomes crime. The domino effect is that young people living in poor communities remain excluded, simply because of how they appear. Like Linden, Damon had tattoos on his forearms, looked weathered and tough, and was always part of a crowd of similar men and women. Deep down I could also see that both men were troubled by what they had seen and lived through. Though whenever I was with members of the business or moochers in places like Gemini Park, strangers always treated each group with caution and hostility. Becker

(1963) suggests crime is a consequence of social interaction, a circular process involving people perceived as deviant, and the criminal justice system which then sanctions public perceptions through the law. Therefore, crime only becomes crime once an act has become criminalised through public perception and reaction. Within the context of my fieldwork, the only people who regarded 'working for yourself' as unlawful were outsiders. Foster (1990: 165) describes a similar contradiction, and the effect a milieu has on how certain activities are defined: 'these were not criminal "careers", just ordinary people whose everyday world took for granted certain kinds of crime'. Local employers saw young adults in Nova as an expendable short-term labour supply: to be worked for long hours on minimum wages. To avoid 'going under', as Linden described, members of the Business and moochers would opt to work together, usually out of the Pub. I would argue that both represent the English working class: even though both groups were self-employed, they were still subject to a system while maintaining class consciousness in order to survive within it (see Thompson, 1968).

Young adults' aspirations are reflected in the relationships people have with one another. To understand why young people become involved in 'mooching' and 'the Business' to achieve their aspirations, you have to appreciate how both activities give form and direction to memory. Barbara Misztal (2003) says memory is representations of the past, in ways that make them meaningful in the present.

Children under a shadow

Young adults could only adapt to exclusion outside of Nova's local economy, as working within it would mean an end to history. In short, young people would lose hope in the idea of community itself through becoming slaves to drudgery and misery associated with workfare. Eric Hobsbawm (1997: 14) argues, 'for the greater part of history we deal with societies and communities for which the past is essentially a pattern for the present'. In the previous chapter, young adults described how at school and in work coming from Nova resulted in being associated as a threat to society. For some young adults I spoke to, being perceived in those terms initially resulted in feeling inferior. Jay describes how he saw himself at school: 'I was quiet at school to a degree. When I was at Greaves I was a bit of a shit 'ead like I didn't smoke or anythin'. I just got me head down and got me subjects done. I didn't wag it or nothin.' Yet, that negative self-perception suggested that among his fellow residents, Jay was exposing himself to the stigma associated with Nova. Other young adults reacted in the same way as Linden when he was confronted with exclusion:

He [Linden's teacher] was callin' out the register one day. When he was callin' out the names he was chewin' a sweet. An' I was there chattin' to my mate. Then he spits out his sweet into the bin but he misses the bin. Then, because I didn't answer to my name he shouts out to me, 'Linden, come and pick this up and put it in the bin'. I just turned round and said 'You can fuck off'. He comes over to me and says to me 'What did you say', thinkin' that I'd say 'Nothin' Sir'. But I just said 'You can fuck right off'. Then he grabbed me to drag me out. But I just jumped back then smacked 'im in the mouth. And they suspended me for that. But I was in school the next day. Me mum wouldn't let me stay at home for weeks; she had me back in there the next day.

Robbie said:

I got chucked out of that school and then they accepted me at Nova Primary. But I got chucked out of that school 'cause I didn't like the teacher. See they were makin' this thing out of egg boxes, like a dragon or summit. Y'know the whole class was makin' this dragon, except me. They wouldn't let me do it, they made me do somethin' else, an' I was dead artistic like.

Jason described how he reacted to being labelled at school:

I was fifteen, just turned fifteen. I went in and 'cause I hardly ever went there they said I weren't getting any exams so I just left. I went down the Education Department to see if I could go to work instead of goin' to school and they said 'No you've gotta keep goin' in'. So, I worked on the sly.

Montana had been to several schools:

I kept gettin' thrown out . . . I got thrown out of juniors [school] for fighting the teachers then when I got to Greaves I got thrown out for hitting a teacher with a chair. Yeah, and the desk. He was standin' over me jabbin' me with his finger. So, I jumped up and the desk fell on his feet then I threw the chair at him. After that I went to Greaves.

Later I describe the structural forces working against young people on leaving school, and how exclusion echoed into the adult lives of Jay, Linden, Robbie and Montana because they were unable to leave the estate. Goffman (1963) describes stigma as a way of coping with a split between how we perceive ourselves and a category others impose upon us. Inside we feel like a human being like anyone else; a person, therefore, who deserves a fair chance and a fair break. Others, in the way they treat us, feel differently. Like Becker's (1963) account of the relationship between insiders and outsiders, for stigma to work, the stigmatised person must believe that others do not really accept him and are not willing to make contact with him on equal grounds. Goffman's (1963) idea of stigma is useful in the way it identifies how we can either reject or assume a label. Many young adults I met in Nova described feeling stigmatised for growing up there. That only occurred when young adults themselves believed how outsiders described them. Growing up, and being together with other young adults in similar situations in Nova, was a form of collective security against that feeling of stigma. Marshall McLuhan's (1964) distinction between an oral and a written history explains how young people were able to maintain a sense of history as a community within a society composed of images (see Olalquiga, 1992). As part of the culture of crime, the history outsiders associated with Nova was a written one, made of consumable images. Young adults told me how they were perceived as caricatures: as 'no good' or 'a waste of time'. Many young adults described feeling that no one was listening; that outsiders already had a ready-made representation of young people from Nova. My argument is that being looked at suspiciously as a member of community, and denied opportunities for the same reason, defined and sustained young people's exclusion in Nova. Linden described when he was unable to find work:

> The dole were heavily on my case. See when I was signin' on there would be four of us that went down. There'd be me, me brother, Liam and Steve. Yeah, we'd go and sign on and they'd always get me to go first. And when I went up they'd always pull out a form, a restart [interview]. They'd go and sign on, 'no problem, no problem'. When I went I got a restart, every week. I used to give 'em loads of grief. I mean, 'why me, why you pickin' on me'. But it was because I 'ad a skill. They knew I 'ad a skill and they thought 'look, you should be workin', there's no reason why you shouldn't be workin''.

The stigma Linden describes seemed to stem from the principle that young people from Nova are inherently bad or evil (see Baudrillard, 1988). Later Linden describes taking workfare jobs and being subject to the same principle, of being dismissed because employers felt that he was hostile and oppressed at work for the same reason. The process itself stemmed from what I describe as a masquerade of crime, whereby outsiders were seduced into treating Linden as different, largely because he was a young African-Caribbean man living in a poor community. Chapter 5 describes how even people sympathetic to the poverty young people faced, such as youth workers, would treat individuals as if they were inherently different from other young people in Ford. Among the young people I met in Nova, a handful seemed to have succumbed to the stigma of crime. Robbie was one of a handful of young adults I met who appeared to be losing hope: his experiences also showed how being unable to maintain self-respect left him exposed to further dangers from within and outside the community he had grown up in.

By winter, it seemed Robbie had fallen victim to the stigma associated with young people from Nova. Even though Robbie still had a good sense of humour and fascination with the world, like every young person I met in Nova, unlike Linden and his friends he was no longer able to participate as a member of a community. The value of Linden's community, which I witnessed and was part of myself, is a process best summed up by Barbara Adam (1995: 38), one that 'makes our lives worthy of being preserved in memory and story, worthy of being kept alive after our death'. Giddens (1991: 237) describes how 'human beings make their history in cognisance of that history', appropriating time rather than 'living it'. Being with younger adults, I was able to see how people were able to make their own history and watch it evolve through friendship.

Younger adults I knew at the Project continued to live by the school routine although they also seemed to be trying to develop their own. For instance, when the Project closed at 5 p.m., Chris, Antoine, Jason and Slim always seemed despondent, though they always managed to overcome that by devising plans for the night ahead. We often confuse routine with habit, both blind compulsions. Giddens (1991) describes routine as evidence of autonomy. To develop our own routine requires creativity and effort. Younger adults seemed more deeply affected by the closure of the Project, because all had invested more time and energy in it, compared with older men and women such as Liam and Linden. The closure also seemed to bring back memories of exclusion among younger men and women, some of whom, such as Slim and Jason, had only recently been expelled.

In interviews with younger people, directly after the Project closed, all spoke bitterly of being subject to unfair treatment. Like Pele, many young people I met at the Project had spent time in the Unit, a special enclosure within Greaves Secondary School. Being sent to the Unit was also usually a precursor to expulsion: Tony, Cliff, Jason and Slim had been sent to the Unit, and then expelled. Olly had been to another secondary school close to Nova, Hillcrest, where he was sent into a home apparently by school, as opposed to his parents. I conducted a group interview with Jason, Olly and Slim in a pub in the centre of Ford on the day the Project closed, and as we spoke it seemed as if the weight of the world was on their shoulders. Olly described his own experience of being passed around at school:

Olly: I got kicked out of Hillcrest [laughs] in the last year.

RM: Why?

Olly: Yeah, I dunno what 'appened as it goes. I got fuckin' stitched up, stitched up for. Dunno what the crack was, some fuckin' teacher dragged me out the lesson. She said I'd set fire to the woods or somethin'. I said 'what you goin on about?' That's why I missed my exams. I was meant to go back there. They put me in Sefton House and they said to me the work's too easy, they ain't got the work there for me. So they said they'd get me back to Hillcrest. That was it. So I was out of there and I never got a fuckin' letter off 'em.

RM: What was Sefton House, like a boys' home?

Olly: Na, it's a school not like a home. It was for kids that fucked about basically. But the work there was too easy, y'know. So they said there's nothin' 'ere for ya and they said they'd get me back in Hillcrest and I never heard fuck all from 'em.

RM: You never got a leaving certificate or anything?

Olly: Na, did I fuck. Said they'd sent a letter and that. I went back and they said it must have got lost.

RM: What was Sefton House like?

Olly: That was fuckin' shit, y'know like no one wanted to do any of the work and that. It was fuckin' shite.

RM: How long did you stay there?

Olly: I only stayed there about three weeks. They said like, 'nothin' 'ere for ya'.

RM: And what did you do when you left there. Did you have any money to live on?

Olly: Na, I 'ad to apply for a hardship allowance. Had that for about eight weeks, went on the dole when I was 17.

RM: Have you worked since you left Sefton House?

Olly: Only fuckin' part time. Like temp jobs and the fuckin' pay's been pretty shit.

Ellie was the only young adult I met who had not been advised to leave school at 16. In the previous chapter, Ellie described how she had been unable to afford studying without working full-time. The contingent nature of employment was reflected in what Willis (1977) describes as 'elements of a culture'. Willis (1977) describes the culture of 'the lads', the young adults in his study who went straight from school into manual jobs. Willis (1977) describes the lads' social world and also the process through which working-class culture is formed: 'the systematic self-preparation of the lads for a certain kind of work'. The problem for younger adults in Nova was that many had been led to believe the same opportunities would be waiting in redevelopments such as Gemini Park. As I described in Chapter 1, this economy thrived on temporary employment. When you read *Learning to Labour*, Nova's local youth labour market seemed a world away from certainties available to 'the lads' (Willis, 1977). Ricky told me about leaving school:

> Ricky: I stayed until I was 16 but I didn't do any exams or anythin'. I didn't go on the last week so I didn't get no certificate for leavin'.
> RM: Did you have a job when you left?
> Ricky: Well, I did like bits of work, just temporary like. Then I did this course a few months ago like to help you with confidence and that in interviews and things like that. Career Choice, that's what it was called.

In contrast to younger adults such as Slim and Jason, older men and women such as Linden, Damon and Montana seemed more certain about the future. Certainty usually comes with age though only because most people's economic circumstances improve in parallel. The fact that older young adults retained faith in themselves and the world reflects the resilience of each individual. In Chapter 5, I describe how leaving Nova to look for a better job often meant being exposed to isolation, and even greater economic and emotional uncertainty. Shortly before the Project closed, Jay, who had been on the workfare merry-go-round for almost ten years, told me he was considering taking up a four-year course to train as an engineer. Like Linden, Jay had left school to work in a factory:

> RM: You said you left when you were 16.
> Jay: Yep.
> RM: And you got a job straight away?
> Jay: Yeah, me Nan died and when she was dying she said she'd get me a job with my uncle.
> RM: And what did your uncle do?
> Jay: He worked in a forge. He was workin' on a press and he got me an office job, which was quite strange seein' that I was doin' engineerin'.
> RM: And what were you doing in there?
> Jay: I was just like office junior, paper work, filing, stuff like that.
> RM: And were you there long?
> Jay: I got made redundant, I was there 18 months. The forge shut down.
> RM: How many people were made redundant?
> Jay: A couple of hundred.
> RM: What happened when you left there?
> Jay: I left when I was 17. I got redundancy pay but not much 'cause I was only getting £40 a week.
> RM: Was it a YTS (Youth Training Scheme)?

Jay: No, because I've never been on a YTS. YTS at the time was £28 but they started me on as office junior. The lad before me went on to become production manager.

RM: And you think you would have progressed?

Jay: Yeah, they would have started another office junior and I would have gone into the main offices.

RM: But it shut down.

Jay: Yeah, they shut it down.

RM: So what did you do after that?

Jay: I just dossed around on the dole. You could sign on when you left school then, sign on when you were sixteen. So I started signing on.

Jay then reflected back to the time when he was made redundant; trying to pinpoint when he became trapped on the workfare merry-go-round of temporary jobs and conditional benefits. Like Martin, Jay was made redundant in the recession of 1990–1. Looking to the future, Jay, like Liam, told me he was considering a four-year course in computer-navigated engineering:

Jay: No, you've gotta be fully skilled. I mean I did City and Guilds at school in Basic Engineerin'. I should of went on to become a pattern maker, fabricator welder, sheet metal worker or whatever if I'd taken a course as soon as I left school. But I didn't. I thought 'I was workin', I'm getting some money' so I'm happy with that. But now, it's hard to get on a course for what you wanna do.

RM: Are there a lot of jobs in engineering?

Jay: There are but you've gotta be fully qualified. I mean if you wanna be a CNC machine operator, I mean you've gotta know how to work a machine through a computer, which they didn't teach us that at school. No, most of 'em now is CNC.

RM: So you're about to start on a four-year course?

Jay: Yeah, I've been down and they said it would take anythin' up to six months to get on the course. But, they've gotta make sure that I'm gonna get on with the course. I mean it's four years. They're gonna put faith in me and I've gotta put faith in them. Obviously I want a job that's gonna pay me well at the end of the day after four years trainin' I should be earnin' a good wage. I dunno, a couple of hundred pound a week and I'll be happy. But, once you're in Nova it's difficult to get out of that regime. Y'know you're like stuck in a rut.

During the year of my fieldwork, only Hannah, Linden's partner, and Ellie had full-time jobs. For everyone else, young men and women were lucky if jobs lasted for more than a month: these were 'long-term temporary' as opposed to short-term, which lasted a week at best. Then young people were dismissed, in what was almost a pattern; individuals were treated with suspicion from the outset then working relations deteriorated further and further. Again there seemed to be need to stigmatise and with purpose, mainly because young adults were looked upon as expendable. To cope, it seemed many young people became very realistic about the nature of the local economy generally. Jay explained what happened after he was made redundant shortly after leaving school:

Jay: In those two years. Basically enjoyin' myself. Mainly it was smokin' the draw [cannabis] like with the lads, 'avin' sessions and that. I was livin' with this girl at the time and she was pregnant, after five weeks. So, basically I was thinkin' 'oh shit'. So I was thinkin' I should do the honourable thing so I stayed with her for a couple of years. I got a job the day me daughter was born. I stayed there for a couple of months. Me missus got pregnant again but she had an abortion cause she said she already had a son. So I had to leave me job because [pause] of the situation we were in and the time. So, I was there for like four months.

RM: What were you doing?

Jay: I was makin' Christmas crackers.

RM: And then, you went back on the dole when you left there?

Jay: Yeah, I went back on the dole again. Stayed on the dole for another couple of years. Went to Tel Vision [electrical distribu- tors], stayed there for two months. Then I got made redundant from there. Left Tel Vision. Then I was on the dole for another couple of years. '95 started workin' at this waste reproduction place. Stayed there for about six weeks, [pause] dirty job, dirty job. You'd get all the skip hire places and they'd tip it all in. Then we'd have to like look through it and get everythin' out of it that was metal. Then we'd stack it up so it could go into a lorry and then they'd take it to a landfill.

RM: Was that the last job you had?

Jay: Na, I stayed there for like six or seven weeks. From there, Huey's brother got me a job at his place. So I went there as a Hand Flatter [metal press operator]. I was doin' that. I was like hand flattin' down all day so. I couldn't do it to the target they wanted me to do it. Basically, they said it had to be bang on [perfect]. Then, 'cause it took so long to get each one bang on they'd say why ain't you done so many. So, that was it. You had to be fast at it and you've also gotta get it perfect.

RM: So they let you go.

Jay: Yeah, I was just there for two weeks. Two weeks training period. Then they said 'look, obviously you can't do it. Would you like to stay behind, make up to what it should be but you won't get paid.' An' I said 'yeah, right. No one in Nova would do that. Workin' for an extra two hours and not gettin' paid for it, you've got no hopes.' So that was the last job I had.

In Chapter 5, young adults describe how employers would use dismissal or intimidation as a way maintaining a trainee workforce: either young people were pressured to leave before the end of their course, or they would be sacked to make way for another candidate. The fact that Jay could maintain his faith that local employers will not continue to discriminate once he had completed his four-year engineering course reflects the resilience young people have in the face of exclusion. Yet, Jay is also a Caucasian man, which means he was free from the experiences Benita, Montana, Tony, Martin and Linden have to face (see Ullah, 1987; Foster, 1990; B. Campbell, 1993). Later, Linden, Tony and Martin describe incidents of racial discrimination, particularly at the hands of local employers and the criminal justice system.

Just thievin'

Martin worked at his uncle's construction firm for 18 months until the industry went into recession at the end of the 1980s. After being made redundant, Martin's £180 a week pay cheque was replaced by £27 a week Income Support; to buy food, utilities and cover the cost of looking for work. During our interview, Martin told me that his life before unemployment was an exciting if momentary time. Within the space of a year after Martin was made redundant he had drifted into what he referred to as 'just thievin'', which finally ended in his arrest for armed robbery. At 18 Martin was sentenced to four years in prison. Finally released shortly after his twenty-first birthday, Martin was set apart from the other young former prisoners I knew in Nova through his determination never to go back. Of course, none of the young adults I knew in Nova wanted to go to jail but only Martin seemed to live a life that could make that aspiration possible. During a series of long in-depth interviews at his flat, Martin described his experiences in prison, its impact on his life and his perspective on it. He said:

For me prison was a good thing. I read my first book when I was in prison and I haven't stopped since. The first book took me to foreign countries; y'know like showed me different perspectives. I read *The Times* in jail. I never read the news or financial pages; I couldn't tell you the best shares to invest your money in [laughs]. Instead I used to read the travel pages and book reviews. They were like the books y'know. Now I'd like to travel and see different countries, before I read these books I used to think everyone 'round the world were the same as the people 'round 'ere.

Martin also described other prisoners:

> One bloke in the cell next door was in for four years for molesting two young girls . . . and he'd already served the same term for the same offence. See I was in for robbery and they put me in with this guy right who's interfered with little girls. And all I did was scare one woman for 30 seconds and she was even told on the job just to hand over the money . . . The justice system is really fucked up if he's seen as the same as me.

Like all young adults I got to know in Nova, Martin lived at the centre of a weak system of interdependence (see Braithwaite, 1989). His family lived on the other side of the city, as did his partner and first son (see Pearson, 1983; Cohen, 1987). During the period of my fieldwork Martin persisted in looking for a worthwhile job though he was focused on trying to gain a lease for a clothes shop in the city centre. Martin was also one of the first people to enrol on an accounting course at Gateways, the adult education centre that opened during the latter half of my fieldwork.

Yet the problem for many young people was that to remain living in Nova, particularly the Precinct area, meant being exposed to continuing exclusion. Martin, like many other young people I spoke to, was also aware that a life outside of Nova was an even more atomised and uncertain world. He explained, 'Yeah, I mean I want to move into a nice area, to a house. There's no point going to another area like this, they're all the same, Sefton, Moorside. I want to be able to send my kids to college. I got a kid, they live in Halford which is just like 'ere. The houses round 'ere are painted in the same colour as prison cells.'

John Braithwaite (1989) argues that shaming offenders is a way of integrating individuals back into society, through policies such as community-based sentences. As I show in Chapter 5, even when individuals were fortunate to escape Nova, that often meant leaving family, friends and community.

Racism

Linden's working life within local companies and for local employers involved being unfairly dismissed repeatedly.

> I started at Weston's when I was 16. Left when I was 20, that's four years. I used to have a car in them days and the car was always

playin' up. It wouldn't start in the mornin' and I'd come in late. I was comin' in late and I got a written warnin'. Then I got a final written warnin'. See the policy there was when you got a final written warnin' you 'ad to come in for six months with no lateness. For four months I got in, the car wasn't givin' me any trouble. Then, one mornin', my car was stolen. So I phoned in and told them me car 'ad been nicked, left them a message. Then I phoned the police, notified them it 'ad been stolen. Then I got the bus in and when I got in the supervisor told me to come into his office. I went in and he told me 'you're sacked'. I said to him 'look my car was nicked; there was nothin' else I could do. I phoned in and left a message that my car 'ad been nicked.' Then he said he didn't believe me so I told him to phone the police station. He did and they told him that I'd reported it nicked. But then he still said you're sacked and he said 'I'll have to escort you off the premises'. I said to him I wanted to go and clear out me locker but he said 'Come on Linden, you know the policy. I have to escort you off the premises in case you do anything stupid.' So he led me out through the factory, everyone lookin' at me knowin' what had happened, and I lost me temper. I turned 'round and battered 'im. Then, that night, I got home and went to the Pub. I 'ad a few pints in there and went back home and they swooped on me. Six cars swooped on me and they arrested me for assault.

Then I got a job at Sedgwick engineerin'. I worked there for a year. I got on all right with the gaffer; I got on all right with the people there. But then the gaffer asked me into his office one day. So he hands me the letter and I read it: 'Dear Mr Davis, blah, blah, blah. I am afraid, due to err lack of work we are going to have to let you go.' So, I read that and thought fair enough, there's no work for me there. So, I went home. I thought it might have been because of me but maybe I was just getting' paranoid. Then, the next day, a mate I knew there phones up and tells me they've only gone and started four new blokes.

So I went to try and get it taken to a tribunal. I went to Citizens Advice and they put me onto this place down the town. But because I hadn't been workin' there for more than two years they reckoned I wouldn't have a chance. I reckon it was because I was black. The other lad I knew there was Manny. They sacked him four weeks later. How they got him was . . . they told him that there was no overtime. He wanted to do overtime but they said no, there's none. So he went home, sayin' that there was nothin' he could do about it, it wasn't 'is fault. So he's gone home and then he finds out the next day that his mate was doin' his job as overtime, that night. So the next night I phones up the unit. No, that's it. I gets me girlfriend to phone up and she asks if me mate is there; 'is so-and-so there please'. Then, when the lad comes on the phone, I pulls it off her and shouts 'Right, I'm comin' down there. You cunts said there was no overtime.' Then I gets in the car and drives down there. And when I gets there all the shutters are down and the police are waitin' for me. I dunno what they thought I was gonna do, go mad or somethin'. But I just said I came down to see why they said there was no overtime. Then I got another [engineering] job.

And then I got grief there. Fuckin' grief again. When I applied for the job it's said on the form 'Do you have a criminal record'? And I've put 'No', no big deal. I get the job. Then on the first day the supervisors showin' me where I'll be workin' and I see this lad I knew at school. Then when he left school he became a copper and he was always stoppin' me when he was a copper. He'd stop me and say 'your exhaust is broken; get it fixed or I'll arrest ya tomorrow'. And when he was at school he was a right tearaway, I know 'cause I used to hang around with 'im. And then he arrested me. Anyway, I asked 'im why he wasn't a copper any more and he said he got bored with it and left. And then what happens, four weeks later, over the tanoy: 'Could Linden come to the office please'. I goes in and the gaffer's standin' there with my application form. He says you wrote down here that you don't have a criminal record and we've found out that you 'ave. You know who told 'em don't ya? I fuckin' hated him.

Gender and crime

Benita and Montana described working in Ford and each woman's account reflects how circumscribed the local service economy was by gender. Most jobs available were working as service providers. Other jobs such as car repair outlets often discriminated in favour of men. Women were clearly 'preferred' in industries such as nursing and cleaning. I found no figures to prove this, only what I observed. Even though jobs had a greater degree of stability, they remained temporary. Montana said: 'I did an NVQ in catering at Ford University. I've had loads of jobs in catering; I worked at the Minster Hotel for two days, the Marsh Hotel for 13 months, and the Hilton for two nights. I worked for Moto's for two months, y'know the service station. They were only temporary jobs.'

The workfare merry-go-round Benita and Montana described seemed identical to opportunities available to young men. Benita was forced to alternate between temporary work and state benefits, a 'low pay – no pay' cycle of temporary employment and unemployment (Giddens, 2000). This also meant Benita rarely had time and we held our interview in a waiting room at Ford's main benefits office two days before

Christmas. When I arrived, it was raining and through the tinted glass of the big building, I saw Benita. Inside room D, almost all of the iron benches were full; young people alone like Benita, couples, and families waiting for a number to be relayed on an LCD screen. As each number appeared, individuals or couples would sit before an advisor. Everyone, staff and clients, looked stressed despite the approaching holiday. Some of the tension was eased by the radio; people lost themselves in songs or sometimes hummed along. I asked Benita how long she had been waiting:

Benita: Since eleven. [I had arrived at 3 p.m.]
RM: What are you trying to get?
Benita: A crisis loan. I will get one.
RM: For Christmas?
Benita: Yeah.
RM: Will you have to pay it back?
Benita: That's what they think.
RM: Don't you find it frustrating being on the dole, without any money?
Benita: No, I can do what I want. And I've always got money.

Benita's comment about always having money personified her own and Montana's self-belief: both were very poor though they never acknowledged it in public. In Chapter 4, I describe the how self-respect and tenacity were strategies that kept Linden's circle of friends together. Throughout that afternoon with Benita, one of the few times I was alone with one person, I felt torn apart by her situation. Staying alive under the shadow of exclusion is reflected in the way Tony and Linden, Montana and Benita are always together. Despite a slight age gap, both had bonded at school through common interests. As Benita explained: 'She lives near me. And we were at the same school. Montana got moved there after bein' expelled from Hillcrest. We'd wag it [truant] together; go down the town and that. Out at night, smoke draw [cannabis] and that. We both like the same things, ragga' music [dancehall], going to dancehalls, black men [laughs].'

Montana had spent a significant part of her adolescence in foster homes, Young Offenders Institutions, and finally prison:

Montana: First time I was fifteen, I got a caution; second time got a caution. Then I was put on remand then probation then I had to do community service then community service again then they put me in a home then they sent me to jail when I was old enough.
RM: You didn't go to jail until you were 16?
Montana: Na, but before that they put me in a home when I'd left Greaves. They put me in this home for boys and girls, but they put me on the boys' wing. Because I was a bit of a tomboy.

About the future Montana said, 'I'm goin' to Tenerife in two weeks for Christmas. But after that I'm just gonna stay there and work. I'll get a job in the clubs at night, to pay the rent then just sit on the beach all day with a bottle of brandy.' I asked Montana if she would miss Ford and her friends. She replied 'Na'; there's nothin' for me here. All the girls I knew at school are all stuck with kids. I don't want that. Na', there's nothin' for me in Ford or Nova, only my mum. You always end up on your arse then you have to go out thievin'.' Montana summed up Nova's local economy and echoed Jay's account of how the responsibilities of parenting seem to count for little on the workfare merry-go-round.

Youthful aspirations

Montana was going shopping with Benita and I asked if I could go with them. Linden had also wanted to come along, simply as a release from Nova. Montana was living with her mother at that time. When we arrive, Linden goes up to the door politely knocks then waits. The door opens and Montana steps out into the brilliant sunshine dressed entirely in black. Linden compliments Montana then escorts her to the waiting car. Once inside, Montana phones Benita on her mobile to arrange where to pick her up. Benita is on a course at the local technical college and asks if we can meet her there as she finishes at noon for the day.

On the way, Montana hands me a bootlegged recording of a reggae night at a local club. The music is dancehall. Dancehall is reggae though gets its name through the fact that many records were censored and labelled unfit for radio airplay, only the dancehall. When the tape goes on, Montana lights a joint and starts getting into the infectious music. After picking up Benita, a backseat party begins, while Linden sits shaking his head in the front seat. The destination was Webster, a peaceful rural town. Like two friendly couples, Benita and Montana went shopping while Linden and I waited in the car.

As we sat chatting a cavalcade of motorbikes burble past: then, I see the two girls appear in the rear view mirror. Montana and Benita are giggling and clutching each other. On the way home, Montana and Benita try on eyeliner pencils and blue and orange hair colour spray. At one point Montana produces a pack of silk G-strings and one pair of knickers. After trying the knickers on my head, she then proceeded to spray blue hairspray over me, 'just to see if it suits you'.

Montana and Benita went on shopping trips; even though the goods they obtained were ephemeral, the occasions allowed both to achieve a sense of excitement and self-respect. Katz (1988) argues such crimes are motivated by a 'sentimental materialism' though I would argue the mixture of material gain and excitement achieved in these crimes was a consequence of the perpetual present of consumer culture, a world within which everyone is trapped. Just like a consumer lifestyle, 'the shift', mooching and 'the session' were all opportunities to step into consumer culture and out of poverty, even for just a day. 'The session' and 'the shift' also regulated time by turning the day into a circadian process of wish-fulfilment. Mooching usually occurred between 9 a.m. and 8 p.m. while sessions usually took place after that, going on until 1 or 2 a.m.

Barbara Adam (1995: 38) describes how we use time to transcend the prospect of death, 'endowed with it, human beings do not merely undergo their presents, and pasts, they shape and reshape them'. With what little resources young people have, each person does the same with culture to shape time, confirming Adam's (1995: 37) statement that 'To relate to birth death origin and destiny is an existential condition of human cultural life.' As with listening to Hip Hop music, which I explore in the following chapter, going out on the shift and the session were times and places where young people could step into a consumer lifestyle. 'The shift' involves getting 'suited and booted', as Linden and Tony described.

> Linden: They'd usually be about three of us. We'd get dressed up, in suits, get in a car; go to London, pull up on an industrial estate. See, they'd be like a team of us, usually three of us. I'd be the driver. So I'd be the driver and we'd 'ave a lad who'd go out for a walk about. He'd go into offices.
>
> Tony: I mean if you're suited and booted you get a lot further. See if I've got a suit on I'm gonna' get through two or three people. But if I've got a tracksuit on someone's gonna' say summit straightaway, see what I'm sayin'. It's part of the blag.

When I was out with Tony, he often drew money from other people's accounts and often seemed to revel in the process itself. In his interview, Tony described his progression into what he described as 'the life of crime'.

> RM: What have you done since you left school?
>
> Tony: Robbin' stuff, robbin' from building societies then just went up the ladder, cheque books, credit cards, industrial estates, defrauding from banks. Fraud mainly. I'll get up, get in my car and drive to an industrial estate. Just walk around seein' what I can take. If you can sell it, I'll take it.
>
> RM: Is it not difficult now?
>
> Tony: Yeah, but I'm really clever. Like the locks they've got on the doors now, the coded locks, I can get past all of them.
>
> RM: So if you get a card you go straight to the bank?
>
> Tony: It all depends. Like if I go out and get a woman's handbag and I've got a bird with me. If the number ain't in her handbag

I'll phone her up, say I'm the bank and eight times out of ten it works. Then, go to the bank get the money out the cash point and that'll do me. If I get like a bloke's wallet and I can do the signature and there's a drivin' licence I'll go into the bank. If the bloke's signature is too hard and there's no drivin' licence I'll phone 'im up. If he gives me the PIN numbers it's sound, if he doesn't it's a waste but I'll carry on.

RM: If you've got a bloke's drivin' licence and a cheque book you can clear the account out?

Tony: Yeah, you go in and get a balance and that is it. The maximum I've ever taken out, £11,000. That was from a cheque. I went to a business and got the cheque from 'round the back out the back of the business account book. Then I went to the front and asked them if they had any jobs. They said no so I asked if the boss could write me a compliments slip so I could show it to the dole. Then I put his signature on the cheque and cashed it.

'Mooching', 'going out on the shift' and 'the session' could be interpreted as habitual, and on the surface Martin fulfilled the stereotype of a repeat offender. However, as I describe in the next chapter, Martin, like many other moochers I met, personified the entrepreneurial spirit of the 1980s. In many ways, that spirit still seemed to define the public culture of the Precinct during my fieldwork. Another was the sense of social disintegration that characterised many of Britain's inner cities during the 1980s (see Carley, 1990).

When the Project closed, all that was left was consumer culture, and it seems that after that point individuals became more exposed to exclusion. The majority of young people I met there literally disappeared into the Precinct. People I was able to stay with seemed more susceptible to crime, because the intermediate space the Project provided, between public and private culture, was no longer there to bracket both.

Herbert Gans (1999: 5) makes the distinction between public and private culture: 'one people create and practice at home', another 'closer to a vicarious than to a lived'. Linden's social world, centred around his flat, was like a chorus involving both, yet with no defined time limit. The word 'chorus' derives from *chora*, a place in ancient Greece where plays and festivals would take place. Plato (1957: 50b–c), described it as a space 'receiving all things, and never in any way takes on any character that is like any other things that enter it: by nature it is there as a matrix for everything, changed and diversified by the things that enter it'. Yet, constituting a social world through consumer culture meant that compared with the concrete certainty that the Project provided, Linden's was a much more fragile place. To borrow another Greek term, the Project was a *topos*: a landscape or container that was permanent to change.

When the Project did close, young people I met were left in the perpetual present Jameson (1998) describes: an everyday world of disposable culture. At the Project, friendship was given continuity by the walls of the building itself. No one had to have a reason to go there, and through that feeling of equanimity, young people were able to make an emotional investment, investing and partaking in one another's friendship. Ray Pahl (2000: 14) describes why friendship needs a reason: 'Friendship exists largely through an involvement in certain kinds of activities, which generates sentiments, which in turn encourage further activities.' The sentiment Linden and Tony shared seem to drive the culture of 'the shift'. Yet the disposable nature of opportunities in that culture was reflected in the way moochers, even successful ones such as Jimmy and Baz, were unable to break the stigma associated with how they appeared and where they came from. My belief, which I evidence in Chapter 5, was a deep psychological need on the part of people living outside of Nova to exclude young residents who tried to work for themselves.

In Chapter 1, I described how status is no longer defined by social class boundaries but through the accumulation of commodities. Jameson (1998) argues the consumer society is a 'perpetual present' because consumers themselves define their existence according to body time. We may think we are being innovative, though the reality is a repetitive cycle of consumption and destruction, of commodities and essentially our own image. As a result, we can never truly belong to a community, because our existence is defined by the pursuit of personal desires. Even though moochers and members of the business were entrepreneurs, each person's life was defined by what the philosopher Heidegger (1927) described as 'being in the world'.

Crime, Youth and Exclusion concludes by showing how thinking about crime gradually shaped government thinking on youth crime, to justify a culture in which consumption is an end in itself (Galbraith, 1985). Policy on 'youth' crime is influenced by the idea of peer associations and the assumption that 'negative associations make young people susceptible to crime' (Elmer and Reicher, 1995: 216). The idea of negative peer associations has clear parallels with policy on anti-social behaviour, whereby unsupervised groups of young people are seen as a threat. In Chapter 7, I show how labelling behaviour in such terms often exposes people to further exclusion such as self-abuse. Interestingly, Edwin Sutherland (1949) claimed that 'white-collar' criminals were less likely to be prosecuted, as employers felt individuals would deteriorate psychologically. I would argue that the affluent resist understanding the relationship between crime and poverty in order to preserve the integrity of a consumer lifestyle.

Writing on the consumer society, Jameson (1998: 7) describes 'the masks and voices stored up in the imaginary museum of a global culture'. The masks imposed on young adults create each person's experience of exclusion. Because the only way young adults are able to survive 'going under' was through friendship, the stigma associated with Nova's young adult community continued. Jimmy told me, 'Yeah, 'cause my parents were poor I had to go out and earn money. I started picture sellin' when I was 13.' The stigma that surrounds picture selling in Ford personifies the exclusion of Nova's young adults when they try to work for themselves. The trade began in the early 1980s: four or five people would try to sell reproduction pictures – from French Impressionists to more contemporary designs – to a growing army of homeowners:

> Steve: Yeah, first term of the fifth year. I got expelled and then I began signing on. Then I went picture sellin'. Yeah, but everyone was at it then. There was like twelve cars goin' out, people were advertisin' in the fuckin' paper it was that fuckin' mad, that easy. But I wasn't any good at it.
>
> RM: So what did you do instead?
>
> Steve: I started the life of crime. Goin' out, doin' fraud, goin' out on the shift.
>
> RM: What does 'the shift' mean?
>
> Steve: Goin out, robbin' people. Robbin' people for their plastic (credit cards) then you work 'em. At first, before cards and that it was post office books. But then, when we first started getting cards we used to just hope for the pin numbers and the cash just hopin'. If we never found the numbers we'd just throw it away. We didn't know how to work cards and shops and shit like that. All that plastic we threw away, all those gold cards, we were only after the pin numbers in those days or cash, nuff cash.

Linden said crime was 'a pattern in Nova' because everyone he knew living there was unemployed and many worked for themselves in an informal economy. Crime, as Linden described it, was a subjective experience shared in a working relationship. For the majority of my respondents, the distinction between crime and work lay between stealing from your own and making money from consumers. There was a strong animosity towards those who 'stole from their own' as they are perceived as creating victims in an already victimised community. Steve told me angrily, 'It's the little rogues give Nova a bad name, the shoplifters and the burglars. Little fuckin' bastards, should bang them all up. They'll all take it up the arse.' Yet, other young people expressed empathy towards those who committed burglaries. Jay said that crimes committed in Nova were often just to escape the desperation many faced (see Chapter 5).

While some young people displayed what Katz (1988) describes as 'sentimental materialism' out on the shift, others were more rational; one moocher described how, 'We'd go out on industrial estates moochin' and I'd just go into a few buildin's gettin' compliments slips sayin' to them "look, I'm just lookin' for work". Showin' proof that I am lookin'. So I'd get compliments slips, signed and dated, show them to the dole.' Moochers who told me about going out on the shift also described looking for 'legitimate' jobs at the same time, and not just to placate the job centre. Out on the shift, moochers frequently talk about the opportunities available at certain companies. Yet, as a participant observer during these conversations, the poverty and exclusion awaiting young people back in Nova seemed a world away from the affluence and prosperity we witnessed out on the shift. Companies were often high-tech, situated in purpose-built out-of-town sites that often appear idyllic and affluent.

Successful moochers, such as Jimmy and Baz, were drawn to what Taylor (1999: 52) describes as a 'market society': 'a society in which everything (from consumer goods to public goods like health and educational opportunity) is for sale', a place where 'the idea of consumption is at the centre of everyday lived experience'. Many moochers I spoke to described being drawn to that world. Chapter 4 identifies the trauma successful moochers experienced in being unable to escape exclusion.

Several American studies on unemployment at a local level echo the intractable situation young people in Nova faced after the Project (see Sullivan, 1989; Williams, 1989; Anderson, 1990; Padilla, 1992; Bourgois, 1995). In each study, young people are faced with a situation in which, on the one hand, there is a lack of decent jobs, and on the other, opportunities in informal markets multiply though they provide none of the securities of regular work.

Ethnographic studies such as Sullivan's (1989) are important as they identify how young people living in economically deprived areas have to rely on themselves and one another. *Gettin' Paid* (Sullivan, 1989) shows how young people have to innovate through culture economies such as drug use and supply. This was the same in Nova too, where drugs were a commodity and a means of managing uncertainty.

How society represents drug use and associates it with crime reflects the image consumers have of themselves. Giddens (1991: 181) describes living in today's shifting present, where 'Feelings of restlessness, foreboding and desperation may mingle in individual experience with faith in the reliability of certain forms of social and technical framework'. Giddens (1990, 1991) also writes about how we try to bracket uncertainty by developing a protective cocoon. For many young people, drug use was an accepted method of protecting against the stigma of crime. Even though use was occasional and rarely problematic, the strategy became part of the dialectical process identified in Chapter 1.

In Rosalind Coward's (1994) mythic landscape of the council estate, drugs are recurring features of what is portrayed as a profane culture.

For J. K. Galbraith (1992), stigmatising poor communities in such ways helps sustain what he describes as a culture of contentment, one where consumption is an end in itself. Baudrillard (1988: 199) describes how the guilt of the consumer is displaced into the object of an underclass: 'It is not desire that we cannot escape, but the ironic presence of the object, its indifference, and its indifferent interconnections, its challenge, its seduction, its violation of the symbolic order (therefore the subject's unconscious as well, if it had one. In short, it is the principle of evil we cannot escape.' In Chapter 1, I described how socially excluded young adults are objectified by policy and the media. Baudrillard (1988: 199) goes a step further to suggest that socially excluded young people are described as evil, providing us with 'a soul and a face', enabling us to divert the shame of excess.

'The life', lived as a community of young people, was a defence against the chaos created by the prospect of a lifetime of exclusion and poverty. Living 'the life' helped sustain the feeling of transcendence that Adam (1995) describes: each day separated between the public culture of 'mooching' and 'the shift' and the private culture of 'the session'. However, as soon as both began to dissolve into one another, such as through the use of drugs in public, users themselves were in danger of becoming outcasts within Nova itself.

Shit Street

Over the time I spent at the Project, I sensed a deep feeling of oppression, which seemed to thread through young people's experience of growing up in Nova. Being excluded from work was clearly a factor in people's sense of frustration, though boredom fails to encapsulate the stress these young men and women must have felt. When young people talked in interviews about their experiences of exclusion, they were always articulated with passion and anger. Drug use is a way of containing that anger though practically all of the young people I met in Nova described how drugs, legal or illegal, only sustained exclusion.

On the rare occasions that young adults in the project smoke cannabis, 'smokin' draw' is a way of neutralising frustrations. Yet, when people were seen to be smoking regularly, something Sean was intolerant of as it put the Project in jeopardy, friends would often intervene, usually by suggesting a game of pool or football outside. The closeness of young people's friendships was one reason why, in the four months I spent at the Project, I never witnessed problematic use. Another was because so few people could afford to maintain a regular supply of cannabis or cigarettes: both were often marked out as last resorts. People sometimes did find the money for a smoke though, as I describe in the following chapter, drug use, outside of the private culture of 'the session', signified a loss of self-respect and disrespect towards friends. Huey, for instance, was helping Jay 'stay off the draw'. Jay himself told me how using cannabis all the time was fundamentally destructive.

> Night comes and most lads will think 'right, time for the session'. I mean I've done that, I've been there, but it gets borin' after a while. I mean I've done it for ten years. I mean I've stopped smokin' draw now an' I've been smokin' for ten years. It's hard but I just thought no it's not for me anymore. I mean I've been smokin' it everyday, it's just a daily occurrence. People say you don't get addicted to cannabis but you do.

Like Jay, many young people described how drug use only seemed to expose people to the chaos Steve spoke of, as Slim testified during a conversation we had about his experiences in Nova's local service industries:

> Slim: Like they're shit jobs, you don't need any skills. But if you want a good job you've gotta get trainin' but the trainin' schemes only pay £35 a week, you can't live on that. £35 a week for two years. And you can't live on that for two years, no way. You can't live on £35 when you're 18. An every time you go and sign on they try and get you on these courses. Thing is the dole don't make you wanna get work, it's like free money. But in Nova you need a fuckin' job. It's a ghost town now. If you're livin' 'round Nova you've gotta be drunk or stoned. If you ain't got a drink or a smoke of draw it ain't worth comin' out is it. You either need girls, drink or drugs or a fuckin' car or summit. You don't wanna be goin' out robbin' and that, but you have to. I virtually know every cunt in Nova and that's what they're all up to. If you ain't fuckin' thievin' you ain't no one, they're fuckin' bored shitless. Even the younger ones, hangin' around the chip shop. That's how I made money, sellin' fuckin' draw, anythin' you can get your hands on. That's what I used to do, but then I smoke it and then you get yourself in debt and then you 'ave to go out robbin'. 'Cause you have to get your money to pay them off somehow. I used to sell the draw and I was rakin' it in. I used to get £700 and then I'd just go out on the piss for three days and I've come back £700 in debt, £1,500 on the session, fuckin' back in shit street.
>
> RM: What about going to jail?
>
> Slim: Yeah that's why I stopped doin' shit. But it's in your face, you see all the moochers with a wedge in your pocket. That's the only opportunity to get makin' money. What you earn in a fuckin' month you can earn in a night, goin' out on the shift and that.

As Slim described this situation, he did so with an incredible sense of anger and frustration. It is also important to say that he was not being literal; this was a taped interview, which I had arranged with Slim in advance. Like many young people I interviewed, I could see that Slim was trying to condense and contain experiences that had been lived and endured for years and sometimes decades.

Young people described exclusion as a lifetime overshadowed by poverty, crime and drugs. 'The life' is a delicate web of friendship between young people that protects against self-destruction. Christmas in Nova highlighted that experience and how young people managed to survive through friendships. This period is generally a time when consumerism penetrates almost every aspect of life under the guise of a cultural occasion. A desire and pressure to buy presents for family and friends combined with the work opportunities available made this a tense time for many young people. Among the young people I was with at that time, friendship was the only way to survive that economic and emotional pressure.

Linden phoned saying Steve had let him down. In the Pub the day before, Linden had found out that a light-engineering company were looking for staff for the Christmas period. Linden, Liam and Martin wanted to start and needed a lift; Steve, who had a car at that time, had agreed to start as well, ensuring a lift for all three. The following day, the day Linden called, Steve called Linden saying he could not make it. Waiting for Linden to get ready in his living room, Liam said how the job provided an opportunity to 'get a wedge for Christmas'. Linden came in putting on layers of clothing for the cold night that lay ahead. I said I might not be able to make every night; Linden had 'got it covered', as the boss of the factory would give them a lift after tonight. Stuffing a big lunch box into his rucksack, we all got up to leave.

The factory was situated on the outskirts of Mowbray, a small industrialised town ten miles north of Ford. As we travelled further and further along the motorway Linden, Liam and Martin commented on the increasing distance. I was nervous about being able to find the factory the following morning. Finally, at ten minutes to six, we arrived at the small engineering plant at the end of a gravel track off a suburban street. I dropped them off to 'cheers Rob, you know where to come in the morning'. I assured them I would find the place. Stepping outside of the tiny industrial unit the following freezing morning into the dark, Martin, Linden and Liam looked pale and physically drained. All piled into the back seat to share heat and I asked how it went. Linden said there was no heating (the temperature that night was −5); Martin added 'we need a fuckin' radio in there'. Later Liam told me he was working on a lathe that had no guard at the bottom and the leg of his jeans was shredded when it caught in the machinery. Back at Nova, I dropped Martin and Liam at Martin's flat so the two could have a smoke. Running towards the Precinct, Martin whispered into the cold air, 'need a spliff [cannabis joint] to knock me out'.

That night characterised the frustrations and inequalities all of the young people I met had experienced while working on Nova's workfare merry-go-round. The desperation created by the lead up to Christmas, a frenzy of consumption generally, was manifest in the fact that all three worked for a week at the firm until it was impossible to make the 40-mile distance to and from Mowbray. Another impossible reality was that all three men were desperate to work. Yet Linden, Martin and Liam all supported one another, and prevented what Linden referred to as 'going under'. In Chapter 4, I show what happened when young people were no longer able to hold onto 'the life'.

Chapter 4

Respect

The previous chapter showed how young people were able to survive exclusion through a strategy many described as 'working for yourself'. I also showed how young adults retained a culture of community in order to sustain hope in the future. As I have pointed out throughout this study, the structural conditions young adults had to survive determined the culture of 'the life'. In this chapter I identify how maintaining self-respect – in the clothes young people wore, their music and outlook – was perceived as a culture of crime among those living outside Nova. Finally, I describe how young people coped with the stigma of crime, and what happened when individuals succumbed to it.

Gangsters

The aim of this study is to identify the processes by which young people's subjective experience of poverty and exclusion is perceived as crime. This interactive process involves the mastery of images that make the consumer society, central to which are images of young people living in deprived communities. This recently occurred in the reproduction of a series of images advertising products for the sportswear manufacturer Reebok. One image depicted the Hip Hop artist 50 Cent (real name Curtis Jackson). In one of the advertisements, a gunshot is heard and 50 Cent counts slowly up to nine – the number of times he was shot outside his grandmother's house in Queens New York in 2000. Curtis Jackson asks: 'who you planning to massacre next?', referring to 50 Cent's new album, *The Massacre* (50 Cent, 2005). 50 Cent then laughs and Reebok's slogan 'I am what I am' appears. Reebok's campaign was dropped after complaints that the advert glamorised gang violence. A similar event occurred just after 50 Cent was shot in 2001: originally signed to

Columbia Records, the label dropped Jackson while he was still recovering in hospital. In a recent interview (Russell, 2003), 50 Cent said: 'Columbia didn't understand 50 Cent; to them, people (like me) only get shot on TV. I was shot three days before I was supposed to shoot my first video. They freaked out. Major labels would prefer to work with "studio gangsta's", it's less of a risk.'

The outrage that surrounded the Reebok campaign characterises 'the life' young people I met lived to escape the death of workfare. *Get Rich or Die Tryin'* (50 Cent, 2003) was the title of the album that launched 50's career and encapsulates the situation faced by many young people I met in Nova. By using Reebok to advertise his own album, Jackson was inserting the subjective experience of living in a poor community into a culture with no meaning. The phenomenal global success of both Jackson's music and the Reebok campaign clearly represents a contradiction, whereby affluent consumers are consuming an experience replicated through consumption. Young people in Nova listened to Hip Hop music that occurred within an entirely different context, as I describe below. Returning to the Reebok campaign, the event shows how, in being seduced by crime, consumers are consuming society itself. Baudrillard (1994) describes post-industrial society as the 'desert of the real' where the only reality is the consumers' own self-image. In this situation, what is the point in looking good or keeping fit if our existence has no benefit to others?

50 Cent's music can only be heard as one person's experience, and the same principle applies to understanding young people's experience of exclusion. Yet Hip Hop music's critics continue to isolate images from the music, just as academics try to explain crime. In both cases, the reflection of people's experience, like an image reflected in a mirror, becomes the object of study. As I show in Chapter 7, research on poverty and crime in Europe and North America epitomises this situation: reflections by academics unwilling to engage with or listen to people living with exclusion. The problem is that given the nature of society, an imaginary place for most people, research creates the mannequins that define people's fear about crime. Since the end of the 1980s, it seems that the biggest demon imaginable is the drug-using criminal.

Drugs and crime

Most research carried out on the drug/crime nexus involves researchers studying the behaviour of large (institutionalised) groups of people; that usually means that individuals themselves become classified as drug users. Sutherland and Cressey (1970), for example, noted that in the United States 'felons are over represented in the addict population'. However, Sutherland and Cressey (1970) concluded that a precise definition by which drugs are related to criminal behaviour had not yet been made. Whether in prison or through drug-referral clinics, researchers, once a person has been defined as a user, try to aggregate a coherent pattern between drug use and factors such as an involvement in crime, age at the onset of crime, or persistence in committing crimes. Therefore, once cases (people) are gathered, researchers try to 'explain' the possible relations between crime and drug use by establishing a direct connection between the two. My own position is that findings based on this objectifying approach are often incorporated into policy on crime because they appear as part of Baudrillard's (1994) 'desert of the real'. That is, the image of the drug-using criminal appears to be a seductive albeit silent explanation in the eyes of policy-makers.

During the 1980s, several quantitative studies were undertaken within prisons and drug rehabilitation centres in the United States (see Chaiken and Chaiken, 1990: 181–2). Analysing the findings, the consensus was that drug use induced income-producing crime largely because addicts required money to buy drugs. This theory was supported by evidence that many serious offenders were drug users and had started using drugs as juveniles. The formula was that while not all users became addicts, continued drug use for some frequently led to a nexus of heroin dependence and income-generating crime. Researchers and policy-makers subsequently assumed a clear causal relation between drug use and criminality, especially for a minority who were disproportionately more likely to become involved in drug use. For this minority their lives supposedly followed a simple linear trajectory: some form of drug use in adolescence, a progression to heroin use, and then an involvement in non-violent income-producing crime to finance that habit. This very specific drug/crime nexus gained consent despite contrary evidence pointing to casual (non-addict) heroin users who were not involved in crime (see Coomber, 1994). During my own discussion with young people, individuals identified how once people were 'caught' using drugs, all were exposed to further exclusion.

Poverty and drug use

Prisoners are stripped of their physical possessions as much as their experience of their own world. Outside the 'unnatural' setting of prison or drug rehabilitation centres, the problem is not necessarily the power of drugs themselves but of exclusion itself (see Polsky, 1971; Adler, 1985). Young adults' shared experience of being in Nova and not being able to get out of it is expressed through the Hip Hop life. Prison research inevitably isolates human beings from a process specific to living in a poor, socially excluded community.

Drug use has to be seen as part of our being, whether it involves alcohol or tobacco, heroin or crack-cocaine: all are taken to soften the pain of existence, and if we consume too much we become a danger to others and ourselves. Heidegger (1927) spoke of 'being in the world' to describe how we participate as human beings to survive in the world. Incarcerated within a total institution, we can no longer be human as the prison itself assumes every inmate's concerns and responsibilities. In his study on asylums, Goffman (1968: 18) describes how institutions assume people's responsibilities: 'the handling of many human needs by the bureaucratic organisation of whole blocks of people . . . is the key fact of total institutions'. The concerns we have about others and ourselves underpin our relationship with society generally. Our concerns for others and ourselves are not static but ongoing. Scott Lash (2002: 105) describes how: 'experience is always mediated through a body, a habitus, which is learnt and infused with intersubjectivity and tradition'.

Without an ongoing concern for others and ourselves, we are in danger of becoming melancholic. The nature of prison means that people sent there are in far greater danger of suffering from melancholy. Prisoners by definition are stigmatised as wrongdoers, and stigma, as a process identified by Goffman (1968), can result in people acting differently. Goffman (1968: 267) describes the process as becoming recalcitrant: 'Where enthusiasm is expected there will be apathy; where loyalty, there will be disaffection, where attendance, absenteeism; where robustness, some kinds of illness.' The experience of stigma raises questions over the value of prison research on the possible relations between crime and drug use. Being stigmatised was an ongoing experience for young people in Nova. Robbie described how he started using heroin in jail to avoid being given 28 days for proving positive to cannabis use:

I went into prison and they'd just introduced the piss test. And I'd only ever smoked fuckin' draw [cannabis]. So, I'd gone in there and I got banged up with this lad. Anyway, I 'ad a bit of draw when they nicked me. But the lad I was in with said, 'you don't wanna' smoke that, they come round to your cell randomly and just take you out and take a piss test'. So he says 'the only way to get round it is that when you take a piss is to put some soap in-between your nail or salt and then flick it in when you're pissin' and then it destroys it'. But I still get done for it anyway; you still get the 28 days anyway because you've tampered with it. So this lad says cannabis stays in the system for 28 days but he says, 'this place is now fuckin' run with smack 'cause if you take smack it only takes three days to get out the system'. So if you have a couple of lines chasin' the dragon three days later it's out of the system so you wouldn't give a fuck if they tested ya'. But, if you smoked a joint you'd be worryin' for 28 days afterwards; thinkin' 'fuckin' 'ell it's still in me fuckin' system'. So I started takin' brown [heroin], y'know the old smack like and that was me I was at it.

Leaving prison, Robbie told me he tried crack and had had difficulties with both ever since he was released: 'See crack to me is more addictive than what brown is because I prefer crack to brown. But if I 'ave the crack I need the brown to come down otherwise I'll be wired all fuckin' day long. I've gotta have it. I say to myself I don't need it but I do.' Robbie was one young adult I met who appeared to be losing hope: his experiences also showed how being unable to maintain self-respect left him exposed to further dangers from within and outside the community he had grown up in. Robbie told me how his problems began once he had left school.

> I stayed 'till I was 16. Then I got a job, YTS straight away at this school of welding. I spent a whole year there then they put me on placement with this hire shop. I was 16 then and I bought myself a moped. I weren't. I wasn't banned then. I got myself a provisional. I went all legal, got all legal. I stuck it out, got myself a moped. Then, when I was 17 I took me drivin' test, passed me drivin' test and it worked for about a year. Then I bought myself a car then it all started going wrong [laughs]. It all started going wrong when I bought a car. I bought a car for three grand, y'know on hire purchase. But in the first year, I thought I was jack the lad. I had a job I had a car, no worries. But I used to go out on the lash and get drunk and all that lot and then I used to drive. Then I got caught, an' I got banned. But I didn't take it in that much, y'know when I came out of court. They just said right you're banned for a year. So, I just carried on drivin'. Anyway, yeah that's it. When I was legal, they always used to stop me. There was this one copper, he used to stop me with one driver then he had another driver so it would be a different producer every time, it was always a different copper. So, I tried to do something about harassment but they said it was just routine. But they used to stop me and search me, and when I was with me family sometimes. Y'know, it was embarrassing. So I started to rebel against that, y'know what I mean, 'cause I'm like that. So, I didn't start to like the police then, I started to get a bit violent with 'em. I then I got banned but I just carried on drivin', yeah but I didn't think anything of it. Then I was out, about three weeks after I got banned I borrowed me sister's car, it was a GTI [sports model] right [laughs]. So, anyway, I went out on the lash [drinking] in the GTI and they waited for me in the car park. Then I came out and then they came after me and then woo, woo. But I thought, I ain't stoppin' so I gave 'em a little chase. They chased me for fuckin' miles, anyway. Anyway, I was comin' down Main Road, y'know where it twists. And I came down from the bridge and I just went for it. But it was freezin' that night, an' I must of hit black ice.

Anyway, I lost the fucker, the two front wheels hit the curb, and it shot up in the air and landed on the roof. It fuckin' all caved in and all the glass shattered. Anyway, I'd lost the police, I'd lost 'em but they must of seen the lights so I was gonna do a runner. But, I 'ad a bird in the car and she had a dog as well, and she was screamin' 'I can't move, I can't move' an I just said 'get out the fuckin' car; get out the fuckin' car'. Anyway, I'm tryin' to drag her out the car and I thought I'll just fuckin' leave her. I said you better not say a fuckin' word so I did a runner. I've gone round to me sister's, and I've tried to explain it to her. Anyway, they just burst into me sister's house and I was out the back, fuckin' on the toilet. So, they burst in and fuckin' arrested me. They gave me six months jail and banned me for three years.

RM: Did you stop driving when you got out?

Robbie: Yeah, but I still used to go out on the lash then get into fights. See, I'm only little see Rob and when I was at school everyone used to beat the shit out of me. But then, when I left I thought right that's it, 'I ain't gonna take anymore of this shit' so I fought back. See, when someone had a go at me all me past would come back and I think I 'ain't gonna take what I used to take at school, I was beaten to fuck then and I ain't gonna let this happen'. Yeah. And there was also me ex-girlfriend as well; I had a bad time with her. I was on this sound engineerin' course and when I got back one night I woke up that mornin' and got up with her. She was cryin' and that, and we took her to the hospital and we found out that she'd got a fractured skull. So, she thought it was me that done it 'cause I got up with her that mornin'. So, we took her to the hospital and I couldn't explain it. So anyway, they decided to take my little daughter off me, y'know social services and nick me for it. So, they took the babby off us 'cause the doctors said it was a 'non-accidental external injury'. So when they'd put her into care I sat down with me girlfriend and then she tells me that five days before she took her round to her sister's. And, when she was there they let her play with her sister's kid and she dropped her on her head. Anyway, Social Services weren't buyin' that 'cause they said they had to go on what the doctor said. So anyway we got this doctor from Sheffield, a bone specialist, and then we took it to appeal and it took about three months to get the case together. But anyway, in the meantime all her family were blamin' me, they kept blamin' me and it was doin' my fuckin' head in. Anyway it was my ex-wife's birthday and we went out and she was still dead miserable and she had a few drinks and she turned round and said 'you fuckin' done this I know you fuckin done this'. So she kept goin' on and I just fuckin' smacked her, I just smacked her right in the head for accusin' me. So anyway she got me done for it and I got fuckin' locked up for it back in prison.

The point in writing this study was to allow young people living in Nova to describe in their own words growing up with exclusion. As I argue in my conclusion, to write an account that judged actions such as those Robbie described would only contribute to the insidious categorisations young people had been subject to all their lives.

Inside out

The prison process means that people are inevitably isolated from the world and being able to participate as a social being. Nina Cope (2000: 184), in her qualitative study on drug use in a Young Offenders Institute, identifies this situation: 'The absence of formal structures, such as family stability, school and employment, frequently left the inmates with an abundance of free time so that even outside, they were faced with the challenge of making an activity out of doing nothing.' *Drug Use in Prison* is one of the few prison studies where the researcher builds a relationship with inmates, instead of relying on inmates' records, and identifies a real relationship between the use of institutional power and drug use (see Liebling, 1992). Cope (2000: 293) describes a culture of drug use played out in what she describes as 'the power game': 'inmates' resistance to staff power is inevitable and increases as rules become more pervasive and punitive'. The relationship Cope (2000) identifies, between offenders primarily from deprived inner-city areas and drug use in prison, related directly to how individuals adapted to specific institutional pressure. Even though 'the life' and 'the power game' are specific to two very distinct spheres of action, both reflected how young people from deprived areas remain susceptible to being stigmatised. In addition, to confuse the life of a community with the life of an institution can only result in the same abstraction. That is, the point of prison is to make people prisoners, a process that begins the moment an inmate begins his/her sentence. The psychologist Goffman (1967: 26) describes how institutions such as prisons often force, deliberately or otherwise, inmates to act differently through what he describes as 'the looping effect': 'An agency that creates a defensive response on the part of the inmate takes this very response as the target of its next attack. The individual finds that his protective response to an assault upon self is collapsed into the situation: he cannot defend himself in the usual way by establishing distance between the mortifying situation and himself.'

It seemed some young adults were susceptible to using heroin in prison through the process identified by Goffman (1968). Robbie had started taking the drug in prison as a response to being imprisoned and continued because, unlike other young people I met, he continued to feel stigmatised, even among his friends. British prisons operate a policy whereby inmates, if found to be using illicit drugs, are immediately convicted to serve another 28 days on top of their original sentence (Roberts and Kidd, 1999). Prisons minister Paul Goggins (2005) outlines the reasoning behind the policy: 'reducing the rate of re-offending is one of the core objectives of NOMS (National Offender Management Service). By effectively confronting problematic drug use among offenders, we can also address other aspects of offending behaviour, which will help us to achieve this goal.' Through assuming inmates who use drugs are inherently criminal, the policy is an attempt to objectify young people's subjective experience; the first stage in the looping effect described by Goffman (1968). Martin, who is not a heroin user, described a similar process:

> I used to smoke draw [cannabis resin] before I went in but 'cause they were tryin' to clamp down on coke [cocaine] and brown [heroin] I had to stop. They were still lookin' for draw when they took the piss test. It's okay if you take coke or brown inside 'cause it only stays in the system for a few days but the draw will stay there for 28 days. You could get rid of it quicker if you drank pints of water, about six pints a day. But then you'd end up 'avin to take a piss all the time. Every time you got caught, they put another 28 days on your sentence. 28 days, *that's a month*.

Social exclusion in action

The justification for mandatory drug testing reflects how decisions are made on assumptions. How and why the policy is able to repeat those experiences relates to modern principles on which policy is formed. Mandatory drug testing seeks to emancipate prisoners without attempting to understand the reasons why young people take drugs. Being with young adults who used drugs, use reflected the realities of exclusion and the desires that lie behind it. Drug use was exclusion though policy continues to objectify a subjective experience of exclusion; the raw anger and frustration Slim described at the end of the previous chapter. The effect of stereotyping young people in such ways is summed up by Jameson (1998: 52) when he says, 'subjectivity is an objective matter, and it is enough to change the scenery and setting, refurnish the rooms or destroy them in aerial bombardment for a new subject, a new identity, miraculously to appear from the ruins of the old'. Through the classification of drug use and 'drug users', young people who use drugs are stripped of their humanity. This process of classification also seemed to encroach on other aspects of youth culture in Nova, including clothes and music, particularly Hip Hop.

Within mainstream culture, Hip Hop, what I regard as the musical expression of exclusion, continues to be associated with crime and drugs; particularly gun violence and its relationship with the sale and distribution of crack-cocaine. All are realities within many deprived areas though why they are disappears under the image we see of them. For instance, Hip Hop is portrayed as a threat through its associations with 'the street', even when the street no longer exists as a social entity for most people. While I was working in Anderson's, it seemed that for most customers the only streets left were those displayed on television, or in the newspapers sold at the cigarette counter. By consuming those images, I believe people were able to consume their own fears about crime. In Chapter 7, I argue that this process now shapes policy on youth crime. One category in the typology of anti-social behaviour is classified as 'youth nuisance' (Home Office, 2004: 26) after the British Crime Survey 2002/03 identified that 25 per cent of the public felt teenagers hanging around was the biggest anti-social behaviour problem in their local area (Nicholas and Walker, 2004).

Hip Hop is categorised in similar terms; signifying gangs and gang violence because Hip Hop represents a reality consumers are trying to escape: an increasingly fragmented society. In response to recent moral panics surrounding Hip Hop music, the Labour MP Diane Abbott (2003) said: 'But let's not pretend that ending gun criminality on the streets of Hackney or Birmingham is as simple as getting people to sing different songs.' Diane's (2003) critique sums up a situation in which images are used as an explanation for the prevalence of crime and drug abuse in certain areas (see Baudrillard, 1988).

Achieving respect

In the previous chapter, I showed how young adults innovate to survive being socially excluded. Cultures always develop in such situations: survival, by definition, is the physical expression of a desire to re-create human existence. For everyone in Linden's circle, each person's aspirations were encapsulated by the term 'the life'. Everyone shared 'the life' in being excluded from securing a financial future, no matter how small. If they did not, Linden, Martin and everyone else would have been free to live a normal life. Instead, faced with what seemed to be an intractable situation, everyone worked as a community to survive. This chapter describes how young adults were able to maintain a sense of self-respect as members of a community, and how that community came to be associated with crime.

Being with Linden and his friends was like being in the presence of an *avante garde*: a group active in the invention and application of new techniques. Not only was everyone trying to physically stay alive,

Linden, Martin, Montana and Benita were all trying to realise their ambitions. Lyotard (1993: 245) describes the difficulties involved in that process, 'the possibility of nothing happening, of words, forms, colours or sounds not coming; of this sentence being the last, of bread not coming daily. This is the misery that the painter faces with a plastic surface, of the musician with the acoustic surface, the misery the thinker faces with a desert of thought.' Martin described the conflict between the sheer desperation many people I met seemed to face, while trying to hold onto a sense of self-respect in the face of that:

> round here people only come up to you when they want something. Money, yeah when they want money. That's the main thing on people's minds in Nova, money. Money and sex. All people care about round ere is getting their hands on money, just to have it in their hands. If you have £1,000 round here, you're regarded as rich. But, £1,000 is nothing, all you could get is a shit car. I want a Lexus or a Merc, not just because they're flash but because they're the best, the best design, the best make. I don't just want money for itself like the people round here. Money is just a means to get what you want, to do things that you want to do, to go out, to travel. Most of the people round here haven't even been out of Nova and they don't even want to go out, their perspective is like that.

Innovation and survival were reflected and expressed in 'the life'. Everyone wore sportswear, though in highly individualised ways. Even though it was the only affordable clothing, sportswear echoes Linden's expression of 'survival of the fittest'. Unlike the images we see advertised, sportswear seemed to have a subjective meaning, of having to survive each day. The clothes young people wore, which were the only clothes they had, reflect that: trainers and tracksuits, which were warm and protective, almost impenetrable to attack. It was winter after the Project closed and most young people I was with at that time wore Puffa or ski jackets to keep out the cold. Boys, such as Martin and Linden, wore jeans and shirts all worn in a 'ragga' style (loose fit). Tattoos were also important, not as an expression of deviance but as signs of faith, strength and self-belief. The designs often involved gothic lettering or Chinese calligraphy, with characters that reflect aspects of people's personality. Also popular are names of partners or relatives in gothic type, and dragons, tigers or other mythical creatures synonymous with courage and strength. Seen as one, young people's individuality seemed to be contained, almost like a second skin, and very different from fashion or subcultural style. The utilitarian aspect of people's appearance was possibly a reflection of the fact that sportswear was the only form of affordable clothing. In Ford at that time there were a number of discount sportswear stores that offered trainers, tracksuits, jumpers, T-shirts and jeans at a very low cost. Young people wore big sizes (or ragga style) usually because these were often the only sizes available.

Floetry

I had always listened to Hip Hop; Linden and Martin introduced me to what has come to be known in the media as gangster rap. At first, I was shocked by the lyrical content, though at the same time I could appreciate the music's subjective meaning in the context of exclusion. Tricia Rose (1994: 36) describes how 'Hip Hop artists use style as a form of identity formation that plays on class distinctions and hierarchies by using commodities to claim the cultural terrain'. The contexts in which young people listened to Hip Hop music reflected the process Rose (1994) identifies. Because no one at that time could afford to buy either compact discs or a compact disc player, the only way people were able to maintain their passion for Hip Hop music was through bootlegging audio-cassette tapes. I never witnessed the recording process though most young adults had boxes of tapes with the labels written over repeatedly. Tapes lasted until they were chewed up, which happened once in my own car, resulting in some very harsh language. Linden, Montana and Martin all liked Snoop Dog. Montana and Martin became partners and had a child together partly through a shared passion for Snoop. Hip Hop music also gave a shape to the day. Hip Hop was played when people were getting ready to go out on the 'shift' or during the 'session'. Hip Hop was also played loud when people were getting ready to go out. When people were chillin' or relaxing, dancehall music was often preferred, particularly when a group decided to have a 'smoke' (of cannabis). Among moochers and young adults at the Project, the Hip Hop life was not seen as exclusive to young black men on the estate. Almost all the young Caucasian men and women I knew were accessing both African-American and Black British culture on a daily basis. The Rhythm and Blues and dancehall style seemed to be particularly significant for young women. Montana and Benita went to dancehall and R & B events, and always dressed in an R & B look that seemed popular at that time: three-quarter length leather overcoats, black outfits and jewellery; epitomised by the late R & B singer Aaliyah.

In terms of language, most young men and women in Linden's circle and at the Project incorporated both African-Caribbean and African-American terms and references. For instance, in conversations about crime and imprisonment, prison was always referred to as the 'Jailhouse' (prison). Other African-American and African-Caribbean terms were also in daily usage in and around the precinct area, 'Nuff' (enough), 'Dis' (disrespect), 'Chill' (relax), and 'Bitches' (women). Only the African-Caribbean men I met used the N word, and the same principle was applied to the term 'bitch', which was only used between women. In both instances, each term was used exclusively; in excluding young Caucasian men or women, depending on which word was being used, the effect was a way of affirming ethnic and gender identities.

'The life's' articulation through language, clothes, and music by young people in Nova never appeared to be contrived to create a reaction. However, many times when I was with Linden, Tony, Montana and Benita outside Nova, there was often a visible reaction from other people. Several times, we went to some of the towns and villages surrounding Ford. On one occasion, Linden and I entered a public house where the predominantly elderly affluent clientele stared at Linden persistently. In a car park one afternoon, Linden asked two women in a car if they were vacating a space. When the couple had driven away, Linden told me that they had threatened to phone the police unless he moved away from their car.

Exclusion through style

Within criminology, how young people dress is the focus of subcultural studies (see Jefferson and Hall, 1976; Hebdige, 1979; McRobbie, 2000). The subcultural studies epoch seems to have been during the post-war period; aspects of 'youth' leisure, especially music and fashion, were identified as part of young people's rituals of resistance against inequalities experienced at school and work. From the late 1950s to the late 1970s, the consensus among subcultural theorists was that subcultures were most common in working-class communities. De-industrialisation, as Taylor (1999: 76) identifies, has represented crises for subcultural studies in the way it has fragmented the once easy transition from school to work for working-class youth. My own fieldwork with young people in Nova suggested that subcultural style no longer had meaning, as there was no identifiable period between childhood and maturity. Ford, along with most cities it seems, no longer works as a culture or organism; instead, the city appears to be consuming itself.

Saturday night at Orpheus showed how consumer culture had consumed a predominantly young working-class club culture, turning what had been a revolutionary underground movement into an indoor shopping mall. It was not that Orpheus had been neutered but that Ford itself had disappeared in the consumer culture. In recent years, a vast indoor shopping arena has been installed in the heart of Ford City centre: containing four corporate nightclubs. Ford Arena also houses a multiplex cinema, skating rink, bowling alley, and a series of themed American diners. Because everything was built in unison and with a singular purpose, the danger and musical mayhem that characterised the early days of Orpheus could never take hold. Instead, because people who enter the Arena are pressured to appear different among one another, the effect is a stylised masquerade of personalised haircuts, clothes and accessories. Prophetically, Stan Cohen (1972: 151) describes how 'the teenage culture makes them (young people who buy into it) into ineffectual outsiders'.

It seems that the appearance of young people living 'the life' posed a threat, because young people themselves appeared as one through wearing the same brands of sportswear. Echoing young people's accounts of exclusion, it seems that gangs of young people hanging around represent a threat to the consumer society generally, simply for having no identity in that society.

Wearing cheap mass-produced clothes available in every town and city, young adults dressed in sportswear and living in poor urban areas represent a menace to society. Yet, living 'the life' is fundamentally different to subcultural style. Moreover, to criticise young people from similar backgrounds wearing sportswear as anti-social potentially condemns a community with very little choice in how they dress. Even though I have described how young people I met in Nova took time in their appearance, this was always a reflection of self-respect rather than a reaction to society. This is because 'the life' belonged to young people, whereas style is a desire to be seen as an object. Any style is, by definition, a form of individual expression achieved through economic freedom: people try to appear subversive in their dress. 'The life' young people described, in contrast, was immanent or inherent to being excluded. It seemed the only choice available to young people was to remain committed to Nova and the public life of the estate. Robbie was one of a handful of people I met who had given up on life. It seemed the only alternative was through 'the life' of community. Jimmy described 'the life'; 'I'm a Nova boy, I was born there; I've lived there for 26 years. When I left school I started shopliftin' to make money; you could always sell them back in Nova, smokes, alarms, suits, anything. Then I left home when I was 16 and moved into a flat with my girlfriend. I'm livin' with her now and the baby.'

My own belief is that Linden and his friends represented such a threat because all were committed to staying alive. This is the social logic of crime in the consumer society; to work in economies such as Gemini Park was perceived as a fatal step among all of the young people I met. Yet people who define their lives spending time in these places depend on the separation between poverty and crime. In Chapter 1, I described how working in Gemini Park people are individualised and made anonymous through the themed costumes workers are required to wear. I also argued that images of crime give a consumer lifestyle meaning. The masquerade of crime may also explain why images of community are often defined through an association with death and blood, as in the myth of the 'gangster rapper'.

The pejorative term came about during concerns among largely white middle-class parents over the nature of Hip Hop lyrics and the 'value' artists had as role models for young people. Parent pressure on policy resulted in the introduction by the RIAA of its black and white universal parental warning sticker, 'Explicit Lyrics – Parental Warning'. Tricia Rose (1994: 1) encapsulates how the subjectivity Hip Hop articulates became the object of attraction and anger for mainstream society in the United States:

> On one hand, music and cultural critics ... defend rap's ghetto stories as real-life reflections that should draw attention to the burning problems of racism and economic oppression. On the other, news media's attention on rap seems fixated on instances of violence at rap concerts ... gangsta rap's lurid fantasies of cop killing and female dismemberment, and black nationalist rappers' suggestion that white people are the devil's disciples.

Tricia Rose (1994) identifies how the outrage surrounding Hip Hop is an attempt to objectify people living in poverty. Yet, the attempt always seems to fail, resulting in demonology instead of simulation. Hip Hop began as a reaction to the disproportionate levels of unemployment and poverty experienced by black people within America's urban centres following the economic crisis of the late 1970s. Hip Hop's roots also go deeper, within African American history itself. Musically, Hip Hop remains diverse, with influences ranging from reggae, gospel and jazz to disco and rock and roll. Commenting on Hip Hop's musical diversity, Paul Gilroy (1993: 33) contends, 'The musical components of Hip Hop are a hybrid form nurtured by the social relations of the South Bronx where Jamaican sound system culture was transplanted during the 1970s and put down new roots'. Hip Hop, and Rhythm and Blues, and the history of both, reflect the dialectics of exclusion experienced by young people in Nova who grew up during de-industrialisation.

Hip Hop's history is a musical chronology of de-industrialisation and its impact on working-class young people. Early Hip Hop was idealistic, and felt by many in its beginnings as a political project. Sampling the work of Black-American political leaders such as Malcolm X, Martin Luther King and Jesse Jackson identified the inequalities experienced by Black Americans during the 1980s and worked to give a sense of hope. By the 1990s, however, the persistence of the realities of exclusion experienced by Black Americans came to be reflected lyrically in the work of artists such as Snoop Doggy Dog and the Wu Tang Clan. The label of 'gangster rappers' has tarred both and they were the most popular musicians for most of the young people I met. Addressing Hip

Hop's critics, Gilroy (1993: 85) contends, 'It is important to emphasise that all three strands within Hip Hop – pedagogy, affirmation and play – contribute to a folk-cultural constellation where neither the political compass of weary leftism nor the shiny navigational instruments of premature black in aesthetics have so far offered very much that is useful'.

Hip Hop culture

Hip Hop's continued resonance for young people living in deprived urban areas only underlines how the dialectics of exclusion continue. The significance of Hip Hop music within Nova is that its lyrics seemed to echo the feeling of survival Linden and his friends lived by. Hip Hop describes a subjective desire to survive, hence 'the life', a term that echoes through artists' lyrics. Living the life is simultaneously a cultural expression of economic exclusion and a survival strategy for it. Yet, without a representative social space such as the Project, 'the life' on its own cannot defend young people from becoming the hollow caricatures of gangs, gangsters and gangster rappers. Outsiders were afraid to enter the Project because it was what Lefebvre (1974) describes as a representative social space. Like other popular youth centres I have been to, the Project worked because it had been made by and for young people. Once that brick-and-cement skin was literally demolished, young people could be isolated and separated, as if they were a virus.

When the Project was closed, people who went there seemed to be exposed to their own insecurities as much as the suspicions of outsiders. For some people what followed was a dialectical process that usually began with confrontations with external agencies. Whether social services, the benefits agency or the police, everyone I spoke to seemed to have regular encounters with all three. After the Project, some people such as Robbie were less able to cope with these interactions. For Robbie, what followed was a process of confrontation, reaction, then self-harm, resulting in a helter-skelter of crime and drug abuse. When I interviewed Robbie he said that he had just sold his video for a bag of brown and when the interview ended he asked me if I wanted to buy some heroin.

'The life' was being excluded by outsiders and at the same time surviving the feeling of stigma outsiders try to impose for living the life of a community. This cultural praxis underlined that all young people had after the Project was consumer culture. Like society as a whole, young people were trapped, oscillating between practical needs and future-orientated aspirations. The difference was that young people had to practise that in a form outsiders perceived to be a gang.

In the remaining chapters, I show how young people achieved a resolution to the perpetual present of consumption through education, in the form of an adult education centre: Gateways. Gateways was created through social capital; residents got together and convinced local companies and agencies to believe in Nova at a time when society itself was modernising. Chapter 6 describes how the feeling of social renewal reflected in the 1997 general election provided the foundation for Gateways. I also show how it then disappeared after 11 September 2001, after which point poor communities once again became a threat to consumers. Even though young people I met can learn skills at Gateways, the stigma that surrounds Nova appears to remain. Young people continue to live 'the life', as I show in Chapter 6, reflecting a wish to be part of society, and living 'the life' means that young people continue to be excluded.

The power of 'the life' is that it reflects a society with only one overriding concern, consumption. Consumption in Nova and outside it demands production and individualism in an excluded community can only be achieved through 'the survival of the fittest'. When a minority of young people I met began to consume for individual reasons, individuals themselves became susceptible to being stigmatised and disrespected among their fellow young adults. To understand the fragility of young people's support networks and the importance of rejecting people who represented a danger to the community, one has to place young people's experience of exclusion within the context of the consumer society.

Watching communities

Social theorists suggest that people are becoming more individualised by the transition to a global consumer society (Bauman, 2000). For people with wealth, self-identity is no longer built as a social relationship; given the nature of consumer culture it seems people's identities are constituted through individual consumption. The inevitable result for people who live a consumer lifestyle is the 'perpetual present' that Jameson (1998) identifies. Consumer culture also suggests a society of individuals in stasis: people feel more uncertain than ever before at a point when individuals generally enjoy greater wealth. For Young (1999), this sense of general uncertainty is reflected in a move 'from a world whose accent was on assimilation and incorporation to one which separates and excludes'. Growing uncertainties about crime also seem to be reflected in the way private security defines the borders of the consumer society (see Wakefield, 2004).

The continuous presence of CCTV in public places such as Gemini Park also reflects how living a consumer lifestyle makes it far more difficult to trust others. To cope, individuals and groups also appear increasingly compelled to create their own exclusive communes, what

Mike Davis (1990) describes as 'gated communities'. For Bottoms and Wiles (1995: I.20), sometimes these manifest themselves as 'bubbles' of technical control such as spaces or cities of surveillance in which space is controlled by business in order to reassure potential customers. While cities have, since the Industrial Revolution, been made up of areas that generated different degrees of risk, late modernity has ensured that businesses and developers have sought to create 'security bubbles', women-only hotels, patrolled car parks and privately policed shopping arcades. Inevitably, such bubbles use exclusion to demarcate between desirable and undesirable, who to trust and who not to trust (Davis, 1990). Bottoms and Wiles (1995) identify the importance of wealth in being able to create the social capital to secure membership. Containing those insecurities through better home protection also requires capital, making consumption a risk and security a privilege. The cumulative effect of these trends has been the creation of what Young (1999) describes as an exclusive society, a world where forms of social support such as insurance, health care and pensions are inclusive to wealth (see Jessop, 1994).

Excluded from these private securities, young people I met had to live as a community. Young adults I spoke to felt that the world beyond the estate was a far more hostile place in the way everything in it had been given a monetary value. Exclusion for every young person I met stemmed from the fact that residents generally, even financially successful entrepreneurs such as Jimmy, were unable to obtain a mortgage. Some older residents I spoke to had tried to buy their homes. However, mortgage providers were unwilling to provide services to any resident as they claimed that construction of homes in Nova was somehow insecure.

In Chapter 7, I describe how home ownership became the foundation of the consumer society that arose during the 1980s in Britain. Writing on the new social divisions created by de-industrialisation, Nick Buck (1992) suggests that those most likely to remain outside the mainstream occupational system in Britain are local authority tenants. Buck (1992: 19) argues, 'this is a stronger predictor than either social class or the level of education'.

What struck me most about listening to young people was the level of friendship men and women shared. In addition, how difficult it was for young people to maintain the lifeblood of trust in a world of diminishing supports and proliferating pressures, internal and external. Residents, young and old, still trusted one another, as Jay described, but trust was predicated by exclusion:

> See Nova's like a little community. It's like a little village. Y'know like you hear things goin' around, who to trust who not to trust. Y'know like you know who the grasses are and things. You don't

want grasses livin' in Nova, y'know everyone's doin' their own thing and whatever and you just don't want that. You can, you can still trust people but. I mean I've never been burgled yet. It's probably because I know everyone. Y'know who's a burglar and who's not a burglar. Obviously, if you got burgled you'd go to them first. I've never been burgled yet, me mum's never been burgled yet. Maybe it's because we've lived down there for so long.

Jay describes how young people form protective communities that provide members with a feeling of emotional security. For Jay there is continuity between the public world of the street and the private.

This study ends by describing how that connection between a public and private culture was sustained each day within social spaces such as the Project and the Nova Centre. When the Project closed, family still provided the connection for Jay, between the private culture of home and public culture of the Precinct. However, Jay was lucky in that many other young adults do not have social support beyond their own generation. This was why the closure of the Project had such a detrimental effect on many young people. For almost twelve years, it had been a frontline between a public and private culture of the Precinct. Many young people describe how, living in the Precinct, both cultures were as violent as each other. When Sean pulled down the Project's steel shutters for the final time, all that remained were the bare boxroom flats that line Nova's southern edge.

Risk and defeat

Everyone shared the experience of exclusion, but because no one had the resources to provide long-term support, people were forced to survive alone. This was what Linden meant when he described how it was 'the survival of the fittest in Nova'. Without the means to buy support such as insurance, pensions and investments, young people had to rely on themselves for protection within Nova. It seemed that a sense of emotional and financial security could only be sustained by taking greater and greater risks outside the estate. Liam told me about the external risks:

Well after bein' in there [prison] for 17 months I decided that I weren't comin' back. So, when I got out, I got a job. But the fuckin' old bill were on me case. See I 'ad this job. Well, when I got out I got done for drink drivin'. And then, see I needed me car to get to work, but then the old bill stopped me again an I never 'ad any insurance. So after that I lost me licence and me job.

When risks went wrong, people's hope in the future was inevitably eroded, though maintaining self-respect remained a prerequisite to 'the life'; what Martin described as 'the code of the street'. Survival and self-respect were processes that underlined how the threat of violence and fear of crime were qualitatively worse for people living in a socially excluded community. Definitions of violence always seem vague, though many, such as Foucault's (1977), stress its physicality; power is achieved by physically harming others. Outside poor ghettoised communities, violence for most people is a distant prospect as they are protected by rules that prohibit it. Martin described how young people in Nova lived according to the rule of the street, and what happened to people who broke it. Jay also described how the threat of being robbed was ever present in a community crumbling under the pressure of exclusion: 'Just as long as they can get money really y'know for a drink or a smoke or whatever or so they can go out'. Linden describes how people were labelled in being unable to cope with exclusion, often as addicts or junkies. Martin, Tony, Montana and Benita shared the same ethos Linden describes: 'See, everyone I know is unemployed but there's one group of people that are unemployed that just do nothin'. Sit around all day, in front of the telly. And there's lads that I know that get up and just go out to find somethin' to make some money.' All of Linden's friends were able to live by this ethos and adhere to the rule of the street. Others were not, as Linden pointed out: 'Yeah see me, I know the top ones. I know the ones right down the bottom.' When I asked him about people who could no longer go on, Linden told me about the motorway flyover near the estate. 'The Arch' is a place that has become popular over the years for people in Nova who decide to take their own lives. Other people lost hope by becoming dissolute; when they did, individuals were quickly perceived as a danger to everyone.

Robbie had retreated; as his heroin and crack use became a daily preoccupation, his friendships diminished. At the end of my fieldwork, Robbie was no longer part of Linden's scene and became increasingly reclusive; on numerous occasions in the final months of my research, I tried Robbie's door. Sometimes I could hear whispers though all the curtains remained drawn and no one ever replied. For extroverted entrepreneurs of Linden's world, dependency was a sign that people were unreliable. Tony's relationship with Robbie at that time also showed how losing self-respect had resulted in Robbie becoming an enemy within the community of young people I spent time with after the closure of the Project. Tony told me how one day, he had spotted Leander standing outside a supermarket in another part of Ford. After pulling up, he approached her just as Robbie and another boy came running out of the store. Realising Leander was being used as a look-out, Tony punched Robbie, sending him to the floor. Tony told me that as Robbie fell to the pavement, his jacket fell open and packets of sweets came falling out.

Seen as being unable to cope with heroin and crack-cocaine, Robbie became stigmatised by friends as an addict. Before he disappeared from 'the scene', Robbie often looked dishevelled compared with many other young people. One aspect of the Hip Hop style was that it made young people look stylish, even though the clothes worn were inexpensive, and that required self-respect. Another aspect of the Hip Hop life was maintaining composure even when drugs or alcohol were being consumed. Rarely did I see anyone drunk or intoxicated as it inevitably exposed individuals to the threat of attack. Also, Linden and all his friends regarded injecting heroin as immoral. Linden told me that some of Robbie's friends had been known to 'dig' or inject. The group, who I was never able to get to know, were regarded as too dangerous to associate with. Linden described how Robbie's friends were often being apprehended in supermarkets for shoplifting. Identifying one of Robbie's friends one afternoon, a stocky young Caucasian man nicknamed Mash, Linden told me he was wanted for stabbing a security guard. Why this group was seen as dangerous is because they are seen as having no respect for one another or the community as a whole. Much to Linden's concern, Leander moved in with Robbie after losing her job at the nursing home and the only way he and Tony could protect her was by threatening Robbie with violence.

Maintaining respect

Violence when it occurred in that year was devastating, as an event and in the way a memory of it eroded the self-respect of its victims and perpetrators. As Bourgois (1997) identified in his own study in East Harlem and Hobbs (1995) in *Bad Business*, in a free-market economy, violence is the only way to ensure trust. Violence as a mechanism for sustaining trust results in 'downside' social capital; even though friendships are motivated by empathy, an understanding young people share is that those friendships can only be sustained through fear. The term 'downside' social capital was coined by Rubio (1997) in his work on crime and drug cartels in which individuals living in socially excluded communities are enslaved through the jobs and security that organisations provide. As Slim identified in his account of the time he had tried to make money 'sellin' draw', suppliers organised the business leaving workers to work or face the consequences. Even then, young people had no guarantees on was being bought and sold; once people stepped into what was a sellers' market maintaining individual integrity was as important as the quality of goods. Pete, a friend of Damon, whom I never met, had been deceived in a business deal, sold a lump of chewing gum instead of what he thought was nine ounces of cannabis resin and lost £600 in the process.

Young people's accounts of the danger of going into business in Nova seemed to suggest an attrition between the enterprise culture of the 1980s and being forced to survive de-industrialisation as a community (see Foster, 1999). In being part of what appeared to be an enterprising gang, young people became sucked into a cycle of exclusion. Young (1999: 13) describes the dialectics of exclusion as a 'pyrrhic process', 'involving both wider society and, crucially, the actors themselves which traps them in, at best, a series of dead-end jobs and at worst, an underclass of idleness and desperation'. Steve describes that trap: 'No, all the jobs for lads like me in this city are shit. You're just shovelling shit all week for nothing, for shit wages.' I asked Jimmy: 'But aren't you poor on the dole as well?' Jimmy replied: 'I'm not. Y'see for me when you're on the dole everythin' is free, free rent, free prescriptions, free food for my kid. That gives me free time to make money. The dole gives you free time to earn money and there's no one tellin' you what to do.'

Jimmy and Linden were able to survive exclusion through what could be described as a collective enterprise culture, though because individuals were denied financial services, people's anxieties and frustrations only seemed to get bigger as they became financially successful. This was why 'going out on the shift' was such a perpetual present because all that young adults could achieve was more rapid consumption. As the realities of exclusion persisted in Nova, when young people returned each day all that remained was an immediate culture, of clothes and cars. Steve's life during my fieldwork personified what seemed like a psychological and economic civil war. Every time we met, he appeared more successful and more frustrated. Jimmy's frustration is that he is highly innovative and earns money though he can never move forward. Like many 'moochers', Jimmy can only contain his frustrations through an immediately disposable culture. Eventually Jimmy's aspirations, realisable in any other situation, spilled out: 'I went to loads of raves, between '89 and '91. I used to take loads of E's, loads. I go partners on this rave club in Hilton. I did the DJin' and he paid for the lights and stuff. Then I lost it one weekend and I had to go into the "psych" [psychiatric ward]. After that, all the lads started callin' me schizo.'

Despite being financially successful, 'top moochers' live in rented accommodation: Jimmy lived in a council flat with his wife and child. This meant 'moochers', like the poorer young people I met in the Project, rarely went outside Nova. All that seemed to remain was the session. I asked young people I know who take drugs why they chose to do so. Even though he was not a habitual user Tony told me that he couldn't breathe without drugs, reflecting how close the relationship is between drug use and aspiration.

Entrepreneurship, even when successful, always seemed like the pyrrhic process Young (1999) describes, involving a handful of money-makers in a community desperate to earn money and respect. Linden described friends who had managed to access the consumer society though who were also to forced, like Baz and Jimmy, to remain living in Nova:

> A lot of the lads I know, four particular lads I know, that 'ave never worked in their life. They're all my age, they've all bought their own house, they've all got nice cars. One's got fuckin' Calibra [Vauxhall sports car]. One's got a fuckin' Jag [Jaguar], know what I mean, 26 never worked; and this is all from moochin'. Fuckin' thousands you can make, thousands. If you've got the front; if you've got the balls.

In retrospect, the most successful entrepreneurs were the most visible and the most vulnerable to risk. As individuals built a reputation for being successful entrepreneurs, so people's identity as a member of a community dissolved. The result was that 'top moochers' appeared be caught in a psychological threshold between consumer society and poor community. Shortly after Linden said this, one of the young men vanished from Nova after fatally shooting another man in an argument.

In their work on juvenile delinquency, Matza and Sykes (1957: 667) identified techniques of neutralisation; beginning as reactions to society though ending as interactive processes: 'by learning to view himself as more acted upon than acting, the delinquent prepares the way for deviance from the dominant normative system without the necessity of a frontal assault'. Matza and Sykes' (1957) theory was validated by the fact that none of the young people I got to know acted out violence on outsiders just for being affluent. Matza and Sykes' (1957: 667) techniques were also being adopted in the way no one within Linden's circle had chosen, or was drawn, to the nihilistic path taken by Robbie. Linden explained 'If you wanna make some good money get in and out, do it quick time'. Yet exclusion and poverty remained: young adults I met were forced into a situation where 'findin' an earner', constantly having to generate an income, was a daily reality. In addition, opportunities available with the local labour economy only left people living in subsistence poverty within a community where no one was able to provide anyone else with financial support. The result was an almost continuous tension between dissolution and respect that could only be neutralised by being part of an excluded community.

Working at Anderson's on a minimum wage ensures you had less money than if you were unemployed. Linden and many of his friends had given up on jobs in local supermarkets and other retail stores because they offered no future. Being unemployed was seen as no different, as Linden explained: 'See I get bored of dossin', I can't doss for fuckin' ever. I like to work. Y'know, just meet new people and that, new faces.' For many of the young people I became close to – Linden, Tony, Montana, Martin, Liam, Robbie, Leander, Ellie, Jimmy, Steve and

Hannah – discrimination and exploitation in the local economy were experiences all did not want to repeat. Even though 'the life' could be dangerous and is chaotic, everyone was able to maintain a sense of self-respect. Nova's local labour market does little to provide a way out of exclusion and often erodes identities constituted within the community itself. The techniques Matza and Sykes (1957) identified seemed to be personified in 'the session', a social space that enabled people to displace the anxiety of being continually exposed to exclusion. 'The session' also seemed to be the only way to neutralise the possibility of violence.

Even so-called public forms of protection such as CCTV are financially expensive: like Ford, many cities are now in the business of selling security (Wakefield, 2004). Violence was a greater danger for everyone in Nova because not only did the entire community represent a threat to the consumer society, the arsenal of technologies used to maintain consumer safety was all directed at residents. The result was that violence became invisible, often occurring outside the scope of cameras that operated in the Precinct day and night. Worse was the way in which the most fragile residents of the Precinct were placed in even greater danger through the way technologies were directed at those thought to pose the greatest threat. Even though that may have been justified, as in the case of Geoff, who I introduce in the next chapter, the counter-intuitive result of devices such as CCTV may explain why the Precinct was such a violent and unpredictable place. Going back to Jay's description of how people protected one another physically and emotionally, the most dangerous people in Nova were, tragically, those who had lost hope. Leander and Robbie had succumbed to the stigma associated with Nova's youth; becoming the threat Ford's consumers seemed to demand in the way both seemed undeterred by the threat of arrest. As Jimmy pointed out, that meant 'bringing it on top for everyone else'.

The enemy within

The day I interviewed Tony at Linden's house, Linden and I went to see Leander. A few days before, Leander's father had told her to leave and she was now staying at Robbie's. Linden had offered to accommodate Leander, though after one night she moved into Robbie's. After that point Linden began to suspect that Leander had started using heroin regularly. When we arrived, I beeped the horn. As Linden got out of the car, Robbie came to the window. Linden shouted, 'where's Leander?' Like a mime artist, Robbie shrugged. As Robbie raised his hands, Leander walked out of the front door at the side of the maisonette, forcing Linden to shout 'you're fuckin lyin' to me'. Red-faced Robbie vanished.

When Leander arrived at the car, she clenched both her fists and jumped up and down: 'I'm really hyper.' Linden scowled and asked her if she had been smoking 'H' (heroin). Leander shouted 'No', indignant. She then asked both of us if we could take her to work and avoid having to make two bus journeys. Agreeing, Leander then asked if we could take her and Robbie to the shop first for some washing powder. She then shouted up to Robbie and he came down the steps, his face still flushed. Both then got in the backseat. As we drove down to the Precinct, Leander and Linden began to argue. Linden: 'You told me that you would be round at ten.' Leander: 'Fuck off Linden, I came round at nine, and you were still in bed.' This continued as I parked outside the shop then stopped as Leander went off for washing powder. When everyone was back in the car and we were heading off to the nursing home, Linden asked Leander if she could lend him £30, knowing that she would be paid today. She agreed, telling him to be outside the nursing home at 4 p.m. At the time, Linden was unemployed, which meant Leander would have to wait a week before Linden would be able to pay back the £30.

Two days later, I was at Linden's flat with Hannah. It had been snowing all morning and Nova was now covered in a thick blanket of white powder. I sat at the window ledge watching huge flakes fall. Linden seemed stressed, pacing around picking big clumps of Hannah's hair off the carpet. Hannah also seemed pensive, standing in front of the gas fire while watching Jerry Springer on the TV, focused on trying to stay warm. I asked Linden why he was tidying up; he replied he was waiting for Leander and her father, Frank, to come round. Leander had phoned before I arrived, insisting on getting her £30 back. I asked Linden if he was bothered. 'Am I fuck', he replied.

As he said this, I noticed Leander and her father trudging through the snow. Despite the harsh wind, Frank was walking with purpose. Frank is a man of medium height, though broad shouldered with big hands, making him look tall. Leander was tiptoeing in his footprints, using her father's broad back as a shield against the driving snow. Both arrived at the stairs leading to Linden's door. I then listened to two sets of footsteps climb the stairs, one heavy, the other light. Frank battered the door. Linden, who was in the kitchen trying to appear busy, walked into the hall and snapped open the door. As he did Frank shouted, 'Are you gonna give her this money back or what?':

Linden: I'm gonna give it her.
Frank: When?
Linden: When I can afford it.

Frank then walked into the hallway and glanced into the front room. Though I was the only person there, my presence seemed to have a disarming effect. Hannah had already vanished into the back bedroom. A controlled calm entered Frank's voice as he said 'look Linden just give her the money before tonight'. Saying this Frank gently kicked Linden repeatedly in the shin. I then heard Leander shout from outside in a loud voice, 'He spent it all on crack'. With this Leander's father turned and said, 'Don't go givin' out money to him then'. They then both walked back down the stairs. Frank got into a white van, which seemed to appear from nowhere, while Leander trudged back in the direction she came, her arms crossed against the blizzard.

Possession of crack-cocaine, even though Linden had none, can incur a jail sentence. Leander had done something that day I had never witnessed before: place a friend in jeopardy by shouting claims in public. Incidents that day led to a break in a friendship that had lasted since childhood. When Leander's parents split up, Linden told me how he was always there for her. The day also showed how without friendship there was little else to protect people; I never saw Linden and Leander together again after that point. Several months later Leander received a custodial sentence after CCTV footage of her was printed in the local paper.

The incident with Leander's father clearly unnerved Linden; when both left, he 'went on the session'. Earlier that morning Linden had been offered a decent job, one that could have freed him from poverty, earning £18,000 a year as a skilled engineer. If Linden had a car or the firm could have provided transport, he could have worked towards a mortgage, possibly start a family. In our interview, I had asked what he felt about settling down:

> RM: Do you see yourself with a house, wife, two kids?
> Linden: House, two kids [pause]. Ooh, I dunno. Maybe I'll be swayed that way in the end.

On that snowy December morning, faced with a job, a million miles away, and a man demanding £30 with violence in his face, that prospect must have seemed distant.

When he returned to the front room, Linden looked at me and declared that Leander was barred from his flat. I looked at Hannah, who was now back in the front room, giving another nervous smile. Linden then asked me if I could take him down town, to 'see about that job'; maybe he was reconsidering the job offer; maybe he wanted to just get out of the flat; I know I did.

We came closer to the cluster of high-rise offices that make up Ford's central business district, then pulled up outside the employment agency door. As soon as I switched off the engine Linden turned to me and said, 'Fuck it Rob, I'm gonna blank it.' Linden then got out of the car and went over to a phone box at the foot of an office block. When he returned seconds later, he said that he had just ordered some 'rock' (crack-cocaine). He asked me to drive him back to Nova.

Back at Linden's flat, a red Alfa Romeo waited at the foot of the stairs with its engine still running. Linden got out, ran over, and jumped into the passenger seat, got back out and ran up his flat. As he did I followed, both of us running to get out of the cold.

Inside, in the living room, Linden had a smoke. He had turned the electric fire on but nothing else. Linden told me to lock the front door, explaining 'I don't want Hannah bargin' in again'. As soon as he had exhaled the smoke, Linden relaxed for the first time that morning. After chatting for a few minutes, Linden set to work preparing another pipe. When the rock was finished, I left saying I would call him tomorrow. Linden said that he would probably make another order in a few minutes and 'have a session'. Ordinarily this would have been the beginning of another of Linden's roller-coaster days, though by noon that day I could not take any more.

During sessions, with Linden and friends, I had a smoke when offered, though only if people present felt it was polite. The function of drug use as a private culture was that it enabled young people to control, either emotionally or literally, the spectre of violence which stalked the Precinct at that time. I also wondered whether society and its consumers were any different. The distinction between Linden and stigmatised users was he was fully aware of the difference between recreational drug use and abuse. So were many of the young adults I met: people would rarely be seen drinking in public or in possession of alcohol, or even cigarettes. Not only did consuming in such ways signal a lack of self-respect, private consumption was to allay the pain of poverty and exclusion.

When father and daughter left, I asked Linden if Frank had a reputation; Linden said he was 'connected'. There did not seem to be a hierarchy of any sort, only members of the community who had a reputation 'for sorting things out'. One sunny afternoon at the Project, Sean explained that if an individual was robbed by a fellow resident: 'you either go up the Pub an' see some people or get a baseball bat'. The tragedy of living in a stigmatised community was that many young people described how resorting to violence was often necessary. Some-times people had to react in order to avoid falling prey to a handful of individuals, described below, who appeared to make a living out of intimidating residents of the Precinct area. Others such as Pele testified how people just exploded under the pressure of poverty and intolerance, either that or withered away into defeat.

Reynolds (1986) describes similar conflicts on the Omega estate in Oxford, where younger families were concentrated in the worst housing. Being placed at the bottom of the housing ladder also seemed to compound the conflicts experienced in the Precinct area in the way too many young people were concentrated together then left alone to survive.

Feeling for one another

Robbie and Leander's lives at that time showed how important it was to retain self-respect. Respect is often referred to in ethnographic studies on socially excluded young people, though it is often described in objective terms. Respect is described as an aspect of entrepreneurship and consumption, achieved through the objects attained through crime or the distribution of illegal drugs. Interpreting respect on the basis of a material culture of crime, in my view, only abstracts from the dreams young people described. Respect described by young people I met in Nova and evoked in Hip Hop was embedded in feelings of self-respect, and the promise of a life free from exclusion. When young people such as Leander and Robbie could no longer maintain that, then they became stigmatised as addicts.

Stigmatising fellow residents, however, seemed to be a consequence of exclusion: unable to hold onto self-respect, Robbie became walking testimony to the intractability of the workfare merry-go-round that nearly all of the young people I met faced. Despite being able to tackle that situation themselves, Linden and others inevitably felt anxious at seeing a friend who had lost hope. During those dark winter months, I could appreciate what Linden meant when he described how living in Nova was the survival of the fittest. Darwin (1859) used the term referring to evolution in the natural world yet it could be interpreted as a being emblematic of life in a consumer society. The result of this post-modern condition on society is entropy, evolution's antithesis, and a process that defines the degenerate nature of consumer culture. Barbara Adam (1995: 83) describes the relation between evolution and entropy: species may become extinct but their evolution cannot be reversed; entropy is expressive of a spontaneous process towards disorder and a decrease in information. Eric Hobsbawm (1997) argues that society today is trapped in this cycle, to the point where all of us are in danger of descending into barbarism. Hobsbawm (1997) describes the growing number of what he refers to as 'disintegral societies' such as Bosnia, Sri Lanka or Rwanda, that re-enact the 'horrors of the ancient slaughter-house' (1997: 334). Hobsbawm (1997) concludes that these atrocities persist because we have all got used 'to the normalcy of what our – certainly my – parents would have considered life under inhuman conditions'. Young adults in Nova are in a similar situation, living in an individualistic society where intolerance seems to be inextricably linked to consumption.

The reality Linden and his friends identified was that everyone was desperate to develop and work out of poverty; to overcome the stigma of crime and modernise their own community. In Chapter 1, I argued that outsiders were unwilling to see beyond the seductive images of crime associated with poor communities (Coward, 1994). For Robbie, drugs became a way of objectifying his own exclusion. As with all the other young adults I know, exclusion is uncontrollable. All that young adults could do was maintain the situation through a sense of self-respect.

Robbie's life had become a dialectical process of self-harm and violence at the hands of others. Becoming stigmatised as an addict he could no longer maintain the culture of community that young adults created each day to survive. Goffman (1963) describes how that label develops into a destructive relationship between people, even those who are friends. Goffman (1963) describes how we believe a person with a stigma is not quite human. On this assumption we exercise varieties of discrimination, through which we effectively, if often unthinkingly, reduce his/her life chances. Robbie's life chances were gradually diminishing as he endangered his friends searching for a release from the pain of the stigma he had been subjected to from an early age.

Faith in the future

Culture is a reactive measure to life's uncertainties. In this chapter, I have shown how Hip Hop's culture of community enables young people to survive poverty, and how necessary and easy it is to imagine 'the life' as a threat to the consumer society. Consumer culture appears to be filled with symbols that signify people's anticipation, or desire to survive a solitary life. In my concluding chapter, I describe how images of young people surviving poverty as a community fulfil that deep psychological need.

Given the terrible tragedies young people described growing up with and the difficulties all faced as adults, it must have been incredibly difficult to maintain a sense of hope. Friendship and a culture of self-respect seemed to be the only way young people could survive exclusion. Surviving, however, did not mean young adults were able to resolve exclusion. That was only possible with the help and support of other residents of Nova, and Chapter 5 describes how that happened.

Chapter 5

Education

Every young person I met in Nova identified how exclusion in education was the cause of poverty, not just for young people themselves but also for the entire community. In this chapter, young people describe the stigma of being associated with Nova at school and of being excluded as young adults by being seen as an educational failure. I also describe how a lack of opportunities in education compounded the poverty experienced by older residents.

Apart from Hannah and Linden, every other young person I interviewed had either been discouraged from staying on or expelled before they could gain a leaving certificate. As I described in the introduction, low educational attainment was a serious problem in Nova when I started my fieldwork, and only one of the young people I subsequently met, Ellie, had been encouraged to take 'A' levels. When the factories around Nova closed, the skills older residents had brought with them to Ford were no longer required. Living in a fully modern city, only to watch that crumble into the post-modern consumer society that characterises Ford today, older residents understood the difficulties young people faced. Like young people I met, older residents had arrived young and with nothing; older residents too had survived together by creating social spaces such as the Nova Centre. One could understand why older residents would want to maintain the community they had built, not just to try to retain young people but also maintain Nova's history. Later in this chapter, I describe how residents were able to build a new space where people could work towards a decent education.

Problem youth

Exclusion from secure jobs was a common experience for many young people; Sean described how outsiders implemented initiatives that only seemed to compound the stigma surrounding Nova's younger residents. In those summer months standing outside the Project, Sean described the factors that had shaped young people's experiences of exclusion, and why a collective sense of alienation had persisted for so long. First, the policies aimed at areas hit by de-industrialisation during the 1980s and 1990s. Second, the conservative administrations of this period required local authorities such as Ford City Council to sell social services to private agencies. Third, the labelling of young people's experiences and attitudes, ranging from 'problem' to 'delinquent'. Finally, once the problem or potential problem had been identified, private agencies would compete to manage younger residents (see Pitts and Hope, 1998). The result was a series of short-lived initiatives, which failed because people who were not residents had designed them: as Sean said, 'they haven't got a clue'. Similar paradoxes characterised the management of other problems in Nova. Often the community was caught between a breakdown of existing amenities and a 'plethora' of private agencies (see Wacquant, 1996). In terms of the management of social housing in Nova, the most vulnerable and excluded (young) adults were often located in the areas such as the spaces in and around Nova's main shopping Precinct. Frustration and desperation, emotions magnified by the dispro- portionate lack of opportunities faced by young people, shaped the public life of the Precinct.

The closure of the Project revealed how outside agencies could easily expose young people to further hardships. Shut down for being perceived as unconstructive for the young people who went there, the Project's closure created a completely new set of problems: young people now had to travel into Ford city centre to search for jobs, either through the central job centre or temporary employment agencies. Then there was the loss of social support from the Project staff, all of whom were forced to find other jobs; Sean moved out of Nova and I never saw Mathew, Eddy or Andy again. Terry, an outreach worker who grew up with Mathew in another part of Ford, told me he left the city after the Project closed.

The Precinct had a negative association for people in Nova generally and young people who I talked to who lived there described hating the experience. Warren, a member of the business who lived in the Precinct after his parents divorced, described the atmosphere, 'Fuckin' music blarin' out of windows, cars tearin' around the street, cars that lads have robbed. All arguments goin' on in the houses, just fuckin' mad.' All of the young people I met who lived or who had lived in the Precinct described how desperate they were to leave. Assessing the impact of high property turnover within 'problem' estates such as Nova, Anne Power (1997, 1999) suggests that directing lettings to those most in need only exacerbates problems such as crime, community conflict and vandalism. Research conducted by Cook (1997) in Wolverhampton and

Hagan (1994) in the United States also suggests a tendency among people living in disadvantaged areas to commit violent crimes nearer their homes than within more affluent areas. Evidence from the British Crime Survey (Mirrlees-Black, Mayhew and Percy, 1996) also highlights the connections between locality, crime and victimisation, revealing that over half of all property crimes recorded in the survey occurred in just a fifth of communities in England and Wales. In Ford, crime is higher in poorer areas such as Nova. However, research seems beset by an unwillingness to engage with people living in such areas, and the gulf of misunderstanding becomes filled with superficial misconceptions such as 'broken windows' where James Wilson (1985) argues that activities like aggressive begging, drunkenness and petty crime precipitate neighbourhood decline.

The nature of the crimes committed by young people in the Precinct reflected the feelings of exclusion and economic frustration young people described. Burglary remained the most common offence, while rates of violence and domestic violence were also among the highest in Ford. What struck me most about going to the Precinct was how visible people's situations were; arguments in the street were common. It reminded me of participant observations and interviews I had conducted with homeless people as an undergraduate. In both cases, it seemed that for people with no stake in society, the only form of self-expression left was the right to be heard. Warren said, 'you can see how bad it is just by goin' there. It's probably worse now than it was when I was livin' there.' Like Warren, Jay had lived in the Precinct though he felt it had grown worse over the years:

> RM: Did you like living in the Precinct? I mean, did you like it then?
> Jay: Yeah, I liked it then but not anymore, it's like Beirut.
> RM: Crime wasn't as bad there when you were younger?
> Jay: No, more people are stealin' off each other now. I mean usually it's just for a drink or summit. That's all they want, just a drink.
> RM: Are people doing more drink and drugs now than they were then?
> Jay: Then we were mainly smokin' cannabis. But over the years it's progressed, takin' ecstasy, speed, trips [LSD].

Martin, who lived near the Precinct at that time, was even more critical of its residents: 'the people are scavengers; they steal from anyone round there. Money, people around here are obsessed with money, I've seen two guys fight over a packet of fags, fuckin' fightin' over £1.80.'

Janet Foster (2000) highlights how ghettoisation can have a devastating impact on both socially excluded young adults and the wider community in which they live. Returning to the North East of England ten years after a study on housing, community and crime (Hope and Foster, 1992),

Foster (2000) highlights how drug use among young adults can wreck any attempt to regenerate neighbourhoods. Foster (2000: 320) found that a failure in the management in social housing allowed the space for a drug-using subculture of young adults to grow and persist. Quoting a local police officer, Foster (2000: 321) found, 'the "radius around the tower blocks" was dominated by "street drug supply, petty crime (and) a lot of nuisance" ... Housing staff felt under siege, reticent and sometimes fearful of encountering difficult and potentially volatile tenants.'

The problems experienced in the Precinct also related to its design and the subsequent ghettoisation of young people living there during the 1980s. At the centre of the Precinct was one long street where most young people in Nova were forced to survive. Even though the young people I met were resilient, each was also vulnerable, and younger adults such as Jason, Antoine and Slim who went to the Project were the most vulnerable.

Ghetto heaven

When we returned from Orpheus, Linden took me out one night 'door knocking' to introduce me to young people and 'open your eyes to Nova'. 'Door knocking' involves knocking on people's doors, hoping they will let you in for a chat, and just shows how close people are in Nova. The night itself was freezing and after a glass of vodka, we left Linden's flat and made for the Precinct. Some of the accounts I had heard about the street from Warren and Jay made me apprehensive. Linden sensed this and advised me to 'behave'.

We arrive at a ground-floor flat. The gantries are dark and empty in the freezing cold, leaving loose newspaper to swirl inside the concrete porticos surrounding doorways. Some of the flats are vacant, sealed off with the terrible steel grills. Others are inviting, with pot plants at the windows, new double-glazing, and stone animals beside doors. Despite the time of night – 3 a.m. – Linden knocks confidently at the door of a more basic flat. I can hear voices inside, and then the door is opened by a very young, slim Caucasian woman. 'Hello Chloe', Linden says with a big smile. Chloe cannot help but smile back despite being conscious of a large bruise circling her left eye. Chloe opens the door and we both tilt to see who is inside. To my amazement Jason, Slim and Pele are all sitting around where a gas fire should have been. All three turn in unison; shout to come in, Pele waving a path. We step in. Linden brandishes the bottle of vodka; all three cheer even though no one takes up the offer of a sip.

The front room is practically empty; a three-piece suite worn and collapsed, a fitted carpet, and a compact disc player on the floor in the

117

corner. The flat is Damon's; a handsome African-Caribbean young man sitting alone in a chair next to the couch that just about holds Pele, Jason and Slim. Chloe comes in behind us and plops down into the last chair. This leaves Linden and me to sit on the floor. 'Just in the middle of a session', Jason grins infectiously even though there is nothing in the room to allow any form of entertainment. Linden introduces me to Chloe and Damon; both smile and say hello. Despite the empty space where a fireplace once was, the room is not as cold as you would expect. Money is too tight for the central heating and that Christmas Liam and Martin told me how they spent Christmas day in bed. Damon, skinnier than the three bigger boys, is wrapped in a duvet. Pele, Jason and Slim are also able to share each other's body temperature, leaving Chloe rubbing her arms and shivering. Linden later told me Damon shares the flat with Norris, who was in bed to keep warm. We stayed for an hour laughing and joking, with the bottle remaining untouched. I rarely saw young people drinking alcohol in the Precinct area. It was only when I interviewed Pele, at his mother's flat, with Jason and Slim drinking tiny bottles of cheap Alsace lager: the context seemed to suggest that outside the private culture of parental space, being seen drinking meant being exposed to attack. When we left for another door, I asked Linden if he knew what had happened to Chloe and he told me, 'looked like someone hit her'.

Do-gooders

Shortly before the Project closed, Stan, a member of the Nova Centre committee, and a member of an outside agency came in several times to try to assess what could be done. At the time, residents belonging to various community groups were putting together a bid to gain funding for Gateways, a new adult education training facility. During that process, residents had been liaising with various outside agencies and it was during those visits I met Stan. A stern, impeccably dressed man who had lived in Nova for most of his life, Stan, like Ralph, had witnessed the difficulties young people faced. The empathy of residents towards young people was reflected in the way Stan, Ralph, Sean and Eddy never prescribed a solution. Spending time with young adults at the Project, all seemed to be aware that the exclusion people faced was deeply individual and radically different from each day to the next. The problem at that time, however, was funding and, more importantly, who controlled it: Sean described working for Ford City Council and gradually being marginalised as youth services came under professional management. Sean also explained how the process resulted in a situation in which 'one hand didn't know what the other hand was doin'', whereby one initiative would often negate the achievements of another.

Loic Wacquant's (1996: 51) research charts the effect of the multi-agency approach of the 1980s and 1990s in Europe and the United States. Identifying an 'over-penetration of state agencies' in housing estates in Paris, Wacquant (1996: 251–4) reveals the consequences of the multi-agency approach. In La Couneurve, 'the over-representation of state agencies and facilities ... contributes to further stigmatising the neighbourhood and to increasing the sentiments of isolation and discontent among residents' (Wacquant, 1996: 254). The process Wacquant (1996) identifies typified the closure of the Project, its impact on the young men and women, and the subsequent battle among various agencies attempting to assume responsibility for a new facility.

A new initiative

During the final months of the Project, two separate youth agencies began to approach Sean, Eddy and the Project's financial backers. Most of the meetings were held at the Project and at a local nursery, a place where agency members could feel more comfortable. I arrived at the meeting early and through the wrong entrance, let in by a polite dinner woman. Leaving the kitchen, I passed through a large play area littered with toys and picture books and decorated with happy jungle beasts. Then, following the tiny painted footprints on the floor, I turned left into a formal office in which were seated a middle-aged woman and her younger female secretary and said I had come for the meeting concerning the Project. As no one else was present in the adjoining room in which eight chairs were arranged in a circle, I strolled through a set of patio doors into a large garden. At the far end of the lawn, a man was tending to border plants. The nursery itself was beautiful, down to the efforts of the Ford City Council who clearly hoped to provide an idyllic environment for children and parents.

I heard voices back in the conference room and I returned to find a large middle-aged woman, Emily, and two men who rarely spoke and never introduced themselves throughout the meeting. All were dressed in a professional manner and were representatives of Youth Concern, a regional agency with a number of centres aimed specifically at unemployed young adults. I sat down while the three discussed agency affairs. Sean, Eddy and Mathew then entered along with Sarah and a tall, slim, stylish woman from the Project's funding agency. Before I started going to the Project, a previous meeting had been held at the nursery, at which a series of 'action plans' were formulated. It became clear that members of the agency hoped to transplant a scheme from another area and had little intention of replicating the Project as a youth centre.

The new Project would involve group 'activities', the development of job and 'inter-personal' skills and incorporate a system of 'mentoring' in which young people would be 'guided' through education, training and eventually work. As a result, this new Project would only be targeted at 16–25 year olds. Sean said he was concerned about the persistent focus on 16–25 year olds. He pointed out that many of the people who came into the Project fell outside this category, such as Tracy, Catherine, Ralph and their respective children. Emily seemed to dismiss these other groups, labelling them as 'long-term unemployed'. She also made clear that when the new Project was relocated it was unlikely that Sean, Mathew or Trevor would be invited to work there. Just before the meeting ended, Emily asked Eddy if she could have a list of the names and addresses of the young people who attended the Project. Eddy had a list of names of people who had an account for teas and coffees supplied at the Project though he never mentioned this at the time and seemed highly reluctant to offer up the list; his expression darkening as the suggestion was made. Pitts and Hope (1997: 43) describe the strategy proposed at the nursery as 'delinquency management'.

Sean described how past attempts to regenerate Nova failed because of the way young people were labelled and treated differently from the outset. Even though policies were well-meaning, having to participate in programmes aimed at 'problem youth' only seemed to compound exclusion. Either way, people, especially young people, living in Nova ended up being excluded or feeling stigmatised in job interviews or when trying to apply for financial services (Goffman, 1963).

Sean identified how exclusion was a shared feeling among a group of young people who grew up together in Nova. For all of the young people I got to know, the backdrop behind everyone's childhood and adolescence was Nova's urban regeneration during the 1980s. During that time, young people in Nova were subject to the schemes designed by government and private organisations, which often presumed at the outset that Nova's youth were susceptible to crime (see France and Wiles, 1997). During that time local groups set up by residents who knew the difficulties all residents had to face were also subject to the same process. Community organisations set up a money advice centre and provided provisions through the Nova Centre and at some of the estate's primary schools. Without adequate financial support, these initiatives seemed to be swept away whenever the regional economy faltered. Closure was often because community-based initiatives were never able to secure a permanent purpose-built space or, as in the case of Sean's table tennis club, Sean himself was constantly forced to move from one location to the next through what seemed like a process of ever-decreasing social space.

Learning to labour

In Chapter 1, I described how work had become more flexible and also more specialised in areas such as Ford during the 1980s. Secure jobs in the city began to require professional qualifications, particularly information-technology skills. Research shows that 80 per cent of the 1.7 million new jobs likely to be created in the next decade will require a professional qualification (Wilson and Green, 2001). Participation by young people in higher education in Great Britain, as measured by the Age Participation Index, has increased significantly over the last decade, from 19 per cent in 1990/91 to 35 per cent in 2001/02 (Archer *et al.*, 2003). In its recent White Paper *The Future of Higher Education*, the government stated its intention to increase participation to 50 per cent for those less than 30 years old (DfES, 2003). Without educational qualifications, people's prospects are far worse now than when there was a more diverse and flexible job market. The greatest obstacle young people faced was trying to find a job in a world where the only decent ones demanded relevant post-16 qualifications or training.

University education is still a privilege. Students from middle-class backgrounds continue to dominate in universities while students from poorer areas and families remain under-represented. This picture relates to the inequalities created and imposed within schools. Although participation in higher education has risen significantly over the past 20 years, participation among students from social classes 3 and 4 remains at 25 per cent nationally while for students from the poorest postcode areas it is only 12 per cent. Equally, non-completion has risen recently to a national average of 16 per cent (Thomas, 2001). Research has identified that some schools have a 'poverty of aspirations' for working-class and socially excluded children, providing pupils with less encouragement compared with students from affluent areas. Pugsley (1998) found that this process manifested itself through the advice given and options made available to pupils. Other studies, where students considering higher education were interviewed, have identified how discouraging young people can lead to a negative perception of university generally. For example, Archer and Hutchings (2000) interviewed students from lower socio-economic backgrounds who perceived higher education as being dominated by the middle class. Many students chose not to go to university as they felt it could be potentially alienating. Evidence also suggests that some universities discriminate during the admissions process. Mudood and Shiner (1994), for example, found that many pre-1992 universities were less likely to accept applicants from ethnic minority and lower socio-economic groups, even when their qualifications were the same as middle-class applicants.

All the young adults I spoke to described discrimination and disincentive at school. Most were required to leave school at 16 because they were perceived to be not good enough by teachers, or that their behaviour was deemed too confrontational. Only Ellie had been given the opportunity to stay on, though she had been unable to. For Ellie, the increasing cost of further and higher education was the main barrier to staying on. Ellie worked in Nova's local supermarket at the time, and described that dual pressure:

> RM: Didn't you want to stay on?
> Ellie: I was gonna, but me sister died just before I left and it did me head in a bit.

Ellie's domestic circumstances could only have made trying to study difficult:

> Ellie: Yeah, I've got two brothers and four sisters. There's nine of us livin' at home now. Two of me nieces as well.
> RM: What's that like?
> Ellie: A bit hectic, 'cause four of 'em share a room. And I think I'm about to get kicked out.

Wanting to leave home and get her own flat, Ellie explained the financial pressures she faced and the effect they would have on her social life. I asked her if she could afford it: 'I won't be able to go out or anythin' y'know. So I'd rather stay at home maybe.' Ellie also told me she had hoped to stay on at school. Staying at home, Ellie, like many young adults I spoke to, had to work full-time. Having to go out and find work at 16, Ellie was in a situation shared by the vast majority of young adults I met in Nova: not just a lack of money but a job that would provide a way out of a day-to-day world of not having enough money to buy food and clothing. Having to survive each day also meant Nova's young adults were denied a freedom the vast majority of young people have. Youth is not simply a freedom to discover, independent from the constraints of family. What many fail to appreciate in their understanding of youth is the importance of a future beyond it. Writing on the importance of work for young people from a working-class community, Willis (1977: 95) says: 'this establishes a clear continuity between disparate situations. We can see this as a continuous base line of experience and response, which informs the whole working class culture in its long arc of adaptation to hostile conditions.'

Another reason why Ellie was unable to stay on at school was that her parents could not afford to look after her once she had turned 16. Unless siblings are in full-time education, child benefits stop at 16 and in an area characterised by low incomes many families were unable to go on supporting their children when they reached that age. Many of the young people I met, including Jason, Olly and Slim, had no alternative but to leave home after leaving school and move into the Precinct.

Leander encapsulated the dangers that threaten young adults who became cut off from friends and had to survive alone. Like every other young person I met, Leander wanted to escape from the stigma surrounding Nova's young adult population. Exclusion was described by young adults as a condition; being surrounded by affluence and affluent, intolerant people, in Gemini Park, in Ford city centre, on television, in the news – even passing along the roads that surround Nova, cars so expensive they appeared other-worldly compared with the situations young people faced. Young adults told me that living in Nova also meant being subject to a process of daily exclusion, whereby all that was available were 'shit jobs' because working within that was how individuals were made to feel. Working at the nursing home and receiving £35 each fortnight, then dismissed by an unfair boss who, I suspect, sacked Leander because she had self-confidence: what seemed to be the only form of protection young people had against exclusion. On the day Linden and I picked her up, through the patio doors of the nursing home we could see how Leander was gaining a lot of attention from older male residents. When Leander told me how the man who was smiling at her later molested her, it was highly probable given the way he was behaving that afternoon. Lodging a complaint, Leander was sacked by her supervisor. Being dismissed also meant that, without references, getting a similar placement was practically impossible. An NVQ in nursing would have allowed Leander to go into a profession where she could have realised her hopes.

Leander's situation personified the exclusion of young people living in Nova. Leander had hopes and dreams like every other young adult I met. After being dismissed from the nursing home, Leander gradually seemed to lose her self-belief. Linden and others described how you have to try to remain composed or 'you lose it'. Finding it impossible trying to find a permanent job with no reference, Leander was left with Nova's local carousel service economy. Like many young adults, 'working for yourself' was the only way to retain hope in the future. Unlike other moochers, however, Leander was very young, only 19. Linden, Montana, Steve and Jimmy, all five years older, seemed to have grown more resilient and resourceful in those years. So too was Leander, though: cut off from the experiences Linden and his friends shared, she seemed more exposed after being barred from Linden's flat. When I spoke with Sean about whether mooching was a durable solution, he told me that without the opportunity to invest, entrepreneurship could never defeat the exclusion surrounding Nova's youth no matter how innovative and resourceful young people were.

Escape attempts

Sadly, the local economy does not provide a way out of the stigma surrounding the estate's young adult population. When I was working in Gemini Park, it seemed that older residents were less able to work for themselves. Residents I met at the supermarket I worked in for three months of my fieldwork were often in middle age and usually had family responsibilities. That is reflected in the fact most of those working in Nova's local service economy are people in their late thirties and older. Having to work in split shifts, which often changed each week, also meant that people had little time to study.

Carol, an adult education worker who I met in Nova at the start of my fieldwork, told me how being excluded from education was a common experience for many residents. Even though the determinants behind exclusion from education differed, the susceptibility of people feeling stigmatised through a lack of educational qualifications transcended age. Unemployment, under-employment, and being denied the qualifications to gain permanent jobs were all processes that residents had been subjected to. The slow collapse of a regional manufacturing economy resulted in unemployment for workers and the stigma of having to claim benefits for one's children. People I met old enough to remember the early 1980s described de-industrialisation's impact on the community, and being made to feel different in its aftermath; young people also told me how the stigma of unemployment echoed at school during the 1980s. Carol told me that older residents felt less confident about studying compared with younger people. Young adults such as Jason and Slim were not inhibited by learning but were defiant against being made to feel different. Jason, Steve and many other young people's experiences of education were characterised by stigma, as Cliff and Tony explained. Tony was unable to get on with teachers at Greaves and described how eventually, 'I 'ad English and maths lessons in the library by myself. Technically I stayed there until I was 15 but I virtually did nothin.' Tony, Cliff and all of the young African-Caribbean men I spoke to apart from Linden had been put into 'the Unit' at Greaves Secondary:

RM: Were you in the Unit?
Tony: Yeah, right. When I weren't doin' lessons.
RM: What was it, what did you do in there?
Tony: It's where no one else would have. It was like The Project, it was a big block where you used to play table football.
RM: Didn't they have any teachers in there?
Tony: Yeah, they had a supervisor in there, that's about it.

Cliff told me when he was placed in 'the Unit':

Cliff: I went into the Unit, then I got thrown out of the Unit.

RM: What happened when you were thrown out of the Unit?

Cliff: See, the Unit was the last resort. They put me in a home then.

Many of the young people I had met were able to survive the stigma of being associated with Nova. Being stigmatised within school only seemed to make Robbie more determined to do well in his final exams:

Robbie: But then, when I left that school I went to Greaves and I stuck it out actually. I was hardly ever there like but I stayed to the end. I did music, I play the drums like, an' I did my exam in music, GCSE, an' I did City and Guilds Engineerin' but I never did the exam but I was too scared.

RM: Really?

Robbie: Yeah, I would've done it but I was just too scared of fuckin' failing y'know what I mean, everyone passin' and I failed that's what I thought.

RM: You shouldn't look at it like that.

Robbie: Yeah, I can remember things but when it comes down to writing it on paper y'know what I mean I just lose track cause I 'aven't got the concentration. I think I'm dyslexic. I can read and write but I don't concentrate that much.

Talking with Robbie during our interview, it seemed that not being able to go on to college had haunted his life ever since. When I met Carol, during the development of Gateways, and told her I was conducting a study of local young people's experiences, she suggested I conduct research within the local labour market. I applied for a job at Anderson's, a large supermarket built several years ago on the edge of Ford and directly next to Nova. Anderson's employed many people from Nova and working there, I could see why the jobs it provided only compounded the conditions residents had to face. Anderson's was divided into sections, fruit and vegetables, fresh meat and fish, household supplies and other commodities you would expect in a big supermarket. Trainee employees had a choice which section to work in though all paid the same, marginally above the minimum wage, which at the time was £3.50 an hour. Most of the jobs were full-time and often involved unsocial hours. For the three months I worked at Anderson's, most days would start at 5 a.m. and finish at 4 p.m. Several days during the week would be free, though most weekends involved twelve-hour shifts and the same applied to all of the people I started with. Judging by the number of people who attended my induction weekend, Anderson's must have had a high staff turnover. Twenty people started when I did and over those three months, half left, usually for other jobs. In our interview, Jay, one of the older young adults I met at the Project, described how the jobs Anderson's advertised only seemed to sustain poverty:

> RM: Compared to being on the dole the pay for these jobs. I mean was it worth it?
>
> Jay: No. If you've got a flat, you've got to pay rent.
>
> RM: The rent really hammers your wages?
>
> Jay: Yeah, the rent's a big 'No'. Y'know like. See no one's really got an education in Nova. A lot of people with families. You've got your own place and you've got to pay rent which is say £60 a week and then you've got to pay council tax, your water, your gas, your electric, food and clothes for the kids, bus fares. Most of the lads in Nova leave school, get jobs through the local paper, and then think 'fuck that'.

Andy, an 18-year-old man from Hillcrest, Nova's neighbouring estate, started with me and left after two months to work in a restaurant. Noel was also 18 and from the other side of Ford and left to work in an electrical store. The induction group I belonged to was made up of older men and women, usually over 40, and young adults the same age as Noel and Andy. Almost all of the older people obtained jobs as checkout operators while young people were allocated to departments on the supermarket floor. A deciding factor in why Noel and Andy left was that they were both treated terribly by supervisors. They never told me themselves, though the counter where I worked faced their departments. Both were constantly verbally abused and intimidated and I was pleased for both when they told me they had found other jobs.

You got no hopes: working on workfare

Even though Carol never said it openly, when she suggested at the start of my fieldwork that I should work at Anderson's she knew I would see at first hand how such industries sustain the economic uncertainties Jay described. Talking about the Project and its value, Carol said that when it closed, the only place left to go was 'the Pub'. Many of the young people I met worked together because service industries within Gemini Park provided no economic future. Carol identified how the Pub acted as an informal self-employment centre, albeit a very dangerous one (see Whyte, 1945). The Pub was demolished with the old shopping arcade during my fieldwork, though Nova's remaining public house, The Cedars, continued as an informal economy. Steve described the Pub:

> Steve: Yeah, the Pub was the magnet, if you go up the Pub and there's nothin' goin on then a lad will come in and say do ya wanna work this.

RM: Someone will get them and bring them in and then someone else will work them?

Steve: Yeah, that's it. Or there's people who will go out and nick 'em then work 'em [obtain goods by deception] themselves but I just think that's piggery.

RM: And like when you're doin' it can you make money everyday or is there like good days and bad days?

Steve: Yeah course there is. They're fuckin' good months and bad months. There's fuckin' right shit months. I mean you can go a month without earnin' any money, it's fuckin' chaos.

Gemini Park, along with companies such as Anderson's, was intended to provide a stable economy to enable residents to revitalise Nova following the recession of the early 1980s: big superstores would provide jobs and investment from the consumers and ancillary businesses who would, in theory, be attracted to move into the area. During my fieldwork, Anderson's was one of the biggest local employers alongside a number of large electrical, DIY and furniture stores that circled Gemini Park. Gemini Park itself was actually split into two areas, one part containing anonymous offices, the other a large retail park.

Carol had watched these industries rise along Ford's border. Throughout the 1980s and early 1990s, Nova and many other socially deprived urban regions were subjected to private property based regeneration initiatives (see Foster, 1999). Successive conservative governments in Britain and the United States believed private or corporate projects would 'trickle down' resources to deprived urban communities. Among residents I spoke to, many believed companies such as Anderson's had deliberately exploited an already poor community.

Urban regeneration

Throughout the 1980s and early 1990s governments had been forced to minimise social services at a point when society itself was collapsing into the economic fissure globalisation had made. As stated above, governments, influenced by what came to be known as the 'American Model' of urban regeneration, believed the private developments would generate profits that would 'trickle down' into deprived communities. During the 1980s, in Europe and the United States, a series of urban regeneration schemes emerged such as museum, leisure and sports complexes, business and retail parks (Fainstein and Gladestone, 1997). In cities such as London, Birmingham and Manchester, initiatives were often purposely built on the foundations of demolished manufacturing works (see Giddens, 1990; Lash and Urry 1994; Taylor, Evans and Fraser 1996; Foster, 1999). The 'American model' was clearly realised in London, where the Docklands area was transformed into an affluent area through the construction of a central financial district and luxury apartments (see Foster, 1999). Within Britain during the 1980s, the 'American model' of urban regeneration came to be replicated in cities such as Birmingham, Glasgow and Manchester, though with differential success (see Fainstein and Gladestone, 1997). Several towns and cities local to Ford survived de-industrialisation through tourism. Often, however, these areas were popular tourist destinations before de-industrialisation. Cities such as York, Lancaster and Oxford, for instance, were already advantaged in being situated in a semi-rural environment (see Lash and Urry, 1994). Ford, however, is a big post-industrial city. Many of the workers in the city's high-tech industries chose to live far away from areas such as Nova and, as a result, did little in terms of inward investment.

Bordering Nova, Gemini Park contains elements of the 'American model', in its design and in the way companies can lease industrial or retail units. Another feature of private property-led urban regeneration schemes was that industries were often divided between high-tech and service-led. Employment opportunities in Gemini Park were divided between highly skilled specialist industries and a string of superstores (see Sassen, 1997). Young people described being restricted to service-sector jobs because of the negative association local employers had about Nova. A survey carried out by Ford City Council found that only a third of those living in Nova were in full-time employment on an estate originally built to house manufacturing workers. Just over half the men were working (53 per cent) while fewer than half of women were in work (48 per cent). Overall, 16 per cent were unemployed, while the study found a further 6 per cent were unemployed and not registered.

In her own research on the opportunities that service industries provide communities adversely affected by de-industrialisation, Patsy Healy (1997: 267) describes initiatives such as Gemini Park as 'job-less growth'. Job-less growth has also been a growing trend over the past two decades, helped by the 'elimination of the human' worker through advances in production technology (see Kumar, 1984). Another trend in urban redevelopments has been the way their insertion into regional economies divides the working population between 'core' high-paid jobs and temporary, menial, low-paid positions. People restricted to service-industry jobs often face greater insecurities: McKnight (2002) found that low-paid work has increased in the last 25 years and the relative earnings of low-paid workers have fallen significantly. In addition, low-paid jobs are now much more insecure than higher-paid jobs. Tracking individuals over time, McKnight (1998) found that low-paid workers are more likely to go on to experience unemployment or periods out of the labour market than higher-paid workers. Many young people described this process of being continuously employed in different positions for years and, for older young adults, decades.

Within private property-led urban regeneration schemes it was felt that employees in high-tech industries would bring wealth that would trickle down to the local community. In addition, service industries that prospered on cheap land rates and low wage costs would feed money back into the community. The difficulties people living in Nova had in attracting a sponsor to redevelop the arcade demonstrated how major retail industries only thought in profit terms (see Foster, 1999). Following the completion of Gemini Park, local services and the local council gained little from the redevelopment of the local area or economy. Faced with continuing deprivation, which I describe in the following chapter, Nova's residents had to rely on one another to regenerate the area. Even though that meant changes were reflective of local people's needs, it also meant change was a long, slow, difficult process.

The workfare carousel

Janet Foster's (1999) study on the regeneration of Docklands identifies how Canary Wharf did little for local people except create a feeling of exclusion and powerlessness. In Gemini Park, Carol describes how initiatives such as Anderson's did little for individual residents or the community as a whole. Local residents were unable to appropriate their own space, even though Gemini Park provided local people with a constant source of jobs, because the economy itself was organised by the principle of workfare. Even though companies such as Anderson's provided incomes less than state benefits, young people I met who never had full-time permanent jobs were required to work there. Every young person I met, with the exception of Hannah, was subject to the workfare initiatives implemented at Ford's local benefit offices. These included frequent and mandatory interviews, work placements and vocational courses designed to eradicate 'dependency' and instil a sense of self-sufficiency. Bob Jessop (1990) describes this process as part of the 'hollowing out' of the welfare state, whereby government is no longer able to fund adequate employment training such as the apprenticeship Linden gained at Weston's. In its place was workfare, summed up by John Lea (2002: 98–101): 'The workfare state is aimed at guaranteeing labour flexibility, creating an attractive "business environment" through vocational training, removal of restrictions on land use etc. rather than guaranteeing universalistic social rights and involves a shift to vocational training, innovation.'

As I described in previous chapters, the re-creation of Nova into a workfare regional economy resulted in the dialectic of exclusion which young people characterised as 'the life'. Not only were opportunities in the local economy prescribed to minimum-wage temporary jobs, the stigma surrounding all young people living in Nova resulted in the destruction of initiatives such as the Project. Also destroyed by workfare was the value of work itself as a means of enabling young people to live a life free from poverty. None of the young people I met worked at companies such as Anderson's because, as I describe below, being there only subtracted the faith and hope young people had in themselves.

The Project was closed because its success contradicted the assumption that Nova's youth were inherently lazy, susceptible to crime and drug abuse. My own experience of the Project was that it allowed people to appropriate their own lives and helped make Nova safer for everyone. Going to the Project, I saw how young people were being given help and support from staff and older residents. The Project was also a place where young people were treated with respect, a process that allowed each person to develop their own self-respect. The problem was that both could not be measured. What followed was a year-long battle between external agencies such as Youth Concern and community organisations trying to build a centre as representative and inclusive as the former Project.

The completion of a new Precinct and Gateways and the eventual appropriation of both into the community were events I never foresaw. This was partly a reflection of my own grounded approach (see Glaser and Strauss, 1967); I knew the Project was there as a community project. I remember it starting as a Job Shop in the mid-1980s when I used to tear around the Precinct as a child, looking in the window and wondering why middle-aged men and women would sit talking in what looked like an empty shop. During my fieldwork, the closure of the Project seemed like a further erosion of Nova's social spaces. The events taking place at the time of my fieldwork were almost as much of a shock to me as they undoubtedly were for the young people who had invested their hearts and souls in the Project.

One afternoon at the Project at the end of September, a representative from Youth Concern came in and described how Gateways would provide programmes and professional guidance for young people who were unemployed or in temporary work. At the meeting, Tracy and Catherine, who were the only young people present, looked pessimistic. They had a right to be: up until then Sean had kept a flame of hope alive – that funding might be obtained to enable everyone to relocate to another building. Stan and other people involved with the Nova Centre had also talked of creating an initiative where local people could take their own steps to achieve a permanent job. At the time, when the representative came in to describe Gateways, it seemed as if yet another local resource had fallen prey to the hostile outside world. After the meeting, Tracy told me she would not be going because, 'it would be just full of middle-class do-gooders'. Over the subsequent months, the closure of the Project and the creation of Gateways only seemed to fulfil everyone's worst fears.

Been here before: repackaging the Project

Many were suspicious as to whether Gateways would make a difference. When it opened, just as the Project was closing, Gateways had a very professional, business-like atmosphere completely antithetical to the homely, lived-in feel of the Project. Compared with the courses being advertised at Gateways' official opening, at the Project Sean structured each day in relation to the collective mood young people seem to express. Living in Nova himself and running activities for under-16s at the Nova Centre meant that Sean knew many of the problems young people experienced. Sean's strategy was inductive, letting young people look for work and providing advice if asked. He never told people what to do and insisted people who worked at the Project do the same. This was why the organisers' description of the Gateway's 'new' strategy came as such a disappointment to everyone. Tracy said after the meeting, 'it sounds like being back at school'. Some older young adults such as Martin and Clive, Linden's older brother, enrolled on courses. Most of the young people I met at the Project had endured years of stigma at school through living in Nova, though only older young adults such as Linden, Montana, Martin and Cliff seemed more able to cope with the feelings of negativity generated in that process. There also seemed to be a correlation between continuous interference and the consolidation of young people's sense of community. After years of successive initiatives, many of the older young men and women I met had gradually disengaged simply to defend their own sense of self-identity.

During those summer months at the Project, Sean explained how the problem was bad jobs, not a lack of them. Another frustration was the way education remained a potential way out of this economy, once Nova had a local initiative where residents could build their own skills portfolio. Throughout Ford, resources for adult education were extremely good. Time and money are often the greatest barriers to accessing it. Ford's transport system connects the entire city, yet Ford remains a sprawling conurbation and getting from one area to the next requires two buses. Day-saver tickets were purchasable, though journeys would still cost a minimum of £1 per day. Ricky at the Project told me how hard it is to keep up a job, ' 'specially without no transport. If I had transport it would be easier to get a job.' Fate has it that most of Ford's adult education facilities remain on the other side of the city. And for residents working in Gemini Park the barriers to education were even greater: people I met at Anderson's who lived in Nova usually worked at night or on split shifts, meaning that no one had a fixed free day every week.

When the Gateways opened, it only seemed to highlight the gulf between a subjective experience of exclusion and its objective classification by outsiders. Gateways was originally intended as a conference facility to attract business to the area, echoing the trickle-down philosophy of the 1980s and 1990s. At a series of events the focus on job opportunities, articulated in a largely external language of business potential and training, only seemed to accentuate young adults' feelings of inadequacy and low self-esteem.

On the opening day of Gateways, Mathew (a youth worker at the Project) and I were invited to attend by representatives from Youth Concern. We were also asked if we could recruit young people from the Project. We both asked Slim and Jason if they would like to come along. Apart from Carol and some members of the Nova Centre committee, many of the people present were representative of external agencies. All four of us, who were dressed casually, confessed to feeling scruffy among the professional assemblage. Jason and Slim's suspicions were compounded by the fact that several present were teachers from Greaves secondary school.

Behind the scenes

During the final weeks of the Project, Stan invited me to sit on the Nova Centre Committee. There I met committee members, including Tom, the director of finance: tall, slim and, like Stan, always impeccably dressed. I also met June, the Nova Centre's events organiser. June was younger than Stan and Tom, in her late 40s, and more concerned with feeling comfortable in her jogging suit. Finally, there was Hilda, the chair of the committee. Along with Tom and Stan, Hilda was always formally dressed. Everyone I met at the Nova Centre lived in Nova and many people had been on the committee since the Centre opened in the early 1950s. Sitting in on committee meetings was such a different experience compared with the liaison process that spelled the final weeks of the Project. Committee meetings seemed to be characterised by a shared subjectivity built around people just listening to one another; a world away from the charts and targets spelled out by outside agencies. Talking with June, Hilda and Tom about the closure of the Project, all knew its end would only mean greater difficulties for young people throughout Nova. Even though it was never said, members also knew that it would be impossible to gain outside support to create a centre that would be representative of what young people wanted. Older residents had worked with the city council and then the agencies created by the privatisation of welfare services during the 1980s. Nevertheless, residents groups were able to eventually gain ownership of Gateways, through a convergence of events that no one could have planned or predicted (see Chapter 6). Neither could I. My own interpretation of events at that time was coloured by the closure of the Project, and I, like many young people who went there, was pessimistic when I witnessed the facility open.

Gradually the committee and other local community groups were able to realise a place where local people would not feel like objects of suspicion just for living in Nova. Today Gateways offers courses that enable local people to break free from the cycle of temporary low-paid jobs and income support. Some of the young people who went to the Project have completed courses there. Gateways does the best it can to offer a safe social space where young people can be themselves, though the Centre was always intended as a training facility. The sense of peace that filled what had originally been an abandoned shop seems to have been lost, though at the time, several young people described a feeling of boredom in relation to the Project. Jimmy and Jason, along with some other young people, referred to the facility as 'the Doss Shop'.

Making history

The transformation of Gateways into a facility representative of local people's experiences was down to the knowledge and determination of Carol, who I met at the very start of my fieldwork. Young, tall, and completely down to earth, Carol had the same intuitive connection with Nova as members of the committee. Growing up in the area and attending Greaves secondary school gave Carol a history and experience of Nova. I met Carol when Gateways was in the final stages of construction and asked if I could conduct part of my study there. I said I had started going to the Project, and Carol told me that that would be the best place to get to know young people who lived in Nova. Carol said I should become part of the furniture. At the time, I took the comment as a metaphor for the approach I should take. Looking back, the phrase encapsulates the embedded nature of Nova as a community. Raymond Williams (1980) conceived the idea of a 'structure of feeling' to describe how individuals organise their lives as a community. Williams (1980: 24) was always critical of the work of Victorian historians, in the way they tried to romanticise history as an evolutionary process of winners and losers. Growing up in a mining village in Wales, Williams' (1989) experience of history was the history of his community: a cyclical feeling of social unity.

The Project was a safe place where people could share common experiences that transcended age, gender and ethnicity. Two regulars at the Project were Ralph, approaching 50, and his daughter Mirabell, nearly five. One sunny afternoon Mirabell was playing pool standing on a plastic chair to enable her to see the balls while holding the cue, which was bigger than she was. Technically, no one under 16 was allowed in the Project though some people, usually very close to Sean, were allowed to bring in their children. Mirabell had just left nursery and was waiting to attend primary school in September. When I arrived that afternoon, she lifted her head, gave me a demonic grin, and demanded that I play. I attempted to do so, though the fact that she could not even connect the cue tip with the cue ball ensured that the game was short-lived. As we played, Ralph was in the back room chatting with Sean. Ralph was a short, thin man with strong forearms and cropped red hair. Like many of Nova's first generation, Ralph had come from another country. Many young adults I met had rarely been outside Nova and during afternoons young men and women listened to Ralph describe his experiences. Ralph testified to the strong oral tradition contained within Nova's spirit of community, passed from Nova's first generation to a third, and the Project and the Nova Centre made that arch possible.

The Breakfast Club

To understand the importance of the Project, it needs to be seen alongside the other social structures that bound Nova's community, and the times they occurred. For many people who went to the Project, young, old and staff members, the day began at the Breakfast Club.

Like the Project, the tables and chairs were basic, like those in a classroom. Because the Breakfast Club was held in the main hall, it had to be a temporary affair. At noon, all the tables and chairs were cleared away to make room for other activities. Despite its makeshift appearance, the Breakfast Club had real social permanence. The room itself, the size of a theatre auditorium, was always very quiet in the morning. People's conversations seemed to ascend into the high ceiling, along with the smell of the boiled milk, hot tea, eggs, baked beans and sausages warming on the griddle. Towers of cups and old sweet jars full of sugar and coffee adorned the shelves behind the breakfast counter. Residents of all ages went to the Centre for breakfast though the atmosphere was always quiet, almost respectful. Its almost sombre quality possibly reflected the fact that older residents decided how the Centre was run. The Breakfast Club was also the Nova Centre's stalwart facility and reflected how Nova's first generation prevailed in the general running of many local initiatives on the estate.

Linden himself had worked at the Nova Centre and his description summed up the eternal struggle between youth and maturity:

> Yeah, I used to do community service in the Nova Centre, cookin' breakfasts. But I fucked that up for everyone else. I used to have lads come up from the Pub, givin' out breakfasts for 2p, 1p, anythin'. My supervisor from community service came out to check on me. And she come out one day and said 'look Linden you'll have to go back to the unit 'cause your friends are comin' down too often'. I said 'look, I've never ever done gardenin', I'm not diggin' gardens'. They

said 'Okay, we've got one other job for ya. But please behave.' They put me down the nursery. And I 'ad to paint the fence, like a white railin' outside it and I 'ad to paint the white railin'. So what I used to do is. I used to bring my car down, do a bit of paintin', sit in my car and listen to some music, burn a spliff. Then one day I was smokin' a spliff in my car and I crashed out. Bang, bang, bang on the window; it was the woman from the nursery, 'right, get back to the unit you'.

Going for breakfast at the Centre every day encapsulated the value of Nova's public culture when it was harnessed in initiatives that represented residents' needs. That time between 9 a.m. and midday, contained within the Centre's main hall seemed to define what young people referred to as being 'born and bred' in Nova. Stan, who worked on the committee at the Nova Centre, told me he went to the Breakfast Club 'to start the day'. Linden said the Breakfast Club was a good place to go for 'a feed', an expression that only underlined how the next meal was as uncertain as life itself. Sean also said it would be a good place to meet people and enjoy the 'great toast'. The Breakfast Club was inevitably more popular in the winter months and Linden took me one cold December morning after the Project had closed.

That day we had planned to go into Ford city centre. Linden had phoned an employment agency advertising an engineering job at a factory 30 miles from Ford. Before we set off, Linden said he wanted to get some 'brekky' (breakfast) at the Nova Centre. I had hoped to stay though Linden 'wouldn't be seen dead in there'. Linden said he often went there for breakfast though he rarely stayed. As I describe below, Linden, along with other young people who go to the Breakfast Club, often display an embarrassment in going there. Even though Nova is such a strong community, bound through the Project and the Nova Centre, the pull of youth culture meant that the Breakfast Club was perceived as boring.

We parked directly in front of the building. There are usually only one or two cars outside as so few people have cars in Nova. As we got out, Linden strode in. Everyone knows Linden and when we walked into the main hall, three women serving breakfast behind the counter all beamed when he entered. Miriam, demure though strong, in her late 30s, puts both hands on the counter. 'Yes Mr Davis, what can I get you?' Linden grinned at the formality and asked if he could have a full English breakfast crammed into a bun. We had arrived just before the Breakfast Club officially closed: Miriam, Helen, in her 20s and with the appearance of a supermodel, and Vera, nearing 40, slim and small, all agree to make an exception. While the breakfast was cooking, we sat with other customers finishing breakfast and chatted in the big auditorium. As we sat, the elders would politely chew their breakfasts while talking.

Younger family members seemed more relaxed: spoon-feeding or placating little infants. Despite the improvised surroundings, a sense of community permeated the air.

Like the Breakfast Club, at the Project older residents provided guidance and protection for young people. Unlike the Project, women managed and ran most events and facilities at the Nova Centre. One could say these facilities were the municipal parents of Nova's young adult population, though only because young people themselves respected the workers at both. In her study of the transformation of London's Docklands, originally a working-class community in the southeast of the city, Janet Foster (1999: 22) describes how 'the matriarchal family structure was central in the creation and maintenance of kinship and neighbourhood networks, especially in the first half of the twentieth century'. Studies by Gans (1967), Rex and Moore (1967) and, more recently, Robert Putnam (2000), all point to the importance of kinship networks in community. Sometimes, however, there is a tendency in community studies to romanticise what can be a cruel and coercive experience (see Pahl, 2000). Even though both generations in Nova were able to live as a community, there were still tensions between young people and their elders. Often that stemmed from the stigma surrounding young people outside Nova.

Demonising community

Throughout *Crime, Youth and Exclusion*, I have argued that modern British society is a social mainstream consuming itself, including those groups forced to survive as communities on its boundaries. Nova remains a community because it is structured in relation to the concern people have for one another instead of through consumption. People's concern for one another is not inherent to being born and growing up in Nova, but part of being human. Attending Greaves secondary school during the 1980s, Carol saw what happened to Nova's community when hundreds of residents were made unemployed by de-industrialisation. Carol was moved to create Gateways as a place for local people through her own experiences with the community. I also feel that writing this study was part of a similar process, though that was never my intention from the outset.

The philosopher Heidegger (1927) described human existence as 'being in the world': we become human beings through the concern we feel for one another. Young people living in Nova personified Heidegger's (1927) definition of being human; everyone described their own experience as 'born and bred' and 'part of Nova'. In addition, that feeling was inscribed into Nova's social spaces, including the Project, the Nova Centre and eventually Gateways (see Chapter 2). Even in terrible situations such as famine and war, people have always made objects with what is at hand that reflect their relationship with the social world. Culture is the expression of our desire to be in the world, imprinted on it to give us hope in the future. The late psychologist Irving Goffman (1967) described the concern we feel for one another as human nature. Goffman (1967: 42) identified how as a purely emotional response, 'human nature is not a very human thing'. Even though we all feel a concern for one another, Goffman (1967) described how that concern needs a space to be expressed. Nova is a place that contains such spaces, where people faced with daily poverty express a concern for one another.

Yet, the Project was forced to close because it seemed to represent an unknowable community. The next chapter identifies the function of stigmatising poor communities in a consumer society.

Chapter 6

Community

During the two years after Gateways opened, Carol and representatives of the Assembly – an amalgamation of local community groups – were able to gain managerial control. In contrast to the corporate atmosphere that pervaded the building when it opened, Gateways now reflects people's experience and provides a framework through which people can gain control of their own lives. Gateways is also a place where people can gain skills and training according to their own design and not one imposed by outsider agencies. This chapter describes the change in society that made Gateways possible and why the stigma surrounding the people of Nova remains.

In 1997, the Labour Party was elected to government, ending 18 years of Conservative rule, and here I want to describe the gains achieved by people living in Nova during that period. I also describe how the sense of optimism that characterised the end of the twentieth century was swept away by new fears concerning global terrorism. *Crime, Youth and Exclusion* ends by showing how people living in Nova continue to be stigmatised by images superimposed on the area by outsiders. Establishing the similarities between the 'war on terror' and public attitudes concerning 'youth crime', I show how objectifying human subjectivity continues to free us from the concern we used to feel for one another.

Living with poverty

None of the young people I met in Nova had the opportunity to move away from the streets that made up 'the Precinct'. Despite the success of initiatives such as Gateways and the regeneration of the arcade, the living conditions young people have to endure remain abject. During my fieldwork, Linden identified the changes needed to improve the public culture of the Precinct: 'Better-quality jobs; fix up the area a bit. 'Ave you seen the state of the Precinct? It's fuckin' terrible, that just depresses people even more.' Most young people I met could only afford second-hand dilapidated furniture, usually obtained through a co-op run by the local council. All young people could afford was the end-of-the-line sportswear available at local discount shops and even though many prided themselves in their appearance, the durability of garments was usually poor. Poverty also affected people's nutrition: fresh fruit and vegetables were too expensive and all young people could afford were biscuits or other cheap processed foods. Because the nutritional content of these products is so bad, I noticed at the Project that young people would have to eat them all the time.

The success of Jamie Oliver's (2005) 'Feed Me Better' school dinners campaign highlights how young people are saturated by the consumer society; also, how the consequences of poor nutrition go unnoticed. Maintaining appearance and eating regularly gives the impression that poverty was not a reality, even though young people wear and eat the by-products of a consumer society. In debates on relative deprivation, one argument is that people living in poverty should work to afford items such as cookers and fridges (see Townsend, 1979).

Why young people were never able to afford these commodities relates directly to the local consumer economy. Employers provided incomes that barely allowed people living in Nova's social housing to feed themselves, let alone maintain a home. Therefore, unless young adults could afford to pay cash for consumer durables, individuals were left with second-hand machines, which were often dangerous and prone to breakdown. During my fieldwork, the nearest laundrette was over five miles away: sometimes I took people who could afford to go. The final alternative, which I witnessed several times, was washing clothes in a sink or bath. In terms of food, the cost of fresh meat and vegetables and the gas and electricity for cooking was often beyond people's means. At a community level, these realities determined the few retail outlets in Nova; the three fast-food outlets were always busy, as was the post office and two newsagents who sold gas, electricity (in cards), sweets, and basics such as bread, butter and milk. Even though Gemini Park was a relatively short distance away, lack of time and transport were practical barriers. In addition, many people seemed reluctant to enter this exclusive space: some of the young people I met at the Project and through Linden explained that they had been barred from Anderson's and some of the other big retail stores in Gemini Park.

Yet, despite the conditions I witnessed young people forced to endure, everyone shared a feeling of identity and belonging with Nova. Talking about living in Nova, many young people described how 'it's part of me' even though so few have any material possessions. Robbie's story shows what happens when young people could no longer hold onto Nova's public culture of community. As Damon rightly identified in his analysis of 'the life', 'there is no alternative, people would be lying if they said there was'. Chapter 1 described how 'the life' of exclusion grew from the stigma imposed by Ford's consumer society. Jimmy described how the infection process began the moment young people stepped outside of Nova at eleven to attend secondary school; Robbie's story testified how the seductions of consumer culture could erode young people's self-respect. Losing control of 'the life' not only left young people exposed to being objectified by outsiders, individuals also represented the death of community.

Stigmatising poor people

Young people's strong sense of community could be interpreted as a solution to exclusion. In line with recent political debates on social capital, described in the following chapter, young people appeared to hold the capacity for innovation and resourcefulness yet chose to act in purely self-interested ways. For many leading policy-makers, social capital is a strategy that can enable communities to develop and integrate into the wider economic and social structure (see Putnam, 2000). Success, however, only seems possible among communities free from the dialectic of exclusion that young people in Nova described (see Fine, 2001; Pahl, 2000). The drug/crime nexus, which consumed Robbie and Leander, was driven by the stigma associated with a poor community. Life remains chaotic in Nova because young people continue to be consigned to the merry-go-round of temporary insecure jobs that characterise Gemini Park. The impression we have of these industries is that they provide a relatively risk-free working environment. However, young people I spoke to described how working within those industries means living in a world of anxiety and poverty, of being paid minimum wages and rarely seeing promotion. As Damon described, 'That's why I left the last job, by the time I'd paid the bills and bought food I 'ad nothin' left. It's like I said before, I can earn more money workin' for myself.' Added to that were accounts and my own participant observations of the physical abuse and exploitation of young people by store managers within Gemini Park. Employed in those industries or trying to survive outside of them, either way young people from Nova were perceived as malevolent towards the rest of society (Baudrillard, 1988).

Gateways was only made possible when that cycle was halted by a change in the way society – all of us – perceives itself. Society exists as a relationship between people who choose to live subject to the concern each feels for one another. In the next chapter, I describe how the sense of shared subjectivity, which characterised industrialisation, gradually declined after the Second World War, when majority populations in

Europe and North America became seduced by a consumer lifestyle. In Chapter 1, I described how a consumer society was only possible through the creation of a simulated landscape; and how communication technologies enabled people to play out a consumer lifestyle within them. Technology creates a distance between ourselves and the world around us; this is characterised by the current 'war on terror', as I illustrate below. Before 2001, however, and during and shortly after the year I spent with young people living in Nova, there was a growing concern that a global consumer society was steadily destroying people's ability to connect socially with others.

Changing times

Towards the end of the last millennium, it seemed that people who had previously enjoyed a consumer lifestyle were beginning to acknowledge how the global consumer economy was endangering everyone's future. The 1990s appear to have been the warmest decade of the twentieth century, and 1998 the warmest year. According to the United Nations (2005), 'the principal reason for the mounting thermometer is a century and a half of industrialisation: the burning of ever-greater quantities of oil, gasoline, and coal, the cutting of forests, and certain farming methods'.

In 1997, the Kyoto Agreement was signed by developed and developing nations across the world, legally binding countries to reduce pollution. Concerns about the predatory nature of globalisation defined the World Trade Organisation summit in Seattle. The summit's main objectives were to relax trade laws so that developing countries could compete against large multinational corporations. Shortly before the summit, Stephen Byers (1999), the UK trade secretary, insisted the best way to tackle inequality in the world remained trade liberalisation:

> We believe the best way of doing that is giving those countries access to the markets of the rich industrialised counties. We're saying that essentially all goods coming from those 49 least developed countries will have access to the European Union with no duties being imposed, giving them access to a market of 370 million people – a radical change that will begin to lift those countries out of poverty, meaning they won't have to resort to child labour.

Yet agreement between participating states was never reached as the summit itself was postponed after demonstrations in Seattle turned to riots. Seattle suffered more than $2.5 million in damage and more than 500 protesters were arrested. Surrounding the summit both in Seattle and across the world was a growing public resentment concerning the relationship between the major industrial nations and global corporations. Many believed that change would never be possible through the World Trade Organisation and the summit became the epicentre for worldwide protests. Thousands of protesters claimed victory as the World Trade Organisation failed to reach an agreement in Seattle. They included environmentalists, anarchists, union members and lobbyists from non-governmental organisations.

In the UK, the feeling that the consumer society of the 1980s was socially regressive seemed to precipitate the election of a New Labour government. Central to the new administration's mandate was the principle that everyone should have a stake in society. Drawing on the idea of social capital, Labour's concept of a stakeholder society follows that not only do people have a sense of responsibility to one another but also that working together, society itself can be improved. The idea of a stakeholder society and its influence on urban regeneration policy was the context that made Gateways possible.

Thinking about society

The policy, in contrast to the centralised corporate approach of the past, contained a belief that people living in deprived areas were the best placed to resolve the conditions residents have to face. *Bringing Britain Together* (Social Exclusion Unit, 1998) describes how, in the past, 'Too much has been imposed from above, when experience shows that success depends on communities themselves having the power and taking the responsibility to make things better'. In Nova, Gateways is successful because residents were given the freedom to realise their own needs and aspirations. A more 'joined-up' approach also spelled less of a reliance on private property-led regeneration. City Challenge and the Single Regeneration Budget (SRB) are explicitly developed to allow a 'three-way partnership' between local authorities and representatives from the voluntary, business and public-sector agencies (Colenutt, 1999). Community groups can apply for their own funding and if bids are successful, projects such as Gateways have been able to organise themselves under supervision of a neighbourhood 'supremo' (Social Exclusion Unit, 1998). At Gateways, Carol has realised this vision. Working there as a volunteer, you could see that the centre is popular with local residents because everyone is given the freedom to choose what they want to learn.

Carol became 'supremo' at Gateways though she never tries to impose on people in the way outside agencies used to. The Assembly also now has much more control over Gateways. Like the Nova Centre, Carol and the people who work there have been able to make it their own and Nova's. When Gateways opened, Sean along with many young people described feeling alienated by its professional corporate atmosphere. Today, Gateways is completely different: colour everywhere, banishing the hostile white space that defined the original centre. Carol and her staff of mainly local young and older residents have also been able to buy and install computers for many of the classrooms. The courses are also reflective of people's needs, as opposed to those of outside agencies. Many of the courses are related to work though there are also many others that allow people to express themselves. Most of the supervision is, when possible, on a one-to-one basis.

These same principles have been applied to the new arcade, in which local residents have more of a say in what services are available and also more opportunities in working there. The arcade is also mixed-use, ranging from public amenities to private business. This means there is no pressure to spend: the design of the arcade is people-friendly, compared with many shopping centres, with no gaudy shop fronts hiding public amenities such as the library and medical centre. Local residents, through the Nova Centre committee, also set up a network of two-way radios that allowed a system of surveillance that still allows people to feel at ease in the arcade. In Gemini Park and many other private retail parks, private security and surveillance camera operators are often advised to target specific categories of people, especially young adults. In Nova's arcade, young adults are free from categorical suspicion. Each facility has its own space, usually its own building, and each building sits at a different angle from the others. Malls and shopping arcades usually follow a linear design, often for maximum security and to prevent people from congregating. The use of escalators as a method of keeping people moving from store to store is probably the extreme example. Being composed in a more haphazard way and with plenty of spaces between shops, people in Nova's new arcade face none of these restrictions. Despite trying to make social spaces different from the theme-park world outside of Nova, Gateways and the new arcade remain subject to the consumer society. That has always been the case since the start of the 1980s when Gemini Park was first built; each initiative created by local residents was squeezed out simply because being part of a community represented a contradiction to consumerism.

Fatal strategies

What erodes Nova as a community is the stigma of crime, imposed each day by Ford's consumer society. In times of economic crisis, as Chapter 1 identified, the people of Nova and the area itself were marked as different, responsible for *them*selves, and gradually fenced off from the rest of Ford. For years, the old arcade encapsulated the exclusion of Nova. When unemployment became an enduring reality, one by one local businesses vacated shops because people no longer had any money. Even though many stores were embedded in the life of the community, as private businesses, owners were forced to find a more viable market. For Nova's residents this meant that a once lively social centre was drained of meaning. The old arcade had a hairdresser, a cafeteria, an optician, fish and chip shop and a bakery. These places were the containers for people's everyday lives. When store holders abandoned the arcade, for local people it was another sign of how Nova as a community was an expendable economic resource. As a result, the old arcade became an object of young people's frustration. Graffiti was an attempt to reclaim Nova's original arcade and inscribe on it people's feelings of abandonment that the area itself seemed to represent. Watching the old arcade being demolished alongside local residents, I could sense a mixture of relief and sadness. Throughout the 1980s and 1990s, the arcade became a daily reminder of being excluded. The arcade was at the centre of Nova, situated like an oasis at the bottom of a deep vale. This meant you could always see it from most parts of the estate. Now that is a good thing as the new arcade is lively, bustling and charming in its design. The old arcade looked like a derelict factory, filled with the echoes of Nova's economic decline.

For almost a decade Ford's city council and local residents tried to gain business support to build a new arcade. In that time, local residents formed groups and associations that represented the issues that stem from exclusion. Sean was part of that process, forming a table tennis club for local young people. Alan, a stocky young man who I met at the Project, was a member. Whenever Alan and Sean played together, they would draw crowds. However, Sean described how he constantly had problems finding a venue for the club. The reason was often the same reason why the Project closed. Money was withdrawn because local initiatives, such as the Project, were said to be failing to meet their targets. Even though the Project's management rarely entered Nova, representatives felt that its users were intransigent. Talking to representatives of initiatives such as Youth Concern (see Chapter 5), few appreciated the value of the Project as a place where young people could negotiate what seemed like an intractable experience. Listening to young people, exclusion touched almost every aspect of life, economic, environmental, social and cultural. Low incomes, debt and unemployment persisted because local employment markets allowed no way out. An overburdened city council also meant poor housing and local amenities. The Project was important for young people because it was a space in which individuals could unravel these pressures, even when they remained at the end of each day. Many young people described exclusion as a pyrrhic process. Families living on low incomes, due to either poor employment or unemployment, meant a difficult environment for young people to grow up in. Yet, even when young people themselves took opportunities to break that cycle, it seemed that no matter what steps people made they often ended up being erased.

As Britain's consumer society has grown, poverty has become progressively more concentrated within areas such as the Precinct. Chapter 1 showed how such inner-city areas in industrial cities acted as zones of transition; secure industries provided an economic springboard enabling migrant communities to move into cities and potentially upwards. The Precinct was a timeless, landless void, resembling what Wacquant (1994: 233) describes as a hyper-ghetto: even when young people did have opportunities, taking them placed individuals and their property at risk because the Precinct was totally disconnected from the rest of society. When I interviewed Olly, who lived in the Precinct at that time, he had just come back from a week at the seaside with his wife and children. The week had been intended as time off for all the family and a break before a new job. Olly was due to start on the Monday, though he returned on Sunday to find his flat burnt out:

> Olly: I was meant to start one last week but I came back from holiday and me flat was burnt out.
> RM: Yeah, I heard about that. How did it happen?
> Olly: Well, I got back then I phoned the police and they said it was an electrical fault. But I said I know it ain't no electrical fault.
> RM: Were you insured?
> Olly: Na.
> RM: And everything's burnt?
> Olly: No, it's just the bedroom that's burnt. Everythin' else has just got smoke damage, just fucked.
> RM: Are you livin' there now?
> Olly: No, I'm stayin' at a mate's house, me and me missus.
> RM: What the council going to do?
> Olly: No, it's a housing association. They said it only take a week and a half. Then they came 'round and said 'all you need to do is put a new window in and put the electric on'. An' I said 'what the fuck am I gonna do about all the smoke and that?' And they said 'Oh you'll get a grant and that to do that'. So I said 'if you get someone to move in anyway you'll 'ave to do all that anyway'. So I'll just get my missus probation officer out to them. Nightmare that was, just came back from holiday.

Recalling Linden's statement of how living in Nova is survival of the fittest, Olly was able to cope with what happened, though to maintain the safety of his family meant passing up the opportunity of a job. For everyone I met who lived in the Precinct, the closure of the Project, shut because it was perceived as a potential threat, could not have been more destructive. Witnessing the consequences of the closure, of increasing crime and drug abuse, young people seemed to be subject to the same entropic process that was consuming the rest of Ford. Barbara Adam (1995: 83) describes entropy as evolution in reverse; as 'a spontaneous process towards disorder and a decrease in information'. The Precinct was caught in a similar process of constant disintegration. Ford City Council regularly made physical improvements such as double-glazing and telecommunication entry systems on the main doors leading into each block of flats. Residents, when finances allowed, also made their own modifications to flats to make them comfortable homes. Constantly working away at both, however, were the corporate strategies imposed by outside agencies. Sean described how Ford's youth services, originally council departments, were privatised during the late 1980s. After that point 'delinquent youth' was subsumed into the workfare state, a cheap source of labour for Nova's new neon coast: Gemini Park (see Zorbaugh, 1929). In *Luke Street*, Gill (1977) maintains that some council estates become delinquent areas because they are at the bottom of the 'hierarchy of desirability': families and older residents are allocated better-quality housing. The problem in Nova was that all of the estate's social housing was in a state of continuous decline. In addition, other housing estates in Ford appeared to be subject to the same process, as Martin testified in Chapter 3.

People power

The Project worked because it allowed people who went there a structure of feeling. The forms that facilitated that structure were fundamental: a cup of tea, coffee, soup and squash at a cost people could afford. Other services could be supplied such as free newspapers and a free phone. As I mentioned in the previous chapter, the Project provided hope. Sean, along with Eddy, Mathew and Andy, were extended family members for many young adults in a community that felt the world was against them. People trusted Sean and Andy because, with them, there was no hidden agenda.

On the official opening of Gateways, both Sean and Andy, like the users of the Project, were deeply cynical. As I stood outside the building with young men and women, watching agency professionals come and go in expensive cars, everyone seemed to view the occasion as another imposed strategy to resolve Nova's problems. I could understand why some young people were reluctant to enter the building at all, after decades of having experiences categorised: crime, unemployment, poor parenting and drug abuse. As I have stated in Chapter 5, young people were also realistic, apprehensive as to whether enrolling on a course would enable them to dispel the stigma associated with Nova's young adults. Again, Gateways continues to be exposed to the pyrrhic process that Young (1999) identifies: even though residents are able to achieve new skills, developing them within a community-run project exposes people to continuing stigma.

Some older residents I spoke to have been unable to obtain a mortgage as banks and building societies were unwilling to provide security for properties in Nova. I heard similar accounts concerning local insurance firms. Nova's local economy continues to keep residents trapped in poverty because it operates on the principle of workfare. Even though the principle of workfare creates poverty and desperation for entire communities, its application gives the impression that residents have the opportunity to earn a living.

Gateways and the new arcade were achieved through the social capital community groups were able to build, pulling in support and investment from outside companies and funding bodies. That required an acknowledgment on the part of people living outside Nova that residents are human beings. In the struggle by poor communities to make such initiatives real, there is often an assumption that businesses are suspicious of investing in areas suffering high rates of unemployment and crime (see Fraser, 1997; Healy, 1997; Dabinett and Ramsden, 1999). What often goes unnoticed is that urban regeneration initiatives often exploit poor areas to the benefit of large multinational industries (see Ritzer, 2004). Nova's local economy, for instance, seemed to determine many of the hardships faced by residents: the creation of a starkly polarised labour market meant people living in an area suffering from low educational attainment and high unemployment were literally forced to work in service industries.

Today, Gateways enables local people to obtain professional qualifications, yet that success continues to be diminished by the workfare merry-go-round. Because the only secure jobs in the region generally are in the third sector, only a minority have a chance for a job in a council department or similar social service. Linden told me how Veronica, his only sister, had to leave Nova, her family and home to get a good job.

> Linden: Yeah, she left Nova; she went to university in Stoke. I'm not sure what she was studying. She works there now though, for the Council.
> RM: She doesn't live in Ford.
> Linden: No, she lives in Stoke. She moved out about twelve years now. She still comes back though, for Christmas, for my birthday, for me brother's birthday. She still keeps in touch.

Like Veronica, Linden was more fortunate than many of the young adults I met in gaining a much sought-after apprenticeship in his final year at secondary school. Yet Linden continued living in Nova. He had to because, unlike his sister, Linden was unable to gain a mortgage.

Then, as he remained in the community he had grown up in, Linden's apprenticeship was pulled away by racism and the stigma that surrounds Nova. All the young Black men I spoke to described persistent racism and all the women I spoke to spoke of sexism and sexual harassment. Overshadowing the ethnic and gender identities of the young adults I met was the stigma associated with coming from a community perceived as having a culture of crime. The only way Veronica could escape all three was through leaving Nova and the family and friends she had grown up with. Outward migration from deprived urban areas is a feature of de-industrialisation: even though leaving means separation from family and community, once people with secure jobs do, areas can sink into further decline. In his influential study *The Truly Disadvantaged*, William Julius Wilson (1987: 46) described the process happening in Philadelphia, New York, Detroit, Chicago and Los Angeles during the 1970s: 'Although the total population in these five largest cities decreased by 9 per cent between 1970 and 1980, the poverty population increased by 22 per cent.' The increase in poverty was caused by outward migration of people with secure jobs, a group Wilson (1987: 56) describes as a 'social buffer' preventing the dialectic of exclusion from beginning:

> In a neighborhood with a paucity of regular employed families and the overwhelming majority of families having spells of long-term joblessness, people experience social isolation that excludes them from the job network system that permeates other neighborhoods and that is so important in learning about or being recommended for jobs that become available in various parts of the city.

This experience seemed common among young people I met in Nova. Linden said to me: 'See, everyone I know is unemployed'. Steve described why: 'all the jobs for lads like me in this city are shit. You're just shovelling shit all week for nothing, for shit wages.' That stigma eclipsed practically all the young people I met. During the twelve months I spent with young people, everyone I met lived by a strong work ethic, though only two people had jobs in which work had a value.

Helping as a volunteer at Gateways, I met Andrew. Tall, Caucasian and slim, Andrew was 18 at the time and was working at a local secondary school in Nova, training to be a teaching assistant. At Gateways, Andrew was studying for an NVQ on a Friday morning and Tuesday evening. For the rest of the week he had a placement at a secondary school in Nova. Like Hannah, who was able to complete an NVQ to become a dental nurse, Andrew was extremely lucky to get a placement. Jason, Slim, Ricky and many of the other young adults I met who enrolled on NVQs were assigned to a local purpose-built training facility or private firms. Working for local employers on placements,

many young adults described abuse and exploitation. Jason had successfully completed his first exam, only to be dismissed just as he was
preparing for level two: 'I finished me course and all that, NVQ level
one. I was goin' on to level two and I got sacked.' At training facilities,
many young adults described being processed with little consideration
taken about people's specific needs. Slim told me: 'But they want me to
go on computer courses. How can I go on a computer course if I'm
dyslexic?' Working towards an NVQ in the third sector is, it seems, the
only way out of Nova. Yet, training placements in health, education and
other public service departments remain scarce.

Township community

What separated Andrew from the rest of the young people I met was
that he was always alone. The tragedy of exclusion is that the feeling of
belonging young people described was perceived as a culture of crime.
Living 'the life' of a community enabled young people to survive
poverty, and the stigma associated with Nova. Then, whenever young
people were seen associating and working together away from the
workfare carousel of Gemini Park, residents from other areas imagined
the worst. In *Work, Consumerism and the New Poor*, Bauman (1998:
65) argues that workfare deliberately compounds exclusion: 'while no
longer supplying the means to reduce poverty, the work ethic may yet
help to reconcile society to the eternal presence of the poor, and allow
society to live, more or less quietly and at peace with itself, in their
presence'.

Service industries, such as those that make up Gemini Park, now form
part of most people's leisure time: a fast-food meal at the weekend, a
game at the bowling alley or film at a multiplex. All are made possible
by a local labour market coerced to work for the minimal rates that
corporations that provide these services pay. This may explain why
many out-of-town retail developments are built close to areas where
unemployment is high. Consumers are also, in my view, facilitated by
concepts such as cultures of crime and anti-social behaviour as they free
people from having to consider the consequences of a consumer lifestyle
on poor communities.

Linden and many others responded to that by creating their own
informal economy, what Cloward and Ohlin (1961: 96) describe as a
differential opportunity structure, 'seeking higher status within their
own cultural milieu'. Living 'the life' enables young people to maintain
self-respect and, understandably, no one wanted to relinquish that.
Working at Anderson's I sometimes called in on Linden during lunch
breaks. When I arrived in my clip-on tie, straw boater and nametag,
Linden, Liam, Tony and Jimmy would all scream with laughter. Yet, for

everyone at Linden's flat on those afternoons, Anderson's and industries like them defined 'the life' most of the young people I met were forced to lead.

Service industries surrounding Nova offer no opportunity structure while the few jobs that do continue to be denied to young adults from Nova. Jay told me one day during my fieldwork: 'That's why most of the jobs you'll get is by word of mouth. They automatically think you're this, you're that. But we ain't like that.' Why employers are unwilling to employ young adults from Nova relates to the culture of crime young adults had had inscribed upon them since school. Nova's informal economy largely involved legitimate forms of self-employment such as painting and decorating, plumbing or electrical work, usually within Nova itself. The problem was that because incomes on the estate were so low and people outside it had a negative association with people from Nova, all that seemed to remain was consumer culture. The inevitable result that had on young people's lives was to further restrict each individual's strategic horizon. Being dismissed just before he was about to take his NVQ level two exam, Jason told me his situation after that:

Jason: I'm getting dole now, I only just sorted it out. Well not dole, a bridge allowance, £33 a week, every two weeks.
RM: Is that enough?
Jason: Not really, 'cause I'm used to like workin' for over £100 a month. I've just been workin' at Torque's (engineering company) for about two months but then after the shut down that's when they laid us off. After that, it's been days here and there. It was industrial cleanin', £4 an hour.

One afternoon at the Project, I gave Ricky a lift to one of Ford's Job Centres. Ricky had been unable to find work at the time and had been sent a letter asking him to attend an interview. During the interview, Ricky was told that unless he enrolled on a vocational course he would lose his benefits: 'Yeah, they said I've got to go on schemes and shit. They want me to go on this one for four weeks and no extra money. I ain't happy about that but you've gotta do it otherwise they stop your money. But I'll just get another temp job to blag them. I ain't doin' that.' Along with many young people I talked with, Ricky identified how the Ford Job Centres would allocate young people onto short courses as a way of managing figures for claimants. The strategy reflects how so many people are unwilling to work in Ford's service sector, as Ricky testified: 'most of the jobs are shit, an' all I'm getting off the dole is £70 a fortnight. I mean that's gone the first and second day you get it.' It seems that in a consumer society, all policy can do is manage an economy organised by service industries that thrive on job insecurity.

When Gateways opened, young people felt that training did not alter the fact that jobs available locally resulted in absolute poverty. Then there was still the likelihood that local employers would continue to discriminate because of a postcode or area address. Employers chose to be seduced by the image of Nova as a rough area containing bad people. Jay said, 'people from Nova ain't like that'. All that remained were the service industries that treated young people from Nova as an expendable resource.

They think you're bad

The economist J. K. Galbraith (1992: 18–26) argues that exclusion is 'deeply functional':

> The underclass is integrally part of a larger economic process and, more importantly, it serves the living standard and the comfort of the more favoured majority. Economic progress would be far more uncertain and certainly far less rapid without it. The economically fortunate, not excluding those who speak with the greatest regret of the existence of this class, are heavily dependent upon its presence.

For Galbraith (1992) the classic Marxist class schema of a proletarian majority in constant conflict with a bourgeois minority fails to account for the new material 'contentment' of modern 'majority' nations and subsequent diminution of older class struggles. Standards of living for such majorities have risen so high comparatively and their life chances appear so seductive globally that disaffection is inevitable (see Davis, 1990). Yet, those at the economic and social margins of these societies increasingly appear politically weak. Sean identified this situation, in which strategies designed to empower people economically only made residents' situations worse, as in the case of Gemini Park. Then there were the imposed strategies Sean described, that resulted in local people feeling stigmatised in the way outsiders would label residents or aspects of people's behaviour as problematic. If you take apart the actual strategies applied by agencies such as Youth Concern, it was in the interests of such organisations to sustain exclusion. For Galbraith (1992), this top-down approach characterises the culture of contentment that currently defines most of the world's leading industrial nations. When you consider the four main characteristics of Galbraith's (1992: 18–26) culture of contentment, his thesis defines Britain's consumer society. First is 'the affirmation that those who compose it are receiving their just deserts'. Second, 'short-run public action ... is always preferred to protective long term action'. Third, for the relatively affluent majority, 'the state is seen as a burden'. Finally, there is a remarkable 'tolerance shown by the contented of great differences in income'.

The new approach in urban regeneration initiatives reflects commitment to a long-term solution, one significantly influenced by Anthony Giddens' idea of a 'third way'. In his critique of modern welfare, Giddens (2000) argues policy could only work if it resolves the perpetual battle between 'left-wing' structural solutions and the idea among conservatives that communities such as Nova exist as cultures of crime. For Giddens (2000), there has to be an acknowledgement across the political spectrum that the welfare state is no longer sustainable through policy alone. What also needs to be accepted is the way private property-led regeneration measures often exploited local people. At the heart of 'the third way' was an attempt to bridge an increasingly exclusive society and an increasingly expedient global economy.

The 'third way' ethos of the New Labour administration was intended to create a bridge between left and right solutions. As a concept, the third way is based on the premise that, for members of a consumer society, people's sense of self becomes a matter of individualism as opposed to maintaining family or social responsibilities. Giddens (1997: 66–74) argues: 'the possession of wealth doesn't necessarily make one happy . . . why not, therefore, attempt to bring the conditions of life of rich and poor closer together.' What Giddens' recent work (2000) identifies is how a global consumer economy has created a world of manufactured risks. For people living in communities where local employment opportunities are restricted to low-paid service industries, state benefits no longer provide a safety net from poverty. Instead, for members of socially excluded communities, welfare becomes another risk, one that can easily enslave recipients because the job opportunities available locally provide less income. Young adults I spoke to all described the benefit trap. Giddens (2000: 113) argues that the welfare state and the nature of work create the merry-go-round many young people identified: 'some groups on the edge of poverty are caught in a low-pay, no-pay cycle – getting into low-paid jobs does not result in stable employment'. The transition to service industries in areas previously reliant on manufacturing often destroyed the economic stability of communities and families (see Taylor et al., 1996). Not only were more secure jobs either nonexistent or made exclusive by the need for specialist skills, workfare meant that in trying to survive through collective enterprise young people were instantly categorised as a gang.

To this day Nova remains an incredibly strong and close community. Residents also continue to endure terrible hardships. The Index of Multiple Deprivation (ODPM, 2004) is a measure used by government to assess poverty by area. There are seven specific domains: income deprivation; employment deprivation; health deprivation and disability; education, skills and training deprivation; barriers to housing and services; crime; living environment deprivation. Nationally, Nova falls within the top 10 per cent, a priority area in which:

- just under a third of people are income deprived

- one in five of women aged 18–59 and men aged 18–64 is employment deprived

- just under half of children live in families that are income deprived

- just under a third of older people are income deprived.

Nova is also rare in Britain's consumer society because it is a place based on common experience. In his book *Imagined Communities*, Anderson (1983: 36) identifies how Nova is an idea as much as a geographical area, one that 'rooted human lives firmly in the vary nature of things, giving certain meaning to the everyday fatalities of existence (above all death loss and servitude)'. I cannot reproduce that same experience: not only is my life free from these fatalities, growing up within a consumer society all I have to remember of the past are simulated media images. In Chapter 1, I described how a consumer lifestyle is a private existence composed of private images: this situation explains why it is easy to objectify the realities of living in poverty. Previous administrations had failed through the way they objectified people experiencing exclusion. The approach was typified by the *Back to Basics* agenda of the final Conservative administration of 1992, which sought to impose a moral culture on an already disintegrating society (see Tester, 1997). At the 1993 Conservative Party Conference in Blackpool the then Home Secretary, Michael Howard, argued:

> All my life in politics I have been utterly convinced that the first duty of government is to maintain law and order . . . You can argue forever about the causes of crime. My approach is based on some simple principles. That children – at home and at school – must be taught the difference between right and wrong. That criminals – and no one else – must be held responsible for their actions (quoted in Young, 1996: 155).

The fact remains that successive Conservative administrations were elected because Britain's consumer society had a stake in objectifying their own waste: communities living and working in poverty. As Britain's consumer society proliferated during the 1980s, the idea of a new urban underclass, along with debates about crime, allowed many people to avoid thinking about poverty (see Lea and Young, 1984). By 1997, society was prepared to elect a political party with the knowledge and ability to reverse the destruction. Labour's strategy for neighbourhood renewal (1998) was a policy statement on the relationship between society and exclusion: 'our goal is simple: it is to bridge the gap between the poorest neighbourhoods and the rest of Britain. Bridging that gap will not be easy. It will require imagination, persistence, and commitment. But I believe that it can be done. Indeed, if we are to bring Britain back together, it has to be done.'

The idea of community captured in *Bringing Britain Together* continues to define Gateways. Yet, after 2001, the realities of living in a socially excluded community continue to be objectified in moral terms.

War on community

I regularly go to Nova and now, in 2005, the new arcade and Gateways both stand as spaces representative of people's experience. Both also signify what can be done when members of society acknowledge the economic and social relationship all of us have with one another in a consumer society. That spirit of optimism has drawn back into Nova itself and remains contained there by a lack of opportunities in the local economy. The atmosphere of hostility and suspicion that haunted the area's borders during the 1980s and 1990s has also returned. Continuing poverty and a new set of cultural fears both mean that the dialectic of exclusion young people describes remains. The concluding chapter of *Crime, Youth and Exclusion* identifies the economic inequalities that continue to be created by globalisation; in addition, how poor communities continue to be stigmatised, primarily through communication technology, enabling consumers to screen out their own connection to an increasingly exploitative global economy.

I described above how the stigma associated with young people from economically deprived areas began to dissolve in the final years of the twentieth century. The result was that one side of the dialectic of exclusion young people identified diminished. Like a wall, the idea that Nova was a criminal community seemed to crumble following the election victory of 1997. For people living in Nova, what seemed like a rebirth of society in Britain provided the freedom to build initiatives reflective of residents' own experiences. Then one year into a new millennium, after the destruction of the World Trade Center on 11 September 2001, that feeling faded away.

The destruction of the World Trade Center resulted in the deaths of over 3,000 people. The viewing of the destruction of the Twin Towers, as an event, was even more destructive as it ushered a war on the idea of community itself. We will never know why a group of people chose to hijack two planes and use them to destroy the World Trade Center because all of its members died during the catastrophe: the reality behind the event disappeared along with both towers and over 3,000 men, women and children. Instead of trying to understand 11 September, nation-states throughout Europe and North America chose to explain what happened through images. In his state of the union address after 11 September, George W. Bush (2002) described Cuba, Iraq, Iran, Libya, North Korea and Syria as an 'axis of evil'. Four of the countries identified as part of the axis of evil are Islamic states. The aftermath of 11 September shows how much we have come to hate and fear the notion of a sense of community (see Levinas, 1994). Why Islam appears such a threat is because it represents the global community that is completely antithetical to the consumer society. Seen territorially, Islamic states are also those most exploited by consumer societies, as they provide the fuel for consumption: oil.

The last frontier

'The life' and Islam represent how destructive consumer societies are on communities living in the developed and the developing world. Consistently, this study has shown how globalisation objectifies human subjectivity to sustain itself, making people and communities expendable and explicable: cheap labour and a criminal underclass. 'The life' and Islam are a collective response to exclusion in a consumer society; defiance against living each day overshadowed by a death. As hard as that must seem for people with secure jobs, this is what living with exclusion means. Some writers have suggested that globalisation is another phase in empire, whereby cultures across the world have been slowly westernised to facilitate and sustain the global economy. Globalisation colonises more than just geographic space. The new global empires such as Nike, Time Warner and Disney no longer wage real wars, steadily consuming territories and communities. The final frontier in the consumer society seems to be our own willingness to imagine other people.

During the creation of the Roman and the British Empires, the last remaining territories to be colonised were deserts, including the Gobi and the Sahara because they contained so few natural resources and were felt to be so inhospitable. This is why nomadic tribes such as the Tuareg, Bedouin and Masai survived, while others were subsumed by Western nations. All three were also warrior tribes, accustomed to the hostile environment in which they lived and acquainted with the terrain, enabling them to counter attacks. Eventually, however, all lands fell prey to the colonial powers and were one by one translated by cartographers into the maps we now use to navigate Africa, Asia and South America. When that happened, the enemy was easier to identify and locate.

The consumer society spelled 'the death of the social' because capitalism has been motivated over the past 30 years to claim the last territory: human subjectivity. Colonising consumers is more a surrender: achieved electronically, chiefly through the television and the computer, enabling consumers to work and live while not belonging. Technology also frees people from community, allowing individuals to draw from their own private well of images, which explains why people choose to remain disconnected from one another to such an extent. Now, when all wars have been fought and all lands conquered, the only enemy left is ourselves. Writing on the war between coalition forces and Iraq in 1994, Baudrillard (1994) contends that in the situation I have just described, the Gulf War did not take place because both forces were 'fighting over the corpse of war'. We have reached a similar conclusion with crime in the so-called developed world. All developed states have reached a point of full employment. Therefore, why do crime and unemployment persist if everyone has the opportunity to work?

Globalisation is not an empire in the traditional sense but a personal empire, consisting of ignorant rulers. The transition to a global economy gave millions of people the freedom to map their own worlds. As I tried to suggest in Chapter 1, that freedom is solitary since all it provides is our own electronic well to gaze at our own reflection. Everything around us, including people, becomes an image of ourselves within that well since the celluloid water it contains objectifies all it reflects. The war on terror has to be seen in those terms, objectifying the communities displaced and excluded by a global economy through the ecstasy of communication. As we sit watching CCTV pictures of suicide bombers, car hijackings or drunken street brawls with vicarious pleasure, reality dissolves behind the screen.

Recently, Linden introduced me to Chris, a short, strong African-Caribbean young man in his mid-20s. Chris works as a bouncer in Ford and, like Linden and his friends, Chris wants to work for himself recruiting and supplying security guards to nightclubs. Self-employed, Chris identified the dangers all the young people I met faced working for themselves. Chris described how men too drunk to be admitted into a club would attack him and how others would deliberately want to 'test' Chris. He showed me the deep scars on his forehead that he had sustained in fights with drunks at the club he worked. Chris explained that owning your own team of security guards is practically a necessity as the career lifespan of a bouncer is so short. Working as a bouncer, Chris described the horror that rages underneath the society he is hired to police. The apathy induced by globalisation also shapes policy in similar ways. People may feel that politics and politicians operate outside their own sphere. Yet the desire people have to dream about crime instead of awaken to the lives affected by it manifests itself in policy through the democratic process. Curfews, electronic tagging and the re-housing of 'problem' families as enforceable through law allow people to avoid confronting how acquisitive mainstream society has become.

Staying alive

Recently, I met up with Linden, Martin, Tony, Montana, Hannah and some of the other young adults I got to know. All are as resilient as ever. What amazes me most of all about the young people I met is how all continue to survive as a community in the face of poverty and exclusion. Linden, Curtis, Liam, Steve, Jimmy, Martin, Tony, Benita and Montana all work for themselves. All are trying to establish themselves. Liam, who was older than his friends, already had a reputation in Nova as a good decorator. Martin and Montana were saving up to start their own catering business. They also have a young daughter. Hannah, who has since left Linden, also has a young son and has her own stall at a local market in Ford. Liam and Fiona, who Liam met after my fieldwork, also have a newborn son and Liam and I marvelled at his size. Most have also moved away from the Precinct and Liam and Martin told me they were happier to be living further from it. Linden and Tony also have new partners and are still incredibly close friends despite the arguments. Linden's flat is still the centre of the universe and last time I was there, he, Tony and Liam were redecorating once again. Some of the younger adults who I met at the Project remain in Nova. Jason is a builder and Olly trains to be a boxer while playing football at a local social club. Leander, the last time I saw her, looked radiant and seemed much happier. Some of the members of the business, who were the oldest of the young adults I met, have left Nova. Most have partners and families. The only business member I still see is Damon, who lives close to Nova to be near his son.

Unemployment, debt, intolerance and racism are still daily realities. Living in and belonging to Nova is something nearly all the young adults I met cherish. A member of 'the business', Nevil, a close friend of Damon, described how, 'whenever you meet someone from Nova, even if you've never met them, you'll get on. There's like somethin' between you.' I have tried to show the strength of Nova's young people; in addition, how the people of Nova were able to overcome what still appears to be a cultural and economic deadlock. The strength of Nova's people must not be seen as a solution to exclusion, just as Chapter 7 should not be seen as an end. Young people's lives, by definition, have just started and Nova's troubles continue to stem from the perception that outsiders have of the estate.

Chapter 7

Society

The idea that we are living as a degenerate society seems to contradict modern Britain. Most people live free from poverty and disease, and have the freedom to communicate with one another and discover the world in ways unimaginable to generations that lived before us. Far more people today are also able to realise their aspirations and live free from status and class, through the expansion of higher education. Higher education is now regarded through the developed and developing world as crucial to both national economies and individual prosperity. In its *White Paper on Higher Education*, the Department for Education and Skills (2003) explains how 'graduates get better jobs and earn more than those without higher education'. Yet, even though higher education grants people access to the consumer society, that world only seems to make sense before a backdrop of fear, about crime, terrorism and contagion. Not only that, consumers must also be oblivious to the poverty they create. This is why societies throughout the developed world are steadily degenerating: in order to live a consumer lifestyle we must work as masters in a slave economy. For our lives to make sense, we must think about crime. Chapter 1 identified how people define their lives in a consumer society and how technologies are used to distinguish between good and evil.

A doll's house

Using communications in our working and daily lives, we become commodities ourselves, no longer human beings, but mechanisms that search out and destroy. We operate like this in our working and leisure life because communications are commodities: computers, televisions, the Internet are not only the methods with which we entertain ourselves;

they are also our tools for work. Using these technologies in work and everyday life, they become weapons to destroy people who contravene the consumer lifestyle. As consumers, our perceptions of crime and poverty personify this process, where we consume and destroy criminals, real or fictitious, to give our own lives meaning. The idea that becoming a victim of crime is a greater danger now than in the past is a necessary mythology in British society. Incidents have risen, though seen in relation to modern economic history, crime has moved from being a consequence of industrialisation to a necessity today; even though the reality of crime is the same as it was during industrialisation: the people most in danger of being victims of crime are residents living in Britain's poorest urban areas. In their own research on crime in deprived urban areas, Pitts and Hope (1997: 39) provide indicators why social housing estates suffer the highest rates of victimisation:

> The estates which experienced the greatest changes – and highest crime rates – saw increasing concentrations of children and teenagers, young single adults, lone parents and the single elderly. Poor young, Black and Asian families constituted a significant segment of the population in some regions. These neighbourhoods also became the last resort for residents who had previously been homeless, hospitalised or imprisoned, and for refugees from political persecution. And these demographic trends often coincided in the same communities with a lack of access to primary job markets for local youth.

According to young people's experiences of exclusion in Nova, crime had a dialectical relationship with work, principally because everyone was excluded from a consumer lifestyle. Even though most people's working lives in Ford's high-tech industries had little social meaning, the working community that redeveloped out of that relationship was perceived as a threat. This chapter describes the result of this process in which crime becomes a seductive image of community, one to which we must aspire, instead of recognise. Not only does the relationship disconnect the real relationship between crime and poverty, our destiny requires images of criminals remaining forever in our minds. Conversely, considering poverty as an intrinsic part of our consumer lifestyle, without thinking about crime this house-of-cards existence would collapse.

In his 'Great Towns' chapter, Engels (1845: 71) described people living in such conditions at the heart of central London, just off Oxford Street:

> Heaps of garbage and ashes lie in all directions, and the foul liquids emptied before the doors gather in stinking pools. Here live the poorest of the poor, the worst paid workers with thieves and the

victims of prostitution indiscriminately huddled together, the majority Irish or of Irish extraction, and those who have not yet sunk into
the whirlpool of moral ruin which surrounds them, sinking daily
deeper, losing daily more and more their power to resist the
demoralising influence of want, filth and evil surroundings.

Engels' (1845) study describes how living in the industrial city meant
living with the experience of poverty. Most people's everyday lives, with
the exception of a small minority, were overshadowed by the prospect
of poverty. In short, poverty could affect most people. As a result,
poverty was understood and acknowledged, and from that public
recognition came a collective belief that cities should be modernised.
That belief characterised the modern city, a place where poverty was
seen as surmountable. Even though many people died from its effects,
entire communities were not expected to be condemned to poverty
forever. Poverty was an evil, as it prevented people from working. To
understand the function of poverty today, we need to appreciate how the
work ethic Bauman (1998) describes is no longer realisable for young
people living in communities like Nova. On one level, young people I
met were the casualties of de-industrialisation: Britain could only adapt
to that by re-creating a slave mode of production, what Lea (2002: 180)
describes as 're-mediaevalisation'.

The irony of globalisation is that Britain's industrialisation would have
precipitated a revolution if slavery had remained lawful. In 1832 the
passing of the Reform Bill narrowly defused a workers' revolt and
universal suffrage subsequently ensured that ordinary people could
work and live free from the terrible social conditions described by Engels
(1845) (see Thompson, 1963).

Cities continue to grow though now based on an utterly different
dynamic; what Beck (2000) refers to as the 'Brazilianisation of work'. In
cities throughout the developed and developing world, the wages
available to people working in service and manufacturing are controlled
to ensure whole populations function as slave labour. This slave mode
of production has allowed many cities to develop into self-contained
city-states. Between 1950 and 2000, the urban populations of most
European cities increased by an average of 80 to 100 per cent. In the
developing world, the growth in urban populations during the second
half of the twentieth century was far more dramatic. In India, for
instance, between 1950 and 1981 the number of urban dwellers increased
by 150 per cent from 61 to 157 million people (Herbert and Thomas,
1990). Parallel to the increase in urban populations has been the growth
in urban poverty in global cities like São Paulo, Mexico City, London and
New York. The World Bank estimates that there are almost a billion poor
people in the world; and over 750 million live in urban areas without
adequate shelter and basic services. A third of people in developing

countries living in cities live in slum/squatter settlements (World Bank, 2004). Yet, the Brazilianisation of work requires people who belong to that third to remain in poverty. In addition, the people forced to survive in such areas remain invisible to those working in so-called core sectors, usually defined by an expert or academic knowledge. The Brazilianisation of work means that, in quantitative terms, the average citizen in big cities in the developing world will die younger and probably die alone, as he or she will be unable to start a family.

Consumers in the developing world are faced with images of these realities, yet people continue to work in pursuit of a consumer lifestyle. Within Ford, this situation was played out each day in local economies such as Gemini Park: a consumer society where work and poverty combined to provide a lifestyle for 'core' workers.

Heroes and villains

The situation, described in these terms, seems intractable. It is not. First, we understand the method – communication technologies – and the control we have over the medium through which we communicate, images. Once we appreciate the power we have over these technologies, we can start using and distributing them so that everyone can represent their own experience. The written word, music and painting are all still central to the creation of culture. What is also significant about this period is that new technologies, specifically radio, photography, and later television, were being used for society, much like developments in industrial and agricultural technology (Giddens, 1990: 77). Modernisation led to universal education, and the use of communications in schools and colleges as educative tools meant that history could be written, spoken and photographed by ordinary people. Photography, sound and film-recording technologies also meant that mass populations and entire communities were able to represent their own lives.

The Mass Observation Project shows how communications can work as methods of representing real situations. Founded in 1937 by a group of non-academic researchers, artists, students and workers, Mass Observation recorded people's experiences of the Depression. During the 1930s, politicians and press often dismissed the realities of poverty and starvation as symptoms of a defected working-class culture (see Orwell, 1937). To identify the realities of unemployment and poverty, Mass Observation conducted a study of Worktown (which was in fact Bolton) involving participant observations over a two-year period. The region itself had shortly before that point been a centre for the production of cotton, though the global depression of the 1930s had resulted in mass unemployment. Initially, interviews with local people and photographs were intended for a four-volume study. However, due to a lack of adequate support from publishers, only one volume was published, entitled *The Pub and the People* (Mass Observation, 1943). Mass Observation's mission of recording the lives of ordinary people was seminal in the tradition of public broadcasting that flourished in Britain after the Second World War, reaching its epoch in the broadcast of *Cathy Come Home* (Loach, 1966).

That tradition, however, was gradually being eclipsed by television and film as forms of mass entertainment. The post-war boom provided many people the freedom to choose a consumer lifestyle or remain part of a community. It was a choice reflected in the battle in British broadcasting, which continues, between a desire to broadcast ideas or to make programmes that could be financially lucrative in appealing to a mass audience. Sociological studies including *The Hidden Persuaders* (Packard, 1960), and *One Dimensional Man* (Marcuse, 1964) identified how more and more people were able to afford a lifestyle promoted on television, in magazines or in film. Television in particular was becoming mass entertainment: each night for millions of people was now organised around programme schedules. The effect of these changes was to make entertainment a daily necessity. In addition, the previous distinction between public and private culture became blurred through the consumption of current affairs and soap operas. Television and magazines became image processors, programming consumers with destinations containing the most desirable objects. The result was that people's social identity became less and less significant. With its roots in the post-war boom, the social disintegration of industrial nations at this time was, paradoxically, accelerated at the end of the 1970s when the global consumer economy collapsed. Chapter 1 identified how the social world of the city gradually diminished as sites of consumption arose on the urban periphery during the 1980s. It was then that the consumer society was fully realised, a hyper-real world in which people and families who had become financially secure during the post-war period could now live private lives. Communication technologies, television, VCR and suddenly personal computers made and marketed by burgeoning companies such as IBM, Acorn, Amstrad and Apple, made this possible, enabling private homeowners to live a privatised existence.

Since their reception among a mass audience, the media have been blamed for ruining society. Yet critics rarely identify precisely how the evil is transmitted (Putnam, 2000). The reality of watching television is of a seduction: images interchange between viewer and screen. Blaming programme makers or the media only makes the medium more seductive, especially if particular programmes or images are deemed sexually offensive. Hip Hop music is the contemporary example of this process, whereby Hip Hop's critics decry artists for promoting gang and gun violence. As a result, even when images represent real people forced to survive poverty and crime, they subsequently become entertainment.

This is how poverty is interpreted as crime: within a society already starkly divided between rich and poor, watching poverty on our screen becomes the interactive masquerade described in Chapter 1. Because we are unable to interact with the people represented, everything is faces and distant voices; even the realities of poverty become television drama (see Valier, 2004).

Ellis Cashmore (1997) describes how a Black culture industry in the United States makes poverty entertainment. As an African American, Cashmore (1997) is highly critical of popular Black culture, arguing that it reinforces negative stereotypes, even when artists are African American. Taking the example of Hip Hop, Cashmore (1997: 154) charts its transition from underground street poetry into a global culture industry. That happened through the success of record labels specialising in Hip Hop, especially the Def Jam label created by Russell Simmons. Cashmore (1997) argues that Simmons, African American himself, translated the poetry of Hip Hop into a business: 'Rap music's slogans of despair were raw and contemporary: it brought a bracing political and artistic radicalism, drawing from other genres with contempt rather than respect. The same music that became the shorthand for the violent implosion of black life was the source of Simmon's extravagant wealth ... Simmon's story is an object lesson in making poverty work for you.' I personally believe Hip Hop is a positive force, in that the musical form rescues young people from the self-destruction of exclusion.

Imagining crime

In Chapter 4, I suggest that Hip Hop artists have no alternative but to live 'the life': 50 Cent sums up Hip Hop's stasis between destitution and a consumer society when he says, 'I just speak on my life' (Russell, 2003). The furore surrounding 50 Cent's Reebok campaign shows how many Hip Hop artists parody the commercial aspects of the industry by disrespecting a legitimate consumer lifestyle. For Gilroy (1994), Jackson's position reflects Hip Hop's 'double consciousness': living a spectacular consumer lifestyle becomes a way of mocking the consumer society for allowing itself to be seduced into believing images are real. To understand how poverty (evoked in Hip Hop music) comes to be interpreted and represented as crime, we need to identify how consumers search and destroy images in and through the media.

What characterised the use of photography, radio and film during the first half of the twentieth century was that they were being used to broadcast ideas. Because broadcasts were intended to inform instead of entertain, watching them occurred in a social time, instead of a body time. Cameras, sound and film-recording equipment were being used in education or journalism to broadcast events, not package them. Even though cinema was mass entertainment throughout the twentieth century, films were often preceded by news broadcasts. Even though Pathé news now appears arcane, its effect was to make going to the cinema less of an abstract experience. Going to the cinema was also often a weekly event, whereas television today is a daily ritual. What distinguished the use of technologies then and now was that up until the mid-1960s, both the form and content of communications was social. This meant that information was subject to a shared language or audience. Today all communications function as methods of entertainment because the context in which they are used relates solely to consumption. To live the consumer society everything we view is entertainment, even within a working environment, because our lives are manifestations of personal gratification.

Search and destroy

Even though a consumer lifestyle has little practical significance, because most of the population of this country live one, British culture is now entertainment. Having everything we need to survive, consumption becomes our destiny. As our object world is perceived through technology and because those technologies are now the most important things in our lives, life only has meaning by surviving other people. As a statement that encapsulates the spirit of modernity, the philosopher Sartre (1947) wrote 'hell is other people'; that people such as family members or similar significant others in our live could limit individual freedom. We now operate in a reverse situation, in which we need other people to survive. Using communication technologies to operate in this way can have deadly consequences.

In her book *On Violence*, Hannah Arendt (1970: 42) distinguishes power and violence: 'the extreme form of power is All against One, the extreme form of violence is One against All'. The holocaust was such an extreme form of violence because people of Judaic heritage were all made to look the same. Hannah (1970: 42) concludes, 'And this latter is never possible without instruments'.

Debates on poverty suggest that in a consumer society, being unemployed is a sign of fecklessness and irresponsibility. So, why do images of poverty and its consequences create such outrage, potentially resulting in a lifetime of exclusion? It seems that the only images (of poverty) that motivate people do so because they have a seductive quality. While this selective strategy is not deliberate, using technology as entertainment always occurs as an oscillation between desire and satisfaction to the point where, over time, our memory of social problems becomes emotional excrement (see Bataille, 1984). This process may explain why young people in Nova told of being treated like shit and left with 'shit jobs'. That always seemed to occur after young people described being perceived as criminal: through images of crime (the gang), young people are literally consumed by society and spat out into poverty.

Consumer protection

Chapter 1 identified how people disappear through communication technology: they choose images, of starving African children or fundamentalist terrorists, because they appear interested then forget when the programme has ended. Viewing the world in this way damages not only our ability to make the connection between social problems and people living through them. In Chapter 1, I showed that over time, the fear of crime consumers generate gradually becomes translated into social policy. Looking back at debates on crime over the past 30 years, that fear has been so powerful that it affects every political party.

Ulrich Beck (1994: 35) distinguishes between rule-directed and rule-altering politics. Rule-directed politics characterise the modern period, whereby social policy is directed towards improving the lives of the majority. In the developed world, we live in societies governed by rule-altering policy. In most cases, policy is created to satisfy consumers, and policy on crime epitomises this. The current war on terror operates as a game; its only objective is to sustain a culture in which consumption is an end in itself. Yet, the cause and effect of the war – oil – and the thousands of people killed in securing its supply are an irrelevance in the application of rule-altering policy. As Beck (1994: 36) describes how consumers define rule-altering politics; 'many demand, and actually begin, to turn the rule system itself inside out, while it remains unclear, to put it figuratively, whether the future game will be bridge, ludo or football'. Whether it is a war on terror or a war on tailors, rule-altering politics enables us to keep developing nations alongside areas in the developed world devastated by de-industrialisation in violent stasis. Then as people tear one another apart to stay alive, we apply technology to make civil wars appear like computer games. This is the post-modern culture of the consumer society, where everyone appears ready to invade the space of our own private existence. We believe this situation to be personal freedom when in fact, living according to what we want, we become as superfluous as the consumer society.

To understand why we live in a society that only makes sense through images of pain, torture and death, we first need to distinguish between a modern community such as Nova and the post-modern world that characterises mainstream Britain. The exclusion of young people living in Nova was one in the collage of images that seem to define Ford's consumer society. Post-modernisation best describes the daily process in which that society is produced, consumed, and then produced again. At a societal level, the effect is what I describe as a crystal maze: roaming individuals looking to objectify and destroy everything and everyone else simply to define their own isolated existence. Even though the people of Nova are subject to that process, everyone still believes in the modernisation of their own community. Modernisation still characterises societies overshadowed by starvation. Even as an outsider, one can see how countries such as India, China and Iran are working to develop a system that allows families and communities to survive.

Modern culture was a process through which people could transcend their own mortality, a process Giddens (1994) describes as the socialisation of nature. For Giddens (1990), managing and coping in what remains a highly volatile natural environment requires trust between people, because existing for ourselves, even in such a technologically proficient period, is a life filled with angst and dread. Like it or not, this is the human condition because every one of us is conscious of our own mortality. Human history, up until recently, has also been characterised by systems formed to enable people to live with the delicacy of life. Most have been a union between economy and psychology; Catholicism, Protestantism, absolute monarchies were all unequal relations between people which worked because believers had a stake in expressing their own beliefs socially, usually through work. There have also been slave modes of production though all were far less successful because the culture through which they were sustained was degenerate. Whether the mass consumer society of today, built and sustained by slave modes of production in Asia, Africa and South America, has a future, time will tell. The point of this conclusion is to identify what brought us to this situation and how it can be reversed.

Faith in the city

We live such isolated lives today because consumer culture is defined by angst and dread. Not only is the consumer society continually trying to mechanise, it also objectifies people who appear to contradict a consumer lifestyle. This is why most cities are now literally diabolical places, filled with theatres of destruction: walk-thru simulated battle zones, outlets selling lethal video games, and films that only succeed if they feature the threat of apocalypse. We convince ourselves, however, that people living in poverty have destroyed city centres, when the reality is that the city is a human farm.

What was significant about life in the modern period was that everyone became subjects within a community in order to survive. Modernity survives in the Islamic world, India and China, mainly because modernisation depends on people working together. Doreen

Massey (1994) describes how the most celebrated spaces of modernism are often urban; Louis Wirth (1938: 69) argued that cities developed because each 'brought together people from the ends of the earth because they are different and thus useful to one another, rather than because they are homogeneous or likeminded'. Emphasising how city's inhabitants, as migrants, have a common destiny, Wirth's (1938) idea of urbanism advocated that by investing in the social life of the city we could transcend our own mortality. Only in belonging to a city could people accept how 'we are exposed to the glaring contrasts between splendour and squalor, between riches and poverty, intelligence and ignorance, order and chaos' (Wirth, 1938: 72). In contrast, once people thought that their own lives were sovereign, cities would begin to appear fearful places and subsequently break down as social entities.

The successful interrelationship between urbanism and modernisation can today be seen in cities throughout the developing world. History is also being written into each city, through innovations designed to improve life in cities themselves, instead of technologies designed for a global market like those produced in Silicon Valley. China's burgeoning car industry, for instance, is not only now a global market but it also provides affordable cars that allow citizens to be more mobile. India, Islamic states and China are unique in the developing world through being able to retain a strong sense of national identity (Gellner, 1983). In contrast, global cities in the developing world today resemble Ford: polarised between an exclusive centre and out-of-town facilities, affluent residential suburbs, and township communities forever under their shadow. Appadurai (1996) describes these as cities that 'hardly require a name anymore, given that they are barely more than stages, holding companies, sites, and barracks for populations with a dangerously thin commitment to the production of locality' (Appadurai, 1996: 192).

The tragedy is that the proliferation of consumerism is beginning to infect and impede the development of so-called 'third world' countries. Like young people's experiences of exclusion in Nova, this is a degenerative process, driven as much by economics as communications: using personal communications as methods of experiencing the city, as consumers, is why people generally have such a lack of commitment. Searching for new markets, especially tourist, often results in the destruction, not modernisation, of developing countries; such is the nature of reflexive accumulation.

Industrialisation, as an attempt to socialise nature, is characterised by the reproduction of the world's natural and human resources. In short, we accumulate – oil, corn, rice, wood – to live. Consumer culture is far more dangerous to the planet and its human population because there is no end, barring the proliferation of superficial needs. The biggest global markets involve the production of goods that are not only superfluous but are also designed to necessitate continuous substitution. The only way companies themselves can meet consumer demand is through the exploitation of poor communities.

Consumer societies are dotted throughout human history, and all were catastrophic. Ancient empires such Rome, Greece and Egypt were forms of consumer society, where status was derived from gold or other precious materials. The previous chapter showed how the slave trade and the appropriation of natural resources from Africa, Asia and the Indian subcontinent financed Europe's period of Enlightenment during the 1700s. Slavery was swept away during the peak of industrialisation and towards its end; empires gave power back to former colonies. It was only after another global economic crisis 20 years later that the process began again. To ensure economic stability in the developed world, corporations moved to countries across Africa and South America. As a result, developing countries in Africa, Asia and South America remain poor and underdeveloped. Even though many former colonies in these regions were granted independence from the former empires of Britain, France, Belgium and Germany after the Second World War, political subjugation instead became economic. Loans supplied by developed nations to the developing world now form part of the global economy whereby interest payments are now a market commodity, alongside corn and oil. Driving this global programme of exploitation is consumption, especially the sale and distribution of communication technologies currently used as methods of personal entertainment. Lash and Urry (1994: 1–17) describe how the global economy spins through the consumption of these goods:

> This faster circulation of objects is the stuff of consumer capitalism. With an ever-quickening turnover time, objects as well as cultural artefacts become disposable and depleted of meaning. Some of these objects, such as computers, television sets, VCRs and hi-fi, produce many more cultural artefacts or signs ('signifiers') than people can cope with.

The reality of reflexive accumulation is that people who do not have the financial means to lead a consumer lifestyle become objects in this maze of consumption. Chapter 1 identified this as a dual process whereby public places became theme parks during the 1980s, which objectified everyone who worked there in making people appear like characters. In addition, during that time, majority populations began to use television and video as methods of entertainment and tools for work. The result was a blurring between people and objects, resulting in the masquerade that now characterises the design of most cities (see Davis, 1990).

The golden years

Affluent societies are often characterised by an entropic, as opposed to evolutionary, movement: once majority populations have everything at their disposal, society itself begins to degenerate. This was noticeable during the late 1970s; a sharp rise in sexual offences in Europe and North America alongside the development of a global sex trade. Both reflect how human desire no longer had an objective meaning, once people were no longer overshadowed by hunger and poverty and replicating family life was no longer necessary. One consequence of the post-war boom was that male heterosexuality became the market for what was one of globalisation's first slave trades. Andrea Dworkin (2000) describes how pornography in the United States is an $8 billion trade. Pornography has been an aspect of many societies, though as Dworkin (2000: 19–39) writes, it 'was always part of a private culture: What has changed is the public availability of pornography and the numbers of live women used in it because of new technologies . . . Until recently, pornography operated in private, where most abuse of women takes place.'

In his essay, 'Barbarism: A User's Guide', Eric Hobsbawm (1994b) suggests that human genocide, in Bosnia and Rwanda, continues because: 'we have learned to tolerate the intolerable'. What concerns me here is the disappearance of these events once they happen: based on young people's accounts, poverty in Nova and the tragedies that flowed from its experience appeared to be subject to the same process. My argument is that genocide, the logic of exclusion, becomes tolerable through communications. Then such events only have significance in that they define a consumer lifestyle. It is not that the media-makers produce consumable movies, but that consumers desire to be entertained. Guy Debord (1967) described this as the society of spectacle, in which every image that passes before our eyes is a commodity, even images of genocide. Living in a 'society of spectacle' must been seen as part of a general shift from a period in which culture was a productive process to one where the exclusion and finally the elimination of human beings is customary. To achieve this, society required the abandonment of tradition, as a process through which people transmitted trust between one another. Debates about post-modernity often describe a loss of tradition in contemporary society though they often confuse content with form. Tradition is not a collection of values to be believed in – trust, hard work, loyalty – but a desire to believe in other people. That can only be socially valuable as believing in the destruction or disappearance of other people is counter-intuitive to being human (Heidegger, 1927).

The creation of a global consumer economy has clearly sent human nature into reverse in that it has made majority populations reflexive or habitual in almost everything they do. Today, countries throughout the developed world are characterised by a society of individuals, connected autonomously to pursue their own desires. Given the nature of contemporary culture in Britain, and the centrality of crime within it, consumption appears to have become the end of society. Looking to the future, the only way that culture can survive is through the creation of poverty and continuance of exclusion. As the previous chapter showed, sustaining poverty in the developed and developing world helps maintain the global economy. Stigmatising communities forced to live in poverty also has the dual function of making a consumer lifestyle appear valuable.

To begin with, reflexive accumulation is made possible by a global operation. That is, exclusion is not simply a matter of stigmatising poor people within the area in which we live. Every consumer in every city throughout the world needs someone to fear, though our fear of crime seems like a local concern because policy makes it appear so – mainly because the state is caught in the same bind as consumers themselves. To give a consumer society meaning, policy is forced to make crime (including terrorism) appear antithetical to work. By supporting the principle of a consumer lifestyle, in practice and in policy, consumers relinquish their own sense of responsibility towards the consequences of consumption, including the events of 11 September 2001. As a result, the state is left having to sustain consumer optimism, and increasingly does so at whatever cost.

Law and order

The political crisis of the 1970s often appears like the political process generally, as events beyond the control of ordinary people. The fact is that the recession of the early 1980s was predicated by the consumer society. To ensure the political support of consumer societies, governments throughout the developed world were forced to abandon modernisation. The tragedy of the 'hollowing out' of welfare institutions was that the process resulted in the rejection of society among the very people the strategy had intended to appease (Lash and Urry, 1994: 13). It seems that by the mid-1980s, consumers still wanted more: instead of pinpointing consumption as the reason behind the crisis, majority populations simply demanded a quicker and cheaper supply of goods to make an already bankrupt existence seem real. To prevent social disintegration, policy had no alternative but to concede to consumer demand.

Governments had been assisted by the fact that, initially, many people had been forced to disengage from the public sphere. Recession meant that most people's private incomes were squeezed and the real social unrest that occurred at the start of the 1980s made many reluctant to venture into the public spaces of the city. Instead, majority populations stayed at home and watched television, as the post-war boom had ensured mass ownership. So they became the silent majority, private homeowners who defined themselves by images of poor communities. The experience young people described, different from past accounts of poverty, is of being excluded from society, and excluded within it.

The feeling of exclusivity that defines consumer culture derives from the ownership of commodities, and the seduction has been sanctioned by policy for the past 30 years under the banner of crime. Throughout the 1980s, in Europe and North America, governments asked people, particularly during elections, to imagine crime. Poster campaigns featured women scared to go out at night and television broadcasts showed how previous administrations had done nothing to halt crime. Irrespective of the actual danger, the effect was to make consumers believe that they are valuable. That was achieved by imagining poor people as criminals. The images had no bearing on the realities of living in poverty, described by young people in this study. Yet, they were believed because for most people life in the post-industrial consumer society had become a lonely existence. These processes, whereby imagining crime became a way of displacing the feelings of guilt and shame associated with a consumer lifestyle, relate directly to de-industrialisation.

After the collapse in the world economy in the late 1970s, societies in developing countries gradually became divided between private homeowners and tenants renting properties usually supplied by local authorities, and in many cases in social housing areas built straight after the war (see Power, 1997; Lupton, 2003). Those with private assets, including many government departments, went underground, leaving the poorest members of society to survive in what was left of the public sphere. Communication technologies sealed the surface between both in that it allowed policy to display inverted images of poverty experienced by people.

The realities of surviving poverty and exclusion described by young people were intensely social: stories of character, friendship and overcoming desperate situations together. As the previous chapter showed, translating the untranslatable reality of community with images only results in stereotypes and caricatures. During the 1980s, in almost every post-industrial society the image of a new urban underclass was devised to make people believe that living a consumer lifestyle was socially and economically valuable. The concept itself derives from an article by American sociologist Charles Murray (1990) entitled *The Emerging British Underclass*, which was published in *The Sunday Times Magazine* in November 1989. Murray's (1990) thesis and the context for its formulation encapsulate the reasons why socially excluding young people is such a necessary part of Britain's consumer society. Not only did the idea of a new urban underclass precipitate the rejection of urban centres in favour of retail parks and malls; its application also continues to be manifest in workfare: supplying retail industries with a cheap and young labour supply.

Back to basics

The UK registered the sharpest growth in economic inequality among nations of the European Union in the 1980s (see Hutton, 1995). To appease voters, many governments after that point became committed to economic deregulation, while retaining and centralising state power. That left governments forced to make the closure of hospitals and schools at a time of mass unemployment appear logical. Therefore, throughout Europe and North America, political leaders argued that the welfare reforms implemented after the Second World War had spawned a 'new' underclass.

Speculation about a new urban underclass had been murmuring for much of the 1980s. It was Murray (1990), however, who gave a circular logic to the idea when he argued that the modern welfare state was a harbinger of social disease. Unemployment relief, Murray (1990) argued, cultivated cultures of crime within communities worst hit by de-industrialisation, communities such as Nova. Because policy-makers and academics now feared deprived urban areas, particularly after the media hysteria surrounding the 1980–1 riots, many preferred to imagine Murray's (1990) thesis was real. Murray (1990) himself had based his thesis on a fleeting visit to a deprived urban area. Formulating his thesis beforehand, Murray (1990) went to Glasgow looking for stereotypes that would make his masquerade appear authentic: the result was a trav-elogue on poverty (see Johnstone and Mooney, 2005).

Murray's (1990) argument was based on the premise that industrial societies such as Britain and America were, for much of the post-war period, organised around a stable nuclear family household. Murray's (1990) household was one in which the man was the principal wage earner while the woman had the main responsibility for domestic life. Having to provide for the family ensured the transmission of a work ethic through generations, specifically from father to son. How the average nuclear family constituted this highly functional life is never clear, probably because Murray (1990) never represents people's experi-ences in his research. Instead, what Murray described in his trip to Easterhouse in Glasgow were characters. I believe Murray's thesis was accepted because mainstream society, including many policy-makers, was already inured by a private culture of television, computers and video. Murray (1990), much like the caricaturist William Hogarth (1738) two centuries earlier, had produced two images that everyone could identify: a single young man and a woman, also alone, pushing a pram.

Picture 3 'The Four Times Of Day – Noon' by William Hogarth

Because each is deliberately presented as different and potentially deviant, both images fulfil the same function of the debauched and drunken caricatures in Hogarth's drawing (see Picture 3, above). In each case viewers were able to mask poverty, subjugation and despair to justify their own affluent lifestyle.

When Murray's (1990) thesis was believed by consumers and policy-makers alike during the 1980s and 1990s, the underclass gradually became hyper-real; an underclass had been created that looked real in an imaginary world. Not only did the idea of underclass stigmatise generations of people living in social housing areas; to avoid contact with the underclass, cities were redesigned as spaces built around a fear of society:

> The city centres explode anew and are demolished; unliveable, unbreatheable, they are depopulated to make room for directional posts (motorways), veritable bunkers of administration, of police, of information. Populations flee or are cast out in disorder towards the outskirts where they find themselves penned in.

Urban areas were re-created, as Virilio (1998: 35–8) identifies, as was the culture of cities, from a public culture of community to a private culture of consumption. Virilio (1998) also highlights how the state was forced to invent new departments and new terms to cope with people's fears. The result, Virilio (1998: 42) defines as the 'suicidal state': consumers and policy running from the idea of society while at the same time trying to consume social problems: in short, a consumer society which 'hates the objects it desires'. To understand why so many people fear society, we need to establish how the consumer society is organised by policy and how policy-makers interpret society.

Intel: crime in an information society

When social services were forced to make job cuts and reduce their budgets, social problems inevitably multiplied. A public loss of faith in policy resulted in what Giddens (1991) describes as 'distanciation'; public institutions became disconnected from the world around them, relying instead on electronic communications. In effect, institutions became what Janet Foster (2006) describes as 'silos': underground structures where ballistic missiles can be stored and fired in the event of war.

Chapter 1 identified how many industrial cities became unsustainable when manufacturing industries closed. I also described the effect de-industrialisation had on the cultural geography of cities, dissolving the borders between working-class community and suburb. Ford remains a city, though its divisions were more psychological than social. Castells (1989: 494–5) describes how the informational city has replaced the industrial city through 'the separation between functional flows and historically determined places as two disjointed spheres of human experience. People live in places, power rules through flows.'

Castells (1989) identifies how invisible communication networks now enable people with access to them, to work and live as individuals. In societal terms, the effect is that beliefs and values no longer bind people to one another. Instead, as young people in Nova testified, everything within the information society is an image or object making people themselves components of the system. Campaigns are designed and produced and then read, making people feel assured. How people living in poor urban areas continue to be seen as a threat reflects how governments were able to retain state sovereignty after the economic crisis. That was only possible through the support of majority populations who, paradoxically, were unwilling to care for others. As a result, the state itself became even more centralised during the 1980s and 1990s.

During Fordism, people invested their lives in cities because the synergy of industry and co-operative society provided everyone with an opportunity to work, live, and start a family. As a result, people could transcend their own mortality. Now cities are regarded as disposable when they start to fail; the variables that compose them are simply imputed somewhere else. Much of the welfare state, referred to today as the 'third sector', now operates as a similar system; trust, respect and responsibility becoming variables in an objective system. Throughout this study, young people described how the realities of exclusion were compounded by strategies imposed by outside agencies, whose members failed to understand the realities of being excluded. Above all, young people described having strategies imposed, of 'people coming down on you; telling you what to do', as Sean described.

Confined within an institution also means social policy programmers are restricted to prescribing measures, even though they are intended as well meaning. In his book *The Birth of the Clinic*, Foucault (1973: 108) describes how welfare institutions developed in seventeenth-century Europe. Taking the example of the medical profession, doctors' capacity to listen and empathise was diminished by the birth of clinical medicine. The creation of medical schools during this time had a radical impact on medical perception. Disease, once defined by listening, became identified through its physical symptoms. Watching and seeing meant that doctors became disinterested. The general feeling was that becoming involved emotionally with the patient, the doctor could miss vital visual clues of disease. Through the invention and use of light, medicine became a process of enlightenment: 'The eye becomes the depository and source of clarity; it has the power to bring a truth to light, as it opens, the eye first opens the truth' (Foucault 1973: xiii). The invention of surgery meant that doctors lost their role as healers, forced to disengage from the communities in which they once lived. Because of that social dislocation, empathy between people was replaced by what Foucault describes as a rational disinterested gaze (Foucault 1973: xiii).

Foucault (1973: xiii) distinguishes between the real world of community – 'the residence of truth in the dark centre of things' – and clinic; a room containing objects saturated with light. Visual perception became the method through which surgeons adopted a disconnection and a dispassionate approach. Another development was a new language, one that ordinary people could not understand. The result was that people with an illness were literally cut out of the conversation, becoming objects. Like visual communications today, such as computers, following the birth of the clinic light was used to make objects: 'This new structure is indicative by the minute but decisive changes, whereby the question: "what is the matter with you?" was replaced by the question "where does it hurt?"' For Foucault (1973), not having to listen gave doctors power over the patient within the walls of the clinic. The new language also meant that surgeons no longer had to enter the dark world of community.

In the late twentieth century, communication technologies fulfilled the same function at a time when policy-makers become institutionally bound; relying instead on the silent images. Watching and making judgements about the best course of action to take are the only options available within the institution. The development of CCTV technology reflects policy's silent gaze, though it needs to be seen in relation to making consumption appear to be both valuable and meaningful. Between 1994 and 1997, the Home Office made available £38 million to fund 585 CCTV schemes. Between 1999 and 2003, they made available a further £170 million for CCTV schemes (Armitage, 2002: 2). Like the language of the clinic, policy was required to invent a new language. In recent years, terms such as 'underclass' and 'welfare dependency' have been substituted by 'anti-social behaviour' and 'disrespect'. Used in welfare and criminal justice policy, the terms objectify people who pose a threat to the consumer society.

In seventeenth-century Europe, medicine was able to become a powerful institution through the patronage it received from those who prospered from a new global trade in slaves from Africa. When the wealth began to flow from the colonies, Europeans began to demand their own private system of protection and care. During the Enlightenment, medical knowledge, along with local knowledge, became expert systems, separating the civilised individual from the community that created him. Like the doctors, lawyers and illustrators during the seventeenth century, policy is forced to objectify people and communities living in poverty to make the consumer society seem real. Even 'social exclusion' becomes an expert system. Writing on how the term is practised, Power and Lupton (2002: 240) suggest: 'the word was simply a different kind of code, in this case for bringing in the emphasis on personal responsibility and policy agenda of workfare . . . At its extreme this discourse condemns the victims of exclusion for deserving their own fate.' Among experts, people living in socially excluded communities, once labelled, are treated like a computer virus: put under quarantine, tracked by electronic tags, or incarcerated. All the time socially excluded communities appear disconnected from the consumer society. In fact, socially excluded communities now function as slave labour for consumers. In between are the emergency services, such as the police, trying to assure those least at risk while trying to save communities being torn apart by poverty and crime.

Being human

To understand people's experiences of poverty we need to establish how we experience the world itself. Understanding globalisation involves not just our experience of the region where we live, as a social entity, but every community across the surface of the earth. Overwhelming as that may seem, the first stage in understanding exclusion is identifying with everyone as people. The first thing that happens when we start to do this is that we are suddenly confronted by a question: but what do people look like? That we can never know.

The problem is that in understanding any experience, images are our primary method of perception (Berkeley, 1709). Chapter 1 identified how exclusion starts when consumers try to imagine people's experiences of poverty. As consumers living in consumer society, we are potentially condemned to exclude people we cannot understand. The key out of that prison is listening to another person's culture, even if the culture appears to make no sense and even if understanding takes time. My fieldwork in Nova spanned twelve months, and in the first months I was unable to appreciate the social world young people were living around me. Then I believe that in actually listening to people's experiences I opened myself to understanding them.

Quilts made by African American slaves seem to reflect the same process. On the surface, the images often appear incomprehensible. Quilts historically are authentic, and one consequence of their authenticity is that the image's appearance is inexplicable. Graffiti, on the walls of buildings as opposed to 'works' shown in art galleries or on the media, are reflections of the same process: created out of appropriated materials originally made by the artist. When we try to make such images explicable, they no longer have meaning even for the people who made them.

Like African American slaves, young people living in Nova tried to symbolise their experience with the only material resources available. Equally, the Hip Hop life represents realities most people in the developed world never experience, one determined by poverty, subjugation and exclusion. This is why, for me, 'the life' remains inexplicable, as someone who has not had to grow up in poverty and under daily suspicion. Young people survived the unimaginable experience of absolute poverty through the desire to live through it, even if that was through the most basic clothes and being with one another for as long as possible. Yet, to make our own consumer existence appear real we give Hip Hop our own subjective meaning. I have shown how young people's desire to survive through 'the life' was objectified into the image of the gang. One argument levelled at young people who dress in sportswear and associate together is that both strategies are intentionally anti-social. This study has described how young people's appearance in Nova was immanent or inherent to being excluded. Young people had no choice in how they appeared in public because only being able to afford cut-price sportswear was a reality of being excluded.

Even though they consist of images, the magic of quilts is that they can never be replicated. To begin with, the experience they contain is real. Reality is that which is possible to give an equivalent reproduction. Quilts do that in the way they evolved with the maker as a bricolage; events on quilts often do not appear in a sequential order, as they are drawn from memory. This is how quilts can have an emotional significance for someone born long after they were made. Because quilts and graffiti represent social time, the surfaces of both echo history. Ethnographic studies are similar in that the texts themselves are impossible to read, partly because of the authors' avoidance of literary realism. Imposing an image of a less troubled world, with a beginning, middle and happy ending, would only make people and situations into entertainment. Ethnographic studies that investigate social problems are often harrowing to read, not because they are designed to be but because they represent something unimaginable: human subjectivity. That does not mean ethnographic studies are doomed to fail. On the contrary, recording, or representing – the stories, music, poetry and painting (including graffiti) created by people – is the only way to understand what it means to live in poverty.

Bibliography

50 Cent (2003) *Get Rich or Die Tryin'* (Shady/Interscope Records: Santa Monica, California).

50 Cent (2005) *The Massacre* (Interscope Records: Santa Monica, California).

Abbot, D. (2003) 'Blunkett Targets Gangster Gun Culture', *BBC News Front Page*, 6 January 2003 (http://news.bbc.co.uk).

Adam, B. (1995) *Timewatch: The Social Analysis of Time* (Cambridge: Polity Press).

Adler, F. (1975) *Sisters in Crime: The rise of the new female criminal* (New York: McGraw-Hill).

Adler, P. A. (1985) *Wheeling and Dealing: An Ethnography an of Upper-Level Drug Dealing and Smuggling Community* (New York: Columbia University Press).

Alexander, C. E. (2000) *The Asian Gang* (Oxford: Berg).

Anderson, B. (1983) *Imagined Communities* (London: Verso).

Anderson, E. (1990) *Streetwise: Race, Class and Change in an Urban Community* (Chicago: University of Chicago Press).

Anderson, P. (1979) *Lineages of the Absolutist State* (London: Verso).

Appadurai, A. (1996) *Modernity at Large: Cultural Dimensions of Globalization* (Minneapolis: University of Minnesota Press).

Archer, L. and Hutchings, M. (2000) ' "Bettering yourself": Discourses of risk, cost and benefit in ethnically diverse, young working-class non-participant constructions of higher education', *British Journal of Sociology of Education*, 21 (4), 555–74.

Archer, L., Hutchings, M. and Ross, A. (2003) *Higher Education and Social Class* (London: Routledge Falmer).

Arendt, H. (1970) *On Violence* (New York: Harcourt, Brace and World).

Armitage, R. (2002) *To CCTV or not to CCTV? A review of current research into the effectiveness of CCTV systems in reducing crime* (London: NACRO).

Atkinson, B. and Hills, J. (eds) (1998) *Exclusion, Employment and Opportunity* (London: Centre for Analysis of Social Exclusion).

Atkinson, P. (1990) *The Ethnographic Imagination: Textual Constructions of Reality* (London: Routledge).

Auletta, K. (1982) *The Underclass* (New York: Vintage Books).

Barthes, R. (1972) *Mythologies* (London: Cape).

Bataille, G. (1984) *Death and Sensuality: a study of eroticism and the taboo* (Salem, New Hampshire: Ayer).

Baudelaire, C. (1821–67) *The Painter of Modern Life and Other Essays* (London: Phaidon Press).

Baudrillard, J. (1988) *Selected Writings* (Cambridge: Polity).

Baudrillard, J. (1988) *The Ecstasy of Communication* (New York: Semiotext(e)).

Baudrillard, J. (1994) *Simulacra and Simulations* (Michigan: University of Michigan Press).

Baudrillard, J. (1995) *The Gulf War Did Not Take Place* (Bloomington: Indiana University Press).

Baudrillard, J. (1998) *The Consumer Society: Myths and Structures* (London: Sage).

Bauman, Z. (1998) *Work, Consumerism, and the New Poor* (Buckingham: Open University Press).

Beck, U. (1992) *Risk Society – Towards a New Modernity* (London: Sage).

Beck, U. (2000) *The Brave New World of Work* (Cambridge: Polity Press).

Becker, H. (1963) *Outsiders: Studies in the Sociology of Deviance* (New York: Free Press).

Benassi, D., Kazepov, Y. and Migione, E. (1997) 'Socio-Economic Restructuring and Urban Poverty Under Different Welfare Regimes', in F. Moulaert and J. S. Allen (eds) *Cities, Enterprises and Society on the Eve of the 21st Century* (London: Pinter), pp. 174–218.

Berkeley, G. (1709/2003) 'An Essay towards a New Theory of Vision', in R. Schwartz (ed.) *Perception* (Oxford: Blackwell), pp. 18–23.

Berman, M. (1988) *All That is Solid Melts into Air* (London: Verso).

Blackman, S. J. (1997) ' "Destructing A Giro": A Critical and Ethnographic Study Of The Youth "Underclass" ', in R. MacDonald (ed.) *Youth, the 'Underclass' and Social Exclusion* (London: Routledge and Kegan Paul), pp. 113–29.

Booth, C. (1889–91) *Labour and Life of the People* (London: Williams and Norgate).

Bottoms, A. and Wiles, P. (1995) 'Crime and Insecurity in the City', in C. Fijnaut, J. Goethals, T. Peters and L. Walgrave (eds) *Changes in Society, Crime and Criminal Justice in Europe, vol. 1* (Antwerp: Kluwer), pp. I.2–I.38.

Bourdieu, P. (1984) *Distinction: A Social Critique of the Judgement of Taste* (London: Routledge and Kegan Paul).

Bourgois, P. (1996) *In Search of Respect: Selling Crack in El Barrio* (Cambridge: Cambridge University Press).

Braithwaite, J. (1989) *Crime, Shame and Reintegration* (Cambridge: Cambridge University Press).

British Youth Council (1992) *The Time of Your Life? The Truth about Being Young in the 1990s* (London: British Youth Council).

Buck, N. (1992) 'Labour market inactivity and polarisation: a household perspective on the idea of the underclass', in D. Smith (ed.) (1992) *Understanding the Underclass* (London: Policy Studies Institute), pp. 9–32.

Bush, G. W. (2002) *The President's State of the Union Address* (http://www.whitehouse.gov).

Byers, P. (1998) 'Space shaping technologies and the geographic dissembedding of place', in A. Light and J. M. Smith (eds) *Philosophies of Place* (Maryland: Rowman and Littlefield), pp. 239–65.

Byers, S. (1999) 'Free trade will boost Third World', in BBC News FrontPage (http://news.bbc.co.uk/).

Callaghan, G. (1992) 'Locality and localism: the spatial orientation of young adults in Sunderland', *Youth Policy*, 39, 23–33.

Campbell A. (1981) *Delinquent Girls* (Oxford: Blackwell).

Campbell, A. (1984) *The Girls in the Gang* (Oxford: Blackwell).

Campbell, B. (1993) *Goliath: Britain's Dangerous Places* (London: Virago).

Carlen, P. (1996) *Jigsaw: A Political Criminology of Youth Homelessness* (Buckingham: Open University Press).

Carley, M. (1990) *Housing and Neighbourhood Renewal: Britain's New Urban Challenge* (London: Policy Studies Institute).

Cashmore, E. (1997) *The Black Culture Industry* (London: Routledge).

Castells, M. (1989) *The Informational City: information technology, economic restructuring, and the urban-regional process* (Oxford: Basil Blackwell).

Chaiken, J. M. and Chaiken, M. R. (1990) 'Drugs and Predatory Crime', in R. Coomber (ed.) *Drugs and Drug Use in Society: a Critical Reader* (London: Greenwich University Press), pp. 281–311.

Charley, J. (1995) 'Industrialisation and the City: Work, Speed-Up, Urbanisation', in M. Miles, T. Hall and I. Borden (eds) *The City Cultures Reader*, pp. 67–9.

Clifford, J. and Marcus, G. E. (eds) (1986) *Writing Culture: The Politics and Poetics of Ethnography* (Berkley: University of California Press).

Cloward, R. and Ohlin, L. (1961) *Delinquency and Opportunity: A Theory of Delinquent Gangs* (London: Routledge and Kegan Paul).

Coffield, F., Borril, C. and Marshall, S. (1986) *Growing Up at the Margins* (Milton Keynes: Open University Press).

Cohen, G. (ed.) (1987) *Social Change and the Life Course* (London: Tavistock).

Cohen, P. (1972) 'Subcultural Conflict and Working Class Community', *Working Papers in Cultural Studies*, 2, pp. 5–52.

Cohen, P. (1986) *Rethinking the Youth Question* (London: Youth and Policy).

Cohen, S. (1972) *Folk Devils and Moral Panics: The Creation of Mods and Rockers*, (London: MacGiddon and Kee).

Colenutt, B. (1999) 'New Deal or No Deal for People-Based Regeneration', in R. Imrie and H. Thomas (eds) *British Urban Policy: A Reader* (London: Sage), pp. 233–45.

Coles, B. (1995) *Youth and Social Policy: Youth Citizenship and Young Careers* (London: UCL Press).

Collin, M. (1997) *Altered State* (London: Serpents Tale).

Connell, R. W. (1987) *Gender and Power* (Oxford: Polity).

Conrad, J. (1902/1988) *Heart of Darkness* (Oxford: Oxford University Press).

Cook, D. (1997) *Poverty, Crime and Punishment* (London: Child Poverty Action Group).

Coomber, R. (1994) *Drugs and Drug Use in Society: A Critical Reader* (Dartford: Greenwich University Press).

Cope, N. (2002) *Drug Use in Prison: a study of young offenders* (Unpublished thesis, University of Warwick).

Corbett, J. (1990) *Uneasy Transitions: disaffection in post compulsory education and training* (Basingstoke: Falmer Press).

Corbett, T. (2003) 'The New Face of Welfare in the US: From Income Transfers to Social Assistance', in *Social Policy and Society* 2, pp. 113–23.

Coward, R. (1994) 'Whipping Boys', *The Guardian Weekend*, 3 September 1994.

Craine, S. (1997) 'The "Black Magic Roundabout": Cyclical Transitions, Social Exclusion and Alternative Careers', in R. MacDonald (ed.), pp. 130–53.

Croall, H. (1998) *Crime and Society in Britain* (London: Longman).

Dabinett, G. and Ramsden, P. (1999) 'Urban Policy in Sheffield: Regenerations, Partnerships and People', in R. Imrie and H. Thomas (eds) (1999) *British Urban Policy and the Urban Development Corporations* (London: Sage), pp. 168–205.

Dadydeen, D. (1987) *Hogarth's Blacks: Images of Blacks in Eighteenth Century English Art* (Manchester: Manchester University Press).

Damer, S. (1974) 'Wine Alley: The Sociology of a Dreadful Enclosure', *Sociological Review*, 22, 221–48.

Darwin, C. (1859) *On the Origin of Species* (Cambridge, Mass.: Harvard University Press).

Davis, M. (1990) *City of Quartz* (London: Vintage).

Davis, N. (1999) *Youth Crisis: Growing Up in the High-Risk Society* (Westport, Conn.: Praeger Publishers).

de Certeau, M. (1984) *The Practice of Everyday Life* (Berkeley: University of California).

Debord, G. (1967) *The Society of The Spectacle* (New York: Zone Books).

Department for Education and Skills (2003) *The Future of Higher Education* (White Paper) (London: HMSO).

Dicken, P. (1992) 'International Production in a Volatile Regulatory Environment: the Influence of National Regulatory Policies on the Spatial Strategies of Transnational Corporations', in J. Bryson, N. Henry, D. Keeble and R. Martin (eds) (1999) *The Economic Geography Reader* (London: Wiley), pp. 115–21.

Dixon, J., Levine, M. and McAuley, R. (2004) *Street Drinking Legislation, CCTV, and Public Space* (London: Home Office Research Study, Home Office).

Douglas, J. D. (1976) *Investigative Social Research* (Beverly Hills, Cal.: Sage).

Downes, D. (1966) *The Delinquent Solution* (London: Routledge and Kegan Paul).

Downes, D. (1993) *Employment Opportunities for Offenders* (London: Home Office).

Downes, D. (ed.) (1989) *Crime and the City* (London: Macmillan).

Downes, D. and Rock, P. (1995) *Understanding Deviance* (Oxford: Clarendon).

Dworkin, A. (2000) 'Against the Male Flood: Censorship Pornography and Equality', in Cornell, D. (ed.), *Feminism and Pornography* (Oxford: Oxford University Press), pp. 19–39.

Eco, U. (1986) *Travels into Hyperreality* (Orlando, Fl.: Harcourt Brace Jovanovich).

Elmer, N. and Reicher, S. (1995) *Adolescence and Delinquency* (London: Basil Blackwell).

Engels, F. (1845) *The Condition of the Working Class in England* (London: Penguin).

Fainstein, S. (1994) *The City Builders* (Oxford: Blackwell).

Fainstein, S. and Gladestone, D. (1997) 'Tourism and Urban Transformation: Interpretations of Urban Tourism', in O. Kalltorp, I. Elander, O. Ericsson and M. Franzen (eds) *Cities in Transformation – Transformation in Cities: Social and Symbolic Change of Urban Space* (Aldershot: Avebury) pp. 119–35.

Family Expenditure Survey (1991) *Family Spending: a Report on the 1990 Family Expenditure Survey* (London: Her Majesty's Stationery Office).

Fine, B. (2001) *Social Capital versus Social Theory: Political Economy and Social Science at the Turn of the Millennium* (London: Routledge).

Flick, U. (1998) *An Introduction to Qualitative Research* (London: Sage).

Foster, J. (1990) *Villains: Crime and Community in the Inner City* (London: Routledge and Kegan Paul).

Foster, J. (1999) *Docklands: Culture in Conflict, Worlds in Collision* (London: UCL Press).

Foster, J. (2000) 'Social Exclusion, Crime and Drugs', in S. MacGregor (ed.) *Drugs, Education, Prevention and Policy* (London: Carfax Publishing), pp. 317–30.

Foster, J. (2002) ' "People Pieces": the neglected but essential elements of community crime prevention', in G. Hughes and A. Edwards (eds) *Community Crime Prevention*, pp. 167–97.

Foster, J. (2006) personal communication.

Foucault, M. (1973) *The Birth of The Clinic: An Archaeology of Medical Perception* (London: Routledge).

Foucault, M. (1977) *Discipline and Punishment* (London: Allen Lane).

Foucault, M. (1979) *The History of Sexuality*, Vol. 1 (New York: Vintage Books).

France, A. and Wiles, P. (1997) 'Dangerous Futures: Social Exclusion and Youth Work in Late Modernity', in J. C. Finer and M. Nellis (eds) *Crime and Social Exclusion* (Oxford: Blackwell), pp. 59–79.

Fraser, P. (1997) 'Social and spatial relationships and the "problem" inner city', *Critical Social Policy*, 16 (4), 43–67.

Galbraith, J. K. (1985) *The Affluent Society* (London: Deutsch).

Galbraith, J. K. (1992) *The Culture of Contentment* (London: Sinclair, Stevenson).

Gans, H. (1999) *Popular Culture and High Culture: An Analysis and Evaluation of Taste* (New York: Basic Books).

Garfinkel, H. (ed.) (1986) *Ethnomethodological Studies of Work* (London: Routledge and Kegan Paul).

Gellner, E. (1983) *Nations and Nationalism* (Oxford: Blackwell).

Gibbons, D. and Jones, J. (1975) *The Study of Deviance* (Engelwood Cliffs, N.J.: Prentice Hall).

Giddens, A. (1979) *Central Problems in Social Theory: Action, Structure, and Contradiction in Social Analysis* (London: Macmillan).

Giddens, A. (1984) *The Constitution of Society: Outline of the Theory of Structuration* (Cambridge: Polity).

Giddens, A. (1990) *The Consequences of Modernity* (Cambridge: Polity Press).

Giddens, A. (1991) *Modernity and Self-Identity* (Cambridge: Polity Press).

Giddens, A. (1994) 'Living in a Post-Traditional Society', in U. Beck, A. Giddens and S. Lash (eds) *Reflexive Modernisation* (Cambridge: Polity Press), pp. 58–110.

Giddens, A. (1997) 'The Two Tony's', Interview with R. S. Boynton in *The New Yorker* 6 October 1997, 73: 66–74.

Giddens, A. (2000) *The Third Way and Its Critics* (Cambridge: Polity Press).

Gill, O. (1977) *Luke Street: Housing Policy, Conflict and The Creation of The Delinquent Area* (London: Macmillan).

Gilroy, P. (1987) *There Ain't No Black in the Union Jack: The Cultural Politics of Race and Nation* (London: Hutchinson).

Gilroy, P. (1994) *The Black Atlantic: Modernity and Double Consciousness* (London: Verso).

Glaser, B. and Strauss, A. (1967) *The Discovery of Grounded Theory* (Chicago: Aldine).

Goffman, E. (1963) *Stigma: Notes on the Management of Spoiled Identity* (Harmondsworth: Penguin).

Goffman, E. (1967) *Interaction Ritual: Essays on Face-To-Face Behaviour* (New York: Pantheon Books).

Goffman, E. (1968) *Asylums: Essays on the Social Situation of Mental Patients and Other Inmates* (Harmondsworth: Penguin).

Goldthorpe, J. H., Lockwood, D., Bechlofer, F. and Plant, J. (1968) *The Affluent Worker in the Class Structure* (London: Cambridge University Press).

Greenstein, R. (1991) 'Universal and Targeted Approaches to Relieving Poverty: An Alternative View', in C. Jencks and P. E. Peterson (eds) *The Urban Underclass* (Washington: The Brookings Institute), pp. 437–59.

Hakim, C. (1987) 'Trends in the Flexible Workforce', *Employment Gazette*, 95 (11), pp. 549–60.

Hall, S. and Jefferson, T. (eds) (1976) *Rituals of Resistance* (Milton Keynes: Open University Press).

Hall, S., Crichter, C., Jefferson, T. and Roberts, B. (1978) *Policing the Crisis: Mugging, the State, and Law and Order* (London: Macmillan).

Hambleton, R. (1990) *Urban Government in the 1990s: lessons from the U.S.A.* (Bristol: University of Bristol, School for Advanced Urban Studies).

Hammersley, M. and Atkinson, P. (1983) *Ethnography: Principles and Practice* (London: Tavistock).

Harvey, D. (1989) *The Condition of Postmodernity* (Oxford: Basil Blackwell).

Harvey, D. (1997) 'Contested Cities', in N. Jewson and S. MacGregor (eds), pp. 19–28.

Haslam, D. (2001). *Adventures on the Wheels of Steel: The Rise of the Superstar DJs* (London: Fourth Estate).

Healy, P. (1997) 'City Fathers, Mandarins and Neighbours: Crossing Old Divides in New Partnerships', in O. Kalltorp, I. Elander, O. Ericsson and M. Franzen (eds) *Cities in Transformation – Transformation in Cities: Social and Symbolic Change of Urban Space* (Aldershot: Avebury), pp. 266–88.

Hebdige, D. (1979) *Subcultures – The Meaning of Style* (London: Methuen).

Hebdige, D. (1988) *Hiding in the Light* (London: Comedia).

Heidegger, M. (1927) 'Being and Time', in W. McNeill and K. S. Feldman (eds) *Continental Philosophy* (1993) (Oxford: Blackwell), pp. 108–22.

Hobbs, D. (1989) *Doing the Business* (Oxford: Oxford University Press).

Hobbs, D. (1995) *Bad Business: Professional Crime in Modern Britain* (Oxford: Oxford University Press).

Hobbs, D. *et al.* (2003) *Bouncers: Violence and Governance in the Night-Time Economy* (Oxford: Oxford University Press).

Hobsbawm, E. J. (1962) *The Age of Revolution 1789–1848* (London: Abacus).

Hobsbawm, E. J. (1994a) *The Age of Extremes 1914–1991* (London: Michael Joseph).

Hobsbawm, E. J. (1994b) 'Barbarism: A User's Guide', *New Left Review*, 206, 44–54.

Hobsbawm, E. J. (1997) *On History* (London: Weidenfield Nicholson).

Home Office (2004) *Defining and Measuring Anti-Social Behaviour* (London: Research, Development and Statistics Directorate).

Hope, T. and Foster, J. (1992) 'Conflicting Forces: challenging the dynamics of crime and community on a "problem estate"', *British Journal of Criminology*, 32, 488–504.

Hughes, G. and Edwards, A. (2002) *Crime Control and Community: The New Politics of Public Safety* (Cullompton: Willan).

Hutton, W. (1995) 'The 30–30–40 Society', *Regional Studies*, 29 (8), 719–21.

Jameson, F. (1991) *Postmodernism, Or, the Cultural Logic of Late Capitalism* (London: Verso).

Jameson, F. (1998) *The Cultural Turn: Selected Writings on The Postmodern, 1983–1998* (London: Verso).

Jargowsky, P. A. (1996) *Poverty and Place: ghettos, barrios, and the American city* (New York: Russell Sage Foundation).

Jencks, C. (1991) 'Is the American Underclass Growing?', in C. Jencks and P. E. Peterson (eds), pp. 28–100.

Jencks, C. and Peterson, P. E. (eds) (1991) *The Urban Underclass* (Washington: The Brookings Institute).

Jessop, R. (1990) 'Regulation Theories in Retrospect and Prospect', *Economy and Society*, 19, 153–216.

Jewson, N. and MacGregor, S. (eds) (1997) *Transforming Cities: Contested Governance and New Spatial Divisions* (London: Routledge).

Johnstone, C. and Mooney, G. (2005) 'Locales of "Disorder" and "Disorganisation"? Exploring New Labour's Approach to Council Estates', paper presented to Securing the Urban Renaissance: Policing, Community and Disorder, Glasgow (16–17 June 2005).

Katz, J. (1988) *The Seductions of Crime* (New York: Basic Books).

Kazepov, Y. and Zajczyk, F. (1997) 'Urban Poverty and Social Exclusion: concepts and debates', in F. Moulaert and J. S. Allen (eds) *Cities, Enterprises and Society on the Eve of the 21st Century* (London: Pinter), pp. 151–73.

Keene, J. (1997) *Drug Misuse Prevention: harm minimisation and treatment* (London: Chapman and Hall).

Kempson, E., Bryson, A. and Rowlingson, K. (1994) *Hard Times? How Poor Families Make Ends Meet* (London: Policy Studies Institute).

Keynes, J. M. (1936) *General Theory of Employment, Interest and Money* (London: Macmillan).

Klockars, C. B. (1974) *The Professional Fence* (London: Tavistock).

Kornhauser, R. R. (1978) *Social Sources of Delinquency* (Chicago: Chicago University Press).

Kumar, K. (1984) 'Unemployment as a problem in the development of industrial societies: the English experience', *Sociological Review*, 32 (2), 185–223.

Lash, S. (2002) *Critique of Information* (London: Thousand Oaks, Cal.: Sage).

Lash, S. and Urry, J. (1994) *Economies of Signs and Space* (London: Sage).

Lea, J. (2002) *Crime and Modernity: Continuities in Left Realist Criminology* (London: Sage).

Lea, J. and Young, J. (1984) *What is To Be Done About Law and Order?* (Harmondsworth: Penguin).

Lefebvre, H. (1974) *The Production of Space* (trans. D. Nicholson-Smith) (Oxford: Blackwell).

LeGates, R. T. and Stout, F. (eds) (1996) *The City Reader* (London: Routledge).

Levinas, E. (1994) *Totality and Infinity: An Essay on Exteriority* (Pittsburgh: Duquesne University Press).

Lewis, O. (1966) *La Vida: A Puerto Rican Family in the Culture of Poverty – San Juan and New York* (New York: Random House).

Lewis, O. (1968) *A Study of Slum Culture: Backgrounds for La Vida* (New York: Random House).

Lewis, O. (1976) *Five Families: Mexican case studies in the culture of poverty* (London: Souvenir Press).

Liebling, A. (1992) *Suicides in Prison* (London: Routledge).

Light, A. and Smith, J. S. (eds) (1999) *Philosophies of Place* (Oxford: Rowman and Littlefield).

Loach, K. (1966) *Cathy Come Home* (London: British Film Institute).

Loader, I. (1996) *Youth Policing, and Democracy* (London: Macmillan).

Lupton, R. (2003) *Poverty Street: The Dynamics of Neighbourhood Decline and Renewal* (Bristol: Policy).

Lyon, D. (2001) *Surveillance Society: Monitoring Everyday Life* (Buckingham: Open University Press).

Lyotard, J-F. (1985) *The Postmodern Condition – A Report on Knowledge* (Manchester: Manchester University Press).

Lyotard, J-F. (1993) 'The Sublime and the Avante Garde', in T. Docherty (ed.) *Postmodernism: A Reader* (London: Harvester Wheatsheaf), pp. 244–56.

MacDonald, R. (ed.) (1997) *Youth, the 'Underclass' and Social Exclusion* (London: Routledge and Kegan Paul).

Malcolm, C. and Wallace, C. (eds) (1990) *Youth in Transition: the Sociology of Youth and Youth Policy* (Basingstoke: Farmer Press).

Madouros, V. (2005) *Labour Market Analysis and Summary, September 2005 Assessment* (London: Office for National Statistics, Labour Market Division).

Marcuse, H. (1964) *One Dimensional Man: Studies in The Ideology of Advanced Industrial Society* (London: Routledge and Kegan Paul).

Marx, K. (1818–83) *Capital: A Critique of Political Economy* (London: Lawrence & Wishart, 1956).

Massey, D. (1994) *Space, Place and Gender* (Cambridge: Polity Press).

Mass Observation (1943) *The Pub and the People: A Worktown Study* (London: Gollancz).

Matza, D. and Sykes, G. (1957) 'Techniques of Neutralisation: A Theory of Delinquency', *American Sociological Review*, 22, 664–70.

McCahill, M. (2002) *The Surveillance Web: The Rise and Extent of Visual Surveillance in a Northern City* (Cullompton: Willan).

McKnight, A (1998) 'Low-Wage Mobility in a Working Life Perspective', in R. Asplund, P. Sloane and I. Theodossiou (eds) *Low Pay and Earnings Mobility in Europe* (Cheltenham: Edward Elgar), pp. 47–78.

McKnight, A. (2002) 'Low-paid Work: Drip Feeding the Poor', in J. Hills, J. Le Grand and D. Piachaud (eds) *Understanding Social Exclusion* (Oxford: Oxford University Press, pp. 98–117.

McLuhan, M. (1964) *Understanding Media: the extensions of man* (London: Pluto).

McRobbie, A. (2000) *Feminism and Youth Culture* (Basingstoke: Macmillan).

Miller, W. B. (1958) 'Lower Class Culture as a Generating Milieu of Gang Delinquency', *Journal of Social Issues*, 4, 5–14.

Mingione, E. (ed.) (1996) *Urban Poverty and The Underclass: A Reader* (Oxford: Blackwell).

Mirrlees-Black, C., Mayhew, P. and Percy, A. (1996) *The British Crime Survey* (London: Home Office Research and Statistics Directorate).

Misztal, B. (2003) *Theories of Social Remembering* (Philadelphia, PA: Open University Press).

Modood, T. and Shiner, M. (1994) *Ethnic Minorities and Higher Education: why are there differential rates of entry?* (London: Policy Studies Institute).

Morris, A. (1987) *Women, Crime and Criminal Justice* (Oxford: Basil Blackwell).

Morris, L. (1994) *Dangerous Classes: The Underclass and Social Citizenship* (London: Routledge and Kegan Paul).

Morris, L. (1995) *Social Divisions: Economic Decline and Social Structural Change* (London: UCL Press).

Muncie, J. (1999) *Youth and Crime: A Critical Introduction* (London: Sage).

Murray, C. (1990) *The Emerging British Underclass* (London: Institute of Economic Affairs).

Murray, C. (1994) *Underclass: The Crisis Deepens* (London: Institute of Economic Affairs).

Nicholas, S. and Walker, A. (eds) (2004) *Crime in England and Wales 2002/2003: Supplementary Volume 2: Crime, Disorder and the Criminal Justice System – public attitudes and perceptions* (London: Home Office Statistical Bulletin 02/04).

National Offender Management Service (2005) NOMS launches new drug strategy. Press Release (www.homeoffice.gov.uk/rds).

Office of the Deputy Prime Minister (ODPM) (2004) *Index of Local Deprivation* (London: Her Majesty's Stationery Office).

Office of National Statistics (1997) *Social Trends* (London: Her Majesty's Stationery Office).

Olalquiga, C. (1992) *Megalopolis: Contemporary Cultural Sensibilities* (Minneapolis: Minnesota University Press).

Oliver, J. (2005) (http://www.feedmebetter.com).

Orwell, G. (1937/1988) *The Road to Wigan Pier* (London: Penguin).

Packard, V. (1960) *The Hidden Persuaders* (Harmondsworth: Penguin).

Padilla, F. (1992) *The Gang as an American Enterprise* (New Brunswick, N.J.: Rutgers University Press).

Pahl, R. E. (1984) *Divisions of Labour* (Oxford: Basil Blackwell).

Pahl, R. E (2000) *On Friendship* (Cambridge: Polity Press).

Park, R. and Burgess, E. (1925) *The City* (Chicago: Chicago University Press).

Parker, H., Aldridge, J. and Measham, F. (1998) *Illegal Leisure: The Normalisation of Adolescent Recreational Drug Use* (London: Routledge).

Parker, T. (1974) *View from the Boys* (Newton Abbot: David and Charles).

Parker, T. (1983) *People of the Providence* (London: Hutchinson).

Pearce, N. and Hillman, J. (1998) *Wasted Youth: raising achievement and tackling social exclusion* (London: Institute for Public Policy Research).

Pitts, J. and Hope, T. (1998) 'The local politics of inclusion: the State and community safety', in J. C. Finer and M. Nellis (eds) *Crime and Social Exclusion* (Oxford: Blackwell), pp. 37–59.

Plato (1957) *Plato's Cosmology: The Timaeus of Plato with a Running Commentary* (New York: Liberal Arts Press).

Polsky, N. (1971) *Hustlers, Beats and Others* (Harmondsworth: Penguin).

Power, A. (1989) 'Housing, Community, and Crime', in D. Downes (ed.), pp. 206–36.

Power, A. (1993) *Hovels to High Rise* (London: Routledge).

Power, A. (1997) *Estates on the Edge* (London: Macmillan Press).

Power, A. and Mumford, K. (1999) *The Slow Death of Great Cities: Urban Abandonment or Urban Renaissance* (York: Joseph Rowntree Foundation).

Power, A. and Mumford, K. (2003) *Eastenders: Family and Community in Urban Neighbourhoods* (Bristol: Policy Press).

Presdee, M. (2000) *Cultural Criminology and the Carnival of Crime* (London: Routledge).

Pugsley, L. (1998) 'Throwing your Brains at it: Higher Education, Markets and Choice', *International Studies in Sociology of Education*, 8(1), pp. 71–90.

Putnam, R. (2000) *Bowling Alone: The Collapse and Revival of American Community* (New York: Touchstone).

Read, P. (1978) *The Train Robbers* (London: W.H. Allen: Alison Press).

Redhead, S. (1991) *Rave Off!* (Aldershot: Avebury).

Rex, J. (1988) *The Ghetto and the Underclass: Essays on Race and Social Policy* (Aldershot: Avebury).

Rex, J. and Moore, R. (1967) *Race, Community and Conflict: A Study of Sparkbrook* (Oxford: Oxford University Press).

Reynolds, F. (1986) *The Problem Housing Estate: An Account of Omega and Its People* (Aldershot: Gower).

Ritzer, G. (2004) *The McDonaldization of Society* (Thousand Oaks, Cal.: Pine Forge Press).

Roberts, J. K. and Kidd, B. A. (1999) 'The treatment of drug users in prison', in C. Stark, B. A Kidd and R. A. D. Sykes (eds) *Illegal Drug Use in the United Kingdom: prevention, treatment and enforcement* (Brookfield, VT: Ashgate), pp. 141–53.

Roberts, K. (1989) 'Youth Unemployment in Liverpool', in D. Downes (ed.) pp. 88–111.

Roberts, K. (1997) 'Is there an emerging British "underclass"? The evidence from youth research', in R. MacDonald (ed.), pp. 39–54.

Robertson, R. (1992) *Globalization: Social Theory and Global Culture* (London: Sage).

Robins, D. (1992) *Tarnished Vision: Crime and Conflict in the Inner-City* (Oxford: Oxford University Press).

Rose, T. (1994) *Black Noise: Rap Music and Black Culture in Contemporary America* (New England: Weslyan University Press).

Rubio, M. (1997) 'Perverse Social Capital – Some Evidence from Colombia', *Journal of Economic Issues*, 31(3), 805–16.

Russell, P. (2003) *Interview with 50 Cent* (http://www.rapnewsdirect.com).

Sartre, J. P. (1947) *No Exit: A Play in One Act: A Play in Three Acts* (New York: Alfred A. Knopf).

Sassen, S. (1991) *The Global City: New York, London, Tokyo* (Princeton, N.J.: Princeton University).

Sassen, S. (1997) 'New employment regimes in cities', in F. Moulaert and J. S. Allen (eds) *Cities, Enterprises and Society on the Eve of the 21st Century* (London: Pinter), pp. 129–50.

Savage, M. and Warde, A. (1994) *Urban Sociology, Capitalism and Modernity* (London: Macmillan).

Scott, A. J. and Moulaert, F. (1997) 'The Urban Question and the Future of Urban Research', in F. Moulaert and J. S. Allen (eds) *Cities, Enterprises and Society on the Eve of the 21st Century* (London: Pinter), pp. 267–78.

Shaw, C. and McKay, H. (1942) *Juvenile Delinquency and Urban Areas* (Chicago: University of Chicago Press).

Sibley, D. (1995) *Geographies of Exclusion* (London: Routledge).

Simons, R. J. (1975) *Women and Crime* (Toronto: Lexington).

Skocpol, T. (1991) 'Targeting with Universalism: Politically Viable Policies to Combat Poverty in the United States', in C. Jencks and P. E. Peterson (eds), pp. 411–36.

Smith, D. (ed.) (1992) *Understanding the Underclass* (London: Policy Studies Institute).

Social Exclusion Unit (1998) *Bringing Britain Together: a national strategy for neighbourhood renewal* (London: The Stationery Office).

Stedman-Jones, G. (1971) *Outcast London: A Study in the Relationship Between Classes in Victorian Society* (London: Peregrine).

Sudjic, D. (1993) *The 100 Mile City* (London: Flamingo).

Sullivan, M. (1989) *Gettin' Paid: Youth, Crime and Unemployment in the Inner City* (New York: Cornell University Press).

Sutherland, E. and Cressey, D. (1970) *Criminology* (8th edn) (Philadelphia: Lippincott).

Sutherland, E. H. (1937) *The Professional Thief* (Chicago: University of Chicago Press).

Sutherland, E. H. (1949) *White Collar Crime* (New York: Holt, Rinehart and Winston).

Taylor, I. (1999) *Crime in Context: a critical criminology of market societies* (Oxford: Polity).

Taylor, I., Evans, K. and Fraser, P. (1996) *A Tale of Two Cities: A study of Manchester and Sheffield* (London: Routledge).

Tester, K. (1997) *Moral Culture* (London: Sage).

Thomas, E. (2001) *Widening Participation in Post Compulsory Education* (London: Continuum).

Thompson, E. P. (1963) *The Making of the English Working Class* (London: Penguin).

Thornton, S. (1997) *Club Cultures: Music, Media and Subcultural Capital* (Cambridge: Polity).

Thrasher, F. (1937) *The Gang* (Chicago: University of Chicago Press).

Townsend, P. (1979) *Poverty in the United Kingdom: a survey of household resources and standards of living* (London: Allen Lane).

Turner, B. (1990) *Theories of Modernity and Postmodernity* (London: Sage).

Ullah, P. (1987) Unemployed black youths in a northern city,' in D. Fryer and P. Ullah (eds) *Unemployed People: Social and Psychological Perspectives* (Manchester: Manchester University Press).

UNICEF (2005) *End Child Exploitation report, Child labour today* (Essex: UNICEF).

United Nations Framework Convention on Climate Change (2005) *Feeling the Heat* (http://unfccc.int).

Valier, C. (2004) *Crime and Punishment in Contemporary Culture* (London: Routledge).

Virilio, P. (1984) 'Critical Space', in J. Der Derain (ed.) (1998) *The Virilio Reader* (Oxford: Blackwell), pp. 59–72.

Virilio, P. (1998) 'The Suicidal State', in J. Der Derain (ed.) *The Verilio Reader* (Oxford: Blackwell), pp. 29–46.

Virilio, P. (1989) *War and Cinema: the logistics of perception* (London: Verso).

Wacquant, L. (1994) 'The New Urban Color Line: The State and Fate of the Ghetto in Post-Fordist America', in C. Calhoun (ed.) *Social Theory and the Politics of Identity* (Oxford: Basil Blackwell), pp. 231–76.

Wacquant, L. (1996) 'Red Belt, Black Belt: Racial Divisions, Class Inequality and the State in the French Urban Periphery and the American Ghetto', in E. Mingione (ed.) pp. 234–75.

Wakefield, A. (2004) *Selling Security: the Private Policing of Public Space* (Cullompton: Willan).

Wasserman, D., Wormesley, M. and Gottliech, S. (1998) 'Can a Sense of Place Be Preserved?', in L. Light and J. Smith (eds), pp. 191–215.

Whyte, W. F. (1945) *Street Corner Society: The Social Structure of an Italian Slum* (Chicago: University of Chicago Press).

Williams, R. (1989) *People of the Black Mountains* (London: Chatto and Windus).

Williams, R. (1958) *Culture and Society 1780-1950* (London: Chatto and Windus).

Williams, R. (1980) *Problems in Materialism and Culture: Selected Essays* (London: Verso).

Williamson, H. (1993) 'Youth Policy in the United Kingdom and the Marginalisation of Young People', *Youth and Policy*, 40, pp. 33–48.

Williamson, H. (1997) 'Status Zero youth and the underclass', in R. MacDonald (ed.), pp. 70–82.

Willis, P. (1977) *Learning to Labour: How Working Class Kids Get Working Class Jobs* (Farnborough: Saxon House).

Wilson, J. Q. (1985) *Thinking about Crime* (New York: Vintage Books).

Wilson, R. and Green, A. E. (2001) *Projections of Occupations and Qualifications: 2000/2001: Research in Support of the National Skills Taskforce* (Sheffield: Department for Education and Employment).

Wilson, W. J. (1987) *The Truly Disadvantaged* (Chicago: Chicago University Press).

Wilson, W. J (1991) 'Studying Inner-City Dislocations', *American Sociological Review*, 26, 1–14.

Wilson, W. J. (1996) *When Work Disappears: The World of the New Urban Poor* (New York: Alfred A. Knopf).

Winlow, S. (2001) *Badfellas: Crime, Tradition and New Masculinities* (Oxford: Berg).

Wirth, L. (1938) *On Cities and Social Life* (Chicago: Chicago University Press).

World Bank (2004) *Urbanization and Cities: Facts and Figures* (Washington: World Bank).

Young, A. (1996) *Imagining Crime* (London: Sage).

Young, J. (1999) *The Exclusive Society* (London: Sage).

Zorbaugh, H. W. (1929) *The Gold Coast and the Slum* (Chicago: University of Chicago Press).

Zukin, S. (1991) *Landscapes of Power – from Detroit to Disneyland* (Berkeley: University of California Press).

Index